Hepburn and Tracy

To their admiring public Spencer Tracy and
Katharine Hepburn were Everyman and Everywoman. By surviving one devastating crisis after
another in private and with dignity, they proved
they were that and much more. It began in the
autumn of their lives and has lasted to this day:
scripted by its actors, played out in the wings—a
love story for the ages.

An Affair to Remember

CHRISTOPHER ANDERSEN

AVON BOOKS
An Imprint of HarperCollinsPublishers

Grateful acknowledgment is made to the following for permission to use the photographs in this book: AP/World Wide Photos: 55; Archive Photos: 51; Corbis-Bettman: 16, 17, 19, 25, 44, 58; Penguin/Corbis-Bettmann: 47, 54; Springer/Corbis-Bettmann: 35; UPI/Bettmann: 7, 14, 15, 18, 24, 29, 36, 38, 53, 56; UPI/Corbis-Bettmann: 13, 21, 28, 30, 31, 46, 49, 52, 59, 61; The Kobal Collection: 1, 26, 27, 32, 33, 34, 39, 40, 42, 43, 48, 50, 57, 60; *Movie Star News*: 10, 37, 41, 62; Rex Features: 45

AVON BOOKS
An Imprint of HarperCollins*Publishers*
10 East 53rd Street
New York, New York 10022-5299

Copyright © 1997 by Christopher Andersen
Cover photo courtesy of The Kobal Collection
Library of Congress Catalog Card Number: 97-5771
ISBN: 0-380-73158-4
www.avonbooks.com

The William Morrow edition contains the following Library of Congress Cataloging in Publication Data:

Andersen, Christopher P.
    An affair to remember: the remarkable love story of Katharine Hepburn and Spencer Tracy / Christopher Andersen.—1st ed.
        p.   cm.
Includes bibliographical references and index.
1. Hepburn, Katharine, 1909-2003—Relations with men.   2. Tracy, Spencer, 1909-1967—Relations with women.   3. Motion picture actors and actresses—United States—Biography.   I. Title.
PN2287.H45A79   1997   97-5771
791.43'028'092273—dc21   CIP
[B]   94-46303   CIP

First Avon Books paperback printing: June 1998

Avon Trademark Reg. U.S. Pat. Off. and in Other Countries, Marca Registrada, Hecho en U.S.A.

HarperCollins® is a trademark of HarperCollins Publishers Inc.

Printed in the U.S.A.

10 9 8 7 6 5 4

For Edward and Jeanette
For Lenny and Bea

You don't pick out who you fall in love with.
There are so few people to love. . . .
— KATHARINE HEPBURN
TO THE AUTHOR

My Kate, she really has me pegged.
— SPENCER TRACY

Preface

It was one of the great romances of our time—arguably the most celebrated long-running affair of the twentieth century. Thirty years after Spencer Tracy's death, the surviving half of Hollywood's most famous couple remains one of the world's most beloved icons.

Yet what did we really know of Katharine Hepburn and Spencer Tracy? For generations they came to symbolize the ideal American male and female—equally matched warriors in the eternal battle of the sexes. They were impossibly witty, endearingly stubborn, and when they fought in the movies, as Kate said of their friends Humphrey Bogart and Lauren Bacall, it was like "two cats locked deliciously in a cage."

As incomprehensible as it seems now, during his lifetime the public knew Tracy and Hepburn only as an acting team, not as lovers. By the time he died in 1967, Tracy had been married to the same woman for forty-four years. Out of respect for all three, the press did something for them it had done for no other figures of their prominence: it jealously guarded their secret.

When they fell in love, Spencer was forty-one and Kate was thirty-three, and each brought a boxcar load of emotional baggage to the relationship. Already married once, Kate also had had passionate, long-running affairs with superagent Leland Hayward and Howard Hughes, among others. Spencer, a raging alcoholic unable to cope with his son's deafness, had already numbered among his extramarital conquests such screen legends as Joan Crawford, Myrna Loy, Loretta Young, and Ingrid Bergman. There would be more—even after he had met Kate.

In the end, Kate and Spencer were everything and nothing like we imagined them to be. Tracy was the antithesis of his Father Flanagan persona: brilliant but tortured, unfathomably complex. Hepburn, shaped by crushing personal tragedies, a string of famous lovers behind her, emerged with the strength to overcome her demons—and fought to vanquish his.

Hepburn and Tracy may not have starred in the film of the same name, but theirs was certainly "an affair to remember." When Garson Kanin published a collection of warm reminiscences about his close friends Kate and Spencer, he stressed that he had not written a complete biography of the remarkable couple—and that he hoped someday someone would. In painting the first full, uncompromising portrait of Hepburn and Tracy, I drew on my numerous and lengthy conversations with Kate that began in 1976. There were also the hundreds of people I interviewed over the years who offered priceless memories: Kate's sister Marion, her secretary-companion, Phyllis Wilbourn, Tracy's only daughter, Susie, Lauren Bacall, Laurence Olivier, James Stewart, Bette Davis, Henry Fonda, Ginger Rogers, Jane Fonda, Angela Lansbury, Joan Fontaine, legendary filmmakers Joseph Mankiewicz (*Woman of the Year, Suddenly Last Summer*), Stanley Kramer (*Inherit the Wind, Judgment at Nuremberg, Guess Who's Coming to Dinner*), Sam Spiegel (*The African Queen*), and Joseph E. Levine (*The Lion in Winter*)—to name only a few. What emerged was a story as exhilarating as it was poignant: a romance carried on in the shadows and shrouded in mystery, only now being pulled fully into the light.

To their admiring public Spencer Tracy and Katharine Hepburn were Everyman and Everywoman. By surviving one devastating crisis after another in private and with dignity, they proved they were that and much more. It began in the autumn of their lives and has lasted to this day: scripted by its actors, played out in the wings—a love story for the ages.

There was total, complete dedication. There was nothing that could happen that would interfere with their relationship or with him. Nothing, nothing, nothing.

—ALICE PALACHE JONES,
KATE'S LONGTIME FRIEND

Let's just say that where change was required, I adjusted.

—KATE

One

❧

Lying on the floor, her head resting on the down pillow she had brought in from her bedroom, Katharine Hepburn pulled the blind back, slid the patio door open a crack, and breathed in the California night air. In the tiny courtyard behind the house she could see the broad leaves of a banana tree casting eerie moonlight shadows. . . .

Stretched out next to her was Lobo, their amiable German shepherd–coyote mix with the floppy left ear and half-missing tail. Kate could hear Spencer Tracy breathing steadily now, deeply. Cautiously raising her head from the floor, she looked over to see Spencer on his bed, the covers pulled up to his neck. His eyes were closed, and the great barrel chest rose and fell in a steady rhythm. Despite the powerful sedative prescribed by his doctor, Spencer could not keep his agile, tortured mind from racing; it had always been so hard for him to surrender to sleep. So there they lay talking night after night–he propped up in the narrow bed positioned just a step or two from the bathroom, she lying on a thick, brightly colored quilt spread out on the hardwood floor.

That night of June 9, 1967, it was Kate who did all the talking as she gently stroked Lobo: about friends and family and food and gardening and the work they had just done on *Guess Who's Coming to Dinner*. Even more restless than usual, Spencer tossed and turned interminably. When she paused for only a moment, he urged her to go on. Even Hepburn's friend Tallulah Bankhead, famous for her own whiskey contralto, conceded that Kate's voice sounded like "nickels dropping in a slot machine." But Tracy found her distinctive Connecticut Yankee clip oddly soothing.

Now that he was asleep, Kate rose slowly, deliberately, to her feet. She tucked her goose down pillow under one arm and gathered up the quilt. Checking one more time to make sure the call button he used to summon her was close at hand on the nightstand, she picked up the emergency buzzer and tiptoed out of the room, Lobo and the buzzer's black cord trailing behind her. For days now this unwieldy, snakelike contraption had been their lifeline; whether she was in the kitchen making her favorite chocolate brownies or out in the garden, Kate carried the buzzer with her everywhere.

In the sparsely furnished maid's room just off the kitchen down the hall, Kate slipped into bed and quickly drifted off. Hours later a noise awakened her: not Spencer's buzzer but the sound of someone shuffling past her door and down the hall. It was Spence, she thought, headed for the kitchen to pour himself some tea from the kettle they kept simmering on the stove. She checked the alarm clock by her bedstead. It was 3:00 A.M. Kate pulled on her robe and slippers and made her way toward the kitchen.

She was steps from the kitchen when she heard it: the teacup shattering, then an ominous thud. *Spencer.* She pushed the swinging door open and saw him there, sprawled on his back, eyes shut, his red flannel pajamas soaked with hot tea. She knelt down and felt for a pulse. Nothing. "He never knew what happened," she thought as she crouched there on the kitchen floor, cradling him in her arms. "Dear, dear friend—gone. Oh, lucky one. That's the way to exit . . . gone. And never coming back . . ."

Even with the love of her life lying dead in her arms, Kate did not allow herself to indulge in grief or self-pity. She did what she had always done at times like these: She sprang into action. Unable to move him herself, Kate brought a small rug in from the living room and somehow slid it under Spencer's body. Then she got on the phone. Within minutes she had called for moral support her devoted secretary and companion, Phyllis Wilbourn, who lived nearby. She phoned the doctor, Mitchell Covel, then to help move the body, Ida and Willie Gheczy, the husband-and-wife housekeeper and gardener from next door. They carried Tracy into his bedroom and placed him gently on the bed. Kate lit candles and allowed herself only a brief moment to study his craggy face in repose. It struck her how in life Spencer had never looked serene, not even while sleeping.

What was he going to be buried in? someone asked. Kate pulled his favorite old brown tweed jacket and gray slacks out of the closet and laid them out on a chair in the living room. When the men from the Cunningham and Walsh Funeral Home arrived, they would find everything in order.

Then, acting purely out of reflex, she ordered Phyllis to help her gather her things and load them into Tracy's black Thunderbird. They frantically yanked all of Hepburn's clothes from the closets, cleaned out the dresser drawers, and emptied the bathroom cabinets. It was Spencer Tracy who rented this cottage on the grounds of George Cukor's Beverly Hills estate, and by the time the press learned of Spencer's death, there would be no trace of evidence that Kate had ever even visited—much less resided on—the premises. This was the classic *Back Street* life they had chosen to share for more than twenty-six years, traveling separately, staying in separate hotels, never appearing together in public—all to protect Tracy's wife, Louise. There was no reason to change the rules now.

But wasn't there? The car was filled with her

belongings when Kate suddenly realized that the rules *had* changed. At that moment, as she looked at her slacks, shirts, toiletries, and mementos piled in the back seat and wondered to herself, "God, God, Kath. What are you doing?" Kate was overcome with shame and righteous indignation. She respected Spencer's Catholicism and the sense of guilt that had made it impossible for him to divorce Louise. But Kate was no longer willing to deny the part she had played in Spencer Tracy's life, and all he had meant to hers.

Back went the clothes, the personal items. She would not hide the reality of their life together from those who loved him, though the world at large was another matter. It would be years before she could speak openly to the press about their affair.

Before she called anyone else—Cukor, their dear friend Stanley Kramer (who had directed Tracy in *Inherit the Wind, Judgment at Nuremberg, It's a Mad, Mad, Mad, Mad World*, and his last film, *Guess Who's Coming to Dinner*), Spencer's brother Carroll, the Tracy children, John and Susie, or even Louise Tracy herself—she phoned Howard Strickling, MGM's publicity chief. He would know how to handle the nosy reporters. To be sure, in its front-page story on Spencer Tracy's death, *The New York Times* would report that he had died of a massive coronary at 6:00 A.M., that he was already dead by the time Carroll Tracy arrived with Dr. Covel, and that Louise and the children were next on the scene.

According to the Strickling-orchestrated coverage, it was 11:00 A.M. before Katharine Hepburn arrived with Cukor and Spencer's business manager, Ross Evans—and only then for the specific purpose of consoling the bereaved Mrs. Tracy.

Within two hours of Spencer's death the house had filled with family and friends. When Garson Kanin and his wife, actress Ruth Gordon, walked into the living room Kate, now dressed in her trademark pants and man's white shirt, rushed up and embraced him. "Oh, Gar," she said before he could utter a word of condolence, "I'm so sorry for *you*." Rejoining Phyllis in the kitchen, she resumed pouring coffee and serving people from platters heaped with bacon, eggs, and toast. Kate served Louise—a palpably awkward moment for both women—then watched as her man's widow moved slowly down the hallway toward the bedroom.

Three men from the Cunningham and Walsh Funeral Home arrived to remove the body. When Kate told them the clothes she had chosen for Spencer were already out in the living room, Louise was indignant. She was still his wife, she said, and she should be the one to decide what he would be buried in.

"Oh, Louise," Kate sighed, "what difference does it make?"

Yet the charade went on. For three nights, scores of friends and admirers made the pilgrimage to the funeral home to pay their respects. Each night after everyone had left, Kate dropped in through a rear door to "chat" with her love. One night she brought along a small still life of flowers that she had painted and slipped it into the coffin, beneath his feet. She wanted to place more mementos in the casket the night before the funeral—a small chunk of Carrara marble he had found on one of their outings, his rosary beads, a tiny statue of St. Christopher he carried on his travels—but when she tried to lift the coffin lid, it would not budge. The family had ordered it sealed.

Kate was determined not to embarrass Louise or the Tracy family by showing up at the funeral. Instead she and Phyllis drove down to the mortuary for one final good-bye. When they got there, preparations were already under way for the trip to the church. The two women asked if it was all right if they pitched in and then helped maneuver the coffin into the back of the hearse.

Then they got in their car and followed the cortege as it made its way down Melrose and eventually onto Santa Monica Boulevard. Ahead they could see the crowds gathered outside Immaculate Heart of Mary Church. One block short of the church Kate and Phyllis turned away for the short, sad journey home.

Although his queen was absent, the reigning king of motion-picture actors was given a royal send-off. The requiem low mass was said by Monsignor John O'Donnell, Tracy's technical advisor on the film *Boys Town*. Among the pallbearers: Kanin, Stanley Kramer, Jimmy Stewart,

John Ford, George Cukor, and Frank Sinatra. There were other show business legends—Jack Benny, James Cagney, George Burns, Jimmy Durante, Edward G. Robinson, and Gregory Peck, to name but a few—scattered throughout the crowd of six hundred mourners inside the church. There were also buddies from college and from Tracy's polo-playing days, a United States senator, and a Supreme Court justice.

During the mass one of the mourners was so overcome that he lurched from his pew and sprawled in the aisle. "Then the poor guy scrambled back into his seat," Kramer recalled. "Spence would have liked that. It could have been a scene from *It's a Mad, Mad, Mad, Mad World.*"

Howard Strickling's role in this particular production provided another touch of irony. The MGM public relations wizard, who for twenty-seven years had so masterfully kept the Hepburn-Tracy Affair out of the newspapers, was the bereaved widow's official escort. Still, Strickling could not take all the credit. Indeed, it was out of a genuine affection and respect for all the parties involved that the Hollywood press corps simply left Hepburn and Tracy alone.

After the body had been interred at Forest Lawn Cemetery, those who were closest to Spencer went straight to the house to offer their condolences to the woman they *truly* regarded as his closest of kin: Kate. "She was devastated, completely numb," Kramer recalled. "She took it *very* hard. I remember Vincente Minnelli, who could always be counted on to make them laugh with his stories about who was sleeping with who, sitting quietly next to her, just totally silent. Nobody knew what to say. Did she ever break down? No, not Kate. That was not her style. But you could see this lost look in those incredible eyes. She knew he had been very, very sick. We all knew it. But still it had taken her by surprise. She was not ready for him to leave. Her heart was broken. It was a sad, sad thing to see."

The next day Kate returned to the refuge of Fenwick, her family's estate on the Connecticut shore of Long Island Sound. For Hepburn, this had been a rare time of quiet introspection. Doubts about the path she and Spencer had chosen now bubbled to the surface in a way they never had when he was alive. "It taught me a lesson," she later conceded. "One must figure out how much you care about this or that. Then put up a fight. Or don't . . . I think now I took the easy road."

One of the things that most upset Kate was the fact that she had never gotten to know John and Susie with their father. After only a few days she took the sort of unilateral step she could never have taken while Spencer was alive. She called Louise and suggested that they try to become friends. "I might be a help with the kids," Kate suggested.

"Well, yes. But you see," Louise replied, "I thought you were only a rumor. . . ."

I was totally unaware that we were the second-rate sex.

—KATE

Her

Two

⚜

*He was sturdily built and full-faced, with freckles, red-*dish brown hair that would eventually turn white, and what Kate Hepburn liked to call a "real man's neck—a bull neck." She was tall and slim, with ramrod-straight posture and the high, aristocratic cheekbones to go with it. Her face was also splashed with freckles, and she wore her reddish auburn hair piled on top of her head. He was stolid, no-nonsense, sometimes brusque— unquestionably a man of intelligence who was nonetheless given to few extraneous words and no pretenses. She was haughty, demanding, lo- quacious, and at times, shrill. He never walked when he could stand or stand when he could sit. She seemed to be in a state of perpetual motion, a mind-spinning blur of ceaseless activity.

Indeed, Dr. Thomas Norval Hepburn and his wife Katharine Houghton were strong-willed, brilliant, and equally matched. Their forty-seven- year marriage, which ended only with Katharine

Houghton's death in 1951, served as their eldest daughter's model for a male-female relationship. Katharine Hepburn aspired to be like her protean mother, and wound up loving a man who in many if not all ways strongly resembled her father.

"The physical resemblance between Dr. Hepburn and Spencer Tracy was striking," said author Cleveland Amory, who dated Kate's sister Peggy and first got to know the Hepburn family in the 1920s. "But more than that, Dr. Hepburn had a patriarchal presence, a sense of power and authority that Tracy also projected. It was obvious to everyone that all the Hepburn women worshiped Dr. Tom, but no one more than Kate. And even though Spencer Tracy was an infinitely more complicated man, she saw a great deal of her father in Spencer. Otherwise I doubt if she could have respected him."

"The single most important thing anyone needs to know about me," Kate Hepburn said, "is that I am totally, completely the product of two damn fascinating individuals who happened to be my parents. I've had a pretty remarkable life, but compared to my mother and father, I'm *dull*."

Anything but. To paraphrase Winston Churchill, Kate Hepburn could be described as an elitist inside a rebel wrapped in an icon. Her complex, often self-contradictory personality was not an aberration, but a logical reflection of the other, equally complex personalities that preceded her. "Kate sprang," a friend once observed, "from the deep end of the gene pool."

Kate and her five siblings were all given their mother's maiden name, Houghton, as a middle name, forever reminding them of their link to one of the nation's most powerful dynasties. "The Houghtons were really something," Kate liked to say, "and Mother was a Houghton." The Houghtons founded (and continue to run) the multibillion-dollar Corning Glass Company and started Houghton Mifflin publishing. Houghtons have been elected to Congress and served as ambassadors to Britain, Germany, and France. At Harvard the family-endowed Houghton Library houses one of the world's foremost collections of manuscripts and rare books.

Descended from Normans who invaded England with William the Conqueror in 1066, Kate's great-great-great-great-grandfather journeyed to the New World toward the end of the seventeenth century. Her great-great-great-grandfather was a soldier in George Washington's Continental Army, and his son Rufus struggled to make a life for himself as a farmer in Bolton, Massachusetts. It was there that Rufus and his wife, Abigail Barnard, raised thirteen children—including Amory, who would not only pull the Houghtons out of poverty but lay the groundwork for the far-flung family empire.

Starting off as an apprentice carpenter, Amory borrowed three hundred dollars to start his own businesses as a builder and contractor in 1833. A

century later his great-granddaughter would in-
furiate directors by insisting on doing her own
stunts—a streak of derring-do perhaps inherited
from Amory. To pay off his debts, he worked
like a man possessed—balancing on rooftops,
hoisting beams, even working by lantern light
into the night—while his creditors fretted that he
would be killed before he could repay them.

By the time he was twenty-three, Amory had
paid off his creditors and had the then-impressive
sum of three thousand dollars left over—enough
to marry Sophronia Oakes, the daughter of a
Cambridge store owner, and start a family of his
own. From the outset their eldest child, Amory Jr.,
was groomed for business—first shipped off to
a Spartan, "character-building" boarding school
in Ellington, Connecticut, and then apprenticed
to Lawson Valentine, America's leading manufacturer of paints, oils, and varnishes. His
younger siblings—Charles, Kate, Alfred, Annie,
and Nellie—all spent their lives in Amory Jr.'s
looming shadow.

Great-Grandfather Amory, meanwhile, was no
longer satisfied with being Cambridge's leading
builder. He rented a wharf on the Charles River
across from Boston and began selling wood, hay,
cement, lime, and coal. The Houghtons' import-
export business flourished, but after fifteen years,
Amory Sr. was eager to tackle a new challenge.
It was then that he met Gaffer Teasdale, an affable British glass factory manager who convinced him to liquidate his existing business and,

in the fall of 1852, start up the Union Glass Company in the Boston suburb of Somerville.

It seemed a daring gamble, but one that paid off handsomely when the Civil War created a seemingly insatiable demand for lanterns, bottles, glass tubing, and other medical supplies. It was not long before Amory had his eye on another prize. In 1864 he sold Union Glass and used the proceeds to buy out the Brooklyn Flint Glass Company of Brooklyn, New York, with himself and Amory Jr. as principal stockholders.

The Houghtons' dream of becoming America's leading glass manufacturer seemed to go up in smoke—literally—when a fire ripped through Brooklyn Flint Glass's main factory building shortly before Christmas 1867. Undaunted, Amory relocated to the town of Corning some three hundred miles to the northwest. Three years later, facing labor and supply problems, Amory Sr. again faced ruin. Corning was forced into receivership in September 1870 only days after filling a thousand-dollar order from President Ulysses S. Grant for White House stemware.

Amory Sr., having suffered one blow too many, retired to a farm in Westchester County. It was now up to thirty-four-year-old Amory Jr., asked by the new plant owners to stay on and run the company, to get Corning Flint Glass back on its feet. He succeeded—brilliantly—and was able to buy back the company before he turned forty.

With his broad face, white beard, and piercing

blue eyes, Amory Sr. bore a strong resemblance to another business titan of the time—Andrew Carnegie. And tall, bearlike Amory Jr. was, with the exception of his round, wire-rimmed spectacles, a virtual replica of his father.

Not so Amory Jr.'s youngest brother, Alfred, whose granddaughter was to gain worldwide fame as an actress. Timid and frail by comparison to his robust siblings, Kate Hepburn's grandfather utterly lacked the drive that Amory Jr. and to a lesser extent Charles had inherited from their father. Alfred, whose moodswings and prolonged periods of listlessness were chalked up to an artistic temperament, had no interest in the family business. He preferred instead to remain in his room, playing the violin and reading poetry. Fearful to the point of paranoia, he locked his bedroom door before going to bed, then made a ritual of checking under the bed and inside closets for bogeymen.

Since neither Amory Jr. nor Charles had gone to college, Amory Sr. had been determined that at least one of his sons would attend Harvard, the most prestigious institution of higher learning. Alfred was the designate scholar. But at the end of his freshman year in 1870 Alfred's academic career was cut short when his father's company went bankrupt. Dragooned into working at Corning, the chronically late Alfred lasted a matter of months before being sacked by his own brother.

Alfred moved back to Brooklyn and in 1872

married Olive ("Ollie") Chestnutwood, nineteen, a family friend whose fragile nature seemed to mirror his own. She gave birth to a daughter, Mary, on August 25, 1873, but never recovered from the strain. Ollie died eight weeks later.

Devastated, Alfred and his infant daughter moved in with Ollie's mother. His brother-in-law John Linen, president of the prosperous Buffalo Scale Company, took Alfred under his wing. Unlike Amory Jr., Linen was a pillar of support and friendly encouragement. By the time Alfred married nineteen-year-old Caroline ("Carrie") Garlinghouse in 1876 and settled on a seven-acre farm just south of Buffalo in West Hamburg, he was already well on the road to becoming Linen's heir apparent.

Alfred, who today might well have been diagnosed as a clinical manic depressive, still experienced the occasional anxiety attack. But thanks to the expansive, upbeat Carrie, he no longer wallowed in his misery. When the "black spells" threatened to overtake Alfred, she forced him to get out of bed and face the world. If nothing else worked, she retrieved his violin from its carrying case, thrust it in his arms, and commanded him to play. Carrie then accompanied him on the piano until the black cloud of depression passed.

Amory Houghton, meanwhile, was savoring the fruits of his success. He paid ten thousand dollars for a neo-Gothic stone manor house occupying an entire Corning city block. He moved in on February 2, 1878, the same day Katharine Houghton was born to Carrie and Alfred. Edith arrived a year later, followed by Marion in 1884.

All three Houghton daughters were strikingly pretty—not that it mattered much to their mother. Exceptionally bright and articulate, Carrie had nonetheless been expressly forbidden by her father to attend college. She did not let that stop her from becoming one of West Hamburg's most outspoken and, by definition, controversial characters. A firm believer in women having their political say, she started one of New York State's first "social discussion" clubs in her front parlor. Conducted in the afternoons because it was thought women should not venture outside after nightfall, these gatherings gave women the chance to keep abreast of events of the day— from the collapse of the Ottoman Empire to the Haymarket Riot in Chicago. Not surprisingly, such meetings were widely regarded as nothing short of seditious.

Alfred admired his wife's freethinking spirit and actually had some heretical notions of his own. In stark contrast with his devoutly Episcopalian brothers, Alfred not only rejected organized religion altogether but became an outspoken atheist.

While Amory's engineers and technicians worked with Thomas Edison on the design for the first electric lamp (Corning soon became the world's leading manufacturer of lightbulbs), Carrie and her daughters remained steadfastly unimpressed. Alfred was doing quite nicely at Buffalo Scale—well enough to afford several servants, and private tutors for the girls. She was careful not to advertise her intentions, but Carrie was determined that Kathy, Edith, and Marion would get the college education she had been denied.

Yet Kathy was only ten years old when her privileged world began to unravel. Within the span of four years, four of her cousins died in infancy, casting a shadow over the entire Houghton clan. In February 1892 Aunt Annie, Alfred's sister, died in childbirth. It did not help that her own father often talked openly of death and, more specifically, about what it might be like to take one's life.

To make matters worse, Alfred's beloved mentor and surrogate father, John Linen, fell seriously ill in early September 1892, leaving Alfred in charge of Buffalo Scale. The burden proved too much for the emotionally fragile Alfred. By October 1892 Katharine Hepburn's grandfather, unable to cope with the added responsibility, had suffered a nervous breakdown.

Carrie's solace did not work this time, and soon a palpable sense of dread permeated the Alfred Houghton household. There was nowhere left to turn but to Corning. Reluctantly, Carrie encouraged Alfred to accept his brother's invitation to recuperate at the Houghton mansion on Third Street. Instead of merely dispatching one of his carriages to pick up his brother, Amory showed the depth of his concern by making the five-hour-long carriage ride to Buffalo and personally escorting Alfred back to Corning. There he remained in an upstairs bedroom, under strict doctor's orders to do nothing but rest. For two weeks, as visitors marched in and out as part of a well-intentioned campaign to buoy his spirits, Alfred seldom stirred from the oversize canopied bed.

Amory and the other family members felt no less helpless than Carrie when suddenly Alfred emerged from his room. Looking rejuvenated, he asked Amory to summon their sister Nellie. For days she had been trying without success to convince him to accompany her on a carriage ride through town. Now, for whatever reason, he wished to take Nellie up on her offer. They rode through the streets of Corning for two hours, then returned to the Third Street mansion, where Nellie dropped Alfred off at Amory's front steps. She waved back at her brother as her carriage pulled away. As Nellie watched him walk toward the front door, she was confident that the worst was over—that, for the time being at least, the crisis had passed.

She was wrong. Apparently Alfred did not actually go into the house but waited until Nellie's carriage had pulled out of sight to set out on his own, this time on foot. When Alfred did not return by dinner, search parties were dispatched and, according to the *Corning Weekly Journal*, "scoured the city and vicinity during the night."

The search parties found nothing, but Fall Brook, New York, railroad man Ira Miller did. Shortly after dawn on October 29, 1893, Miller was helping run a boxcar through Walker's Lumberyard to Denison's warehouse. Walker's Lumberyard was just west of the Chemung River, only two or three blocks from the Corning glassworks where Amory ruled his workforce with an iron hand.

As the boxcar rolled slowly through the lumberyard, Miller spotted Alfred sprawled faceup on a pile of two-by-fours. Blood oozed from a pistol shot through Alfred's right temple. A revolver was still clenched in his right hand.

Nothing could have prepared Carrie Houghton or her daughters for the telegram that arrived later saying that Alfred had been found, an apparent suicide. The body, the telegram continued, had been taken to Fletcher & Cook's undertaking establishment pending instructions from the family of the deceased.

That same Saturday afternoon, at precisely 5:03, the Lackawanna express train carrying Alfred's body departed Corning for Buffalo. Resisting pressure from Amory and the rest of the family to inter Alfred alongside his first wife, Ollie, in an Episcopal ceremony, Carrie had him buried in a different cemetery altogether—and, in keeping with his atheist beliefs, without clergy.

The stigma attached to suicide was perhaps never greater than during the late nineteenth century, when it was deemed not only an unpardonable sin but a probable sign of insanity—a form of mental illness, it was widely presumed, that ran in one's family. But given the Houghtons' status and power, the press was uncharacteristically restrained in its coverage of the event. In Buffalo only one paper carried the story. A brief account ran beneath the headline A.A HOUGHTON SHOOTS HIMSELF—ONE OF THE OWNERS OF THE BUFFALO SCALE WORKS KILLS HIMSELF IN A FIT OF DESPONDENCY.

Alfred's suicide filled his widow with anger. Carrie blamed her overbearing brother-in-law for somehow pushing Alfred over the brink, and herself for having sent Alfred to Amory in the first place. Yet she could not wallow in self-pity. Having opted out of the glassworks at an early stage, Alfred had managed to amass only a modest estate by the time of his death. If Carrie was going to raise her three daughters in some degree of comfort, she would have to swallow her pride, sell off her assets—right down to the furniture—and allow Amory to invest the proceeds. In return Carrie listened dutifully to her brother-in-law's pious admonitions and interminable lectures.

She would not, however, back down on the promise she had made to herself that her daughters would be the first women of their generation to go to college. Carrie was intrigued by the new Bryn Mawr College for women and particularly by its visionary young president, M. Carey Thomas.

Wealthy Quaker physician Joseph Wright Taylor founded Bryn Mawr as "a place for the advanced education of our young female Friends, affording them all the advantages of a college education which are so freely offered to young men." Yet when Carey Thomas, fresh from earning her doctorate in German philology summa cum laude at the University of Zurich, asked to become Bryn Mawr's first president, the Board of Trustees chose a man instead. They did, however, agree to hire the persistent Thomas as Bryn Mawr's first dean of the faculty.

It was nine years before Thomas ascended to the presidency, but during this time she shaped Bryn Mawr's reputation for academic excellence. Thomas insisted that entrance exams be as tough as those administered at Harvard and Yale, and made no concessions to traditional "female" subjects like domestic science. Boasting a young history professor named Woodrow Wilson on its first faculty, Bryn Mawr became the first women's college to offer a Ph.D.

Carrie believed her daughters were destined to attend Bryn Mawr. But she was also concerned that, if they continued to be tutored at home in Buffalo, they would be ill prepared for the college's famously stringent entrance exams. Her solution was to enroll Kathy and her sisters in the Baldwin School, situated only steps away from the Bryn Mawr campus. Baldwin's singular purpose: to prepare students for the Bryn Mawr entrance exams.

Over Amory's vocal objections, Carrie rented a small house for herself and the girls in Bryn Mawr. She looked forward to the prospect of starting a new life in Pennsylvania and escaping the all-pervasive influence of Uncle Amory. But that summer, scarcely eight months after her husband's death, Carrie was dealt another horrible blow. At first she chalked up the stabbing pains in her abdomen to stress. When she finally did see a doctor, it was too late. His diagnosis: inoperable stomach cancer.

Typically, Carrie's first thoughts were not for herself but for her children. She drew up a will that named Amory and her brother Fred Garlinghouse as a joint executors of her estate, with the proviso that—just as she had planned—Kathy, Edith, and Marion not live with relatives but instead move into the house she had rented for them in Bryn Mawr. Carrie even arranged for the services of a housekeeper who would care for the girls while they attended Baldwin in preparation for entering Bryn Mawr.

In the end Carrie realized that if her plan were to be implemented, sixteen-year-old Kathy would have to outwit her onerous uncle Amory. In August 1894 Carrie asked Kathy to take a walk with her on the wooded grounds of the sanitarium in Hornellsville, New York, where she was being treated. Carrie reminded her eldest daughter that it was her duty not only to attend Bryn Mawr but to make certain that Edith and Marion went there too. "You must all get an education," she said. "You'll have some money, but not as much as the rest of the family. *Don't be drowned by the rich relatives.* Keep your independence. Be your own person, and never, never be afraid of anything."

On September 2 Kathy, Edith, and Marion sat at their mother's bedside as she slipped away. Now it was up to Kathy to fulfill Carrie's dream for her daughters. "All three girls viewed their mother's last wish as sacrosanct," Kathy's own actress daughter Katharine Hepburn said years later. "It was more of a command than a wish, and they were headstrong enough to stand up to their uncle and win."

Toward that end Carrie was careful not to appoint Amory—or, for that matter, anyone—to be Kathy's legal guardian. It scarcely mattered to Amory. Now with a reputation for ruthlessness that was rivaling the robber baron likes of Henry Clay Frick and John D. Rockefeller, Kathy's uncle was accustomed to getting his way. He promptly dismissed many of the will's provisions as impractical, canceled plans for the girls to move to Bryn Mawr, and ordered them to live with Carrie's cousins Mack and Nettie Smith in Canandaigua, a town in upstate New York's Finger Lakes district.

"Uncle can run a big factory," Kathy told her sisters, "but he can't run *me*." Her plan: to make her relatives *want* to get rid of them. The girls shared a bedroom directly above the Smiths' parlor. Each night after they had gone to bed, Kathy stood guard at the door while Edith and Marion pounded on the floor with their hands. Mack Smith would then bound up the stairs to find the three young women sitting primly in their room, listening as Kathy read to them.

After two weeks of this the Smiths shipped the Houghton sisters back to Corning. Uncle Amory tried to get himself appointed Kathy's legal guardian, but again she outmaneuvered him. A court date was set, and when the judge went through the "formality" of asking Kathy to choose a guardian, she produced a handsome young attorney—not just any lawyer, but one with a local reputation as both a crusader for women's education and a notorious ladies' man. Faced with such an objectionable choice, Amory relented. In exchange for her agreeing to his becoming her guardian, Amory would permit Kathy to fulfill her mother's dying wish. The following September, Kate Hepburn's mother enrolled in Bryn Mawr.

"They said Mother had the longest neck, the tightest collar, and the smallest waist of anyone at Bryn Mawr," Kate recalled. She also shared Carrie Houghton's admiration for the school's guiding spirit. "Mother was influenced greatly by Carey Thomas," Kate said. "All the women of her generation idolized her. And they were right to."

Unlike Edith, who followed her sister to Bryn

Mawr, Kathy Houghton was far from a model student. She scandalized Bryn Mawr's staid residents by galloping down Main Street at night astride and not sidesaddle, the only socially acceptable way for a lady to ride horseback in the 1890s. Defying a campus rule against smoking—something respectable young women simply did not do—Kathy and her friends would steal away to a nearby cemetery and sneak cigarettes.

Part of Katharine's appeal as a campus rebel was derived from her status as a Houghton. Although she had always been a thorn in Uncle Amory's side, Kathy told anyone who would listen that she was from the family that owned and ran the famous Corning glassworks. There was nowhere to hide, then, when newspaper headlines blared the news of another tragic death in the family. On March 29, 1897, Kathy's other Houghton uncle—Amory's surviving brother, Charlie—was found dead in the sand shed at the Glassworks, the victim of a self-inflicted gunshot wound to the temple.

The suicide, eerily similar to Alfred's, was cause again for speculation that some form of insanity might run in the family. For her part, Kathy abruptly stopped rebelling and concentrated on her studies. Still, when she graduated in 1900 with a degree in history and political science, Kathy did not conceal her desire to shake things up. In the Bryn Mawr yearbook she stated her main postgraduate goal succinctly: "To raise Hell with established customs."

Kathy went on to earn an advanced degree at Radcliffe and then to tour Paris for a year before returning to the United States in 1901. While visiting Baltimore, where the brilliant Edith was in her second year at Johns Hopkins Medical School, Kathy was introduced to Edith's fencing partner, a husky, redheaded Virginian named Tom Hepburn. "Boy, that's for me," she told Edith once he was out of earshot. "He's the most beautiful creature I've ever seen." It didn't matter that Hepburn was dirt poor. "I'd marry him," Kathy said, "even if it meant I'd die in a year— *and* go to hell!"

The object of Kathy's affection was actually born Norval Thomas Hepbron (pronounced Hebron) on December 18, 1879. When he was two, his father adopted the Hepburn form of the family surname; it was not until he reached Johns Hopkins that Tom took it upon himself to make another adjustment, switching the Norval and the Thomas.

The dashing young medical student with the gentle Virginia accent was nearly two years younger than Kathy. But he had the self-assured bearing of a man twice his age. "It was the whole package Mother fell in love with," Kate recalled. "From the beginning there was no question in her mind that he was the one and that he'd come first." Kathy moved into her sister's apartment and took a job teaching at Baltimore's exclusive Calvert School. "Mother," Kate said, "was determined to get to know this Hepburn fellow."

To be sure, the Hepburns were as poverty-stricken as the Houghtons were rich. They could, however, trace their genealogy back to sixteenth-century Scotland and James Hepburn, fourth Earl of Bothwell and third husband of Mary, Queen of Scots. (Kate Hepburn was to play the doomed queen opposite Fredric March as her ancestor in John Ford's 1936 screen version of *Mary of Scotland*.)

Tom's father, Sewell Stavely Hepburn, had migrated from Missouri to Virginia's Hanover County in 1860. He was studying at Virginia Theological Seminary in Alexandria when he met Selina Lloyd Powell, one of the Richmond Powells. Both slaveholding families, the Hepburns and the Powells had lost everything in the Civil War.

After they had married in 1871, Sewell Hepburn took the respectable, if low-paying, position of rector in St. Paul's Episcopal parish. Selena supplemented their income by taking in boarders.

"My grandfather was a country preacher," Kate Hepburn later recalled. "A simple man with a very simple philosophy of life." Tall and bony with a bushy mustache and gold-rimmed spectacles, "Parson Hep" rode throughout Hanover County on horseback, spreading the gospel to black as well as white congregations in the segregated region. When the county's only physician, a Dr. Macon, died, Parson Hep was left to take his place. A sort of nineteenth-century paramedic, he bandaged wounds, treated fevers, and even pulled teeth.

Not surprisingly, Parson Hep wanted the youngest of his five children to follow in his footsteps. By the time he was a young man, Tom was outspokenly critical of all organized religion. But he did want to emulate his father, not as a cleric but as a healer.

After graduating from Virginia's Randolph-Macon College in 1900, Tom headed for Johns Hopkins—and the headstrong Miss Houghton. For whatever reasons, the normally affable Tom was tongue-tied. After innumerable teas and walks in the park, Tom had still not made his move. "He's more of a sitter," Kathy complained to Edith, "than a suitor."

Finally she confronted Tom. "The best thing about our relationship," Kathy told him almost matter-of-factly, "is that whenever one of us marries it won't hurt the relationship at all."

"How can you say such a thing?" he shot back. "I'll never marry anyone if I don't marry you!"

Amory Houghton grudgingly gave his blessing, though he made no effort to conceal his growing resentment toward his independent-minded niece. "My opinion of you," he wrote to her on February 4, 1904, "is the same as it always has been—that you are an extravagant, deceitful, dishonest, worthless person. . . . When you see Tom, please tell him I do not think he could do worse."

On June 6, 1904, Uncle Amory, limping from

a persistent case of gout, gave Kathy away in a small ceremony conducted by Parson Hep in Baltimore. The bride, always eager to flout convention, dressed her bridesmaids in white. She wore black.

"How goddamn lucky I was," Kate Hepburn later said, "to be dealt that pair out of the shuffle." Leading up to Tom's brief surgical fellowship at the University of Heidelberg, the newlyweds made a whirlwind tour of Europe. On their return to the United States, Tom and Katharine Houghton Hepburn (as she insisted on being known) mulled their options. "Dad had been a brilliant student and now he had a wonderful future ahead of him," Kate said. "He could have gone anywhere, but he did not want to function in Baltimore because he hated the thought of having family—namely my mother's sisters—around. And he didn't want to function in New York or Boston because he liked to live in the country, and both he and Mother wanted a big family. . . ."

Indeed Kathy was already four months pregnant when they moved to Connecticut, where Tom began his internship at Hartford Hospital. They moved into a thirty-dollar-a-month apartment directly across the street from the doctors' entrance—which proved especially convenient when, on the morning of November 8, 1905, Kathy gave birth to Thomas Houghton Hepburn.

Some seventeen months later, on May 12, 1907, Kathy gave birth to the couple's second child and first daughter. Since the firstborn boy was named after his father, it seemed only fitting that the firstborn daughter be named after her mother. Little Tom had her dark eyes and hair, so Katharine hoped their little girl would have her father's coloring. "Hold her up to the window," she instructed the nurse. "Hold her up to the light so I can see. . . . Yes, it's red." Dad called her Redtop. To her brothers she was Kathy, Kath, or Kat, and to her sisters, Catty. The rest of the world would come to know her best as Kate.

Kate would recall the unique environment that shaped her early life: "Some people are New York or London or—God help them—Los Angeles. I am Hartford." As soon as he completed his residency, Tom moved his family into the section of Hartford known as Nook Farm. The intellectual and artistic heart of the city, Nook Farm had numbered among its celebrated residents Harriet Beecher Stowe and Samuel Clemens (Mark Twain). Twain, who published *The Prince and the Pauper, A Connecticut Yankee in King Arthur's Court, Tom Sawyer*, and *The Adventures of Huckleberry Finn* during his thirty-one years at Nook Farm, had grown especially close to his neighbor, *Hartford Courant* editor Charles Dudley Warner. The two even collaborated on Twain's first work of fiction, *The Gilded Age*. Shortly after Warner died in 1900, Twain sold his turreted mansion to the president of the Hartford Fire Insurance Company and moved to New York.

Kate was less than a year old when the Hepburns bought and moved into the Warner house at 133 Hawthorn Street. A gravel drive wound up to the three-story red-brick Victorian Gothic "cottage," with its three gables bordered in lacy black trim. Surrounded by two wooded acres and bordered on the south by a brook, the grounds were dotted with tiger lilies and daffodils. There was a doghouse with a shingle roof, and a wooden garden swing. Off the front parlor was a plant-filled glass conservatory with a domed ceiling.

It was in this storybook setting that Kate Hepburn lived until the age of ten. What she would most vividly recall about the house were the words Charles Dudley Warner had inscribed over the mantel in the study: "Listen to the song of life." "I saw that every day for as long as I can remember," Kate recalled. "First, when I was maybe four or five, I'd stare at it and stare at it and ask Mother and Dad over and over again what it meant. It got to be a joke. Then it hit me: Oh, *that's* what it means! We all believed that was the only way to live. From the moment she set foot in that house, Mother knew this was a perfect place for her to raise her family. And that's all she wanted to do with the rest of her life. At least, that's what Mother *thought*."

It had taken only a few months for Tom Hepburn—"Hep" to his colleagues at the hospital—to find a cause. The young doctor was stunned to find how many young men and women were coming to him with symptoms of venereal disease. In one of the most poignant cases a leading businessman had contracted syphilis during a bachelor party at a local brothel and transmitted the disease to his socially prominent bride. She in turn passed the disease on to their baby. All three eventually died.

Nationally, deaths from venereal disease ran into the tens of thousands, with an equal number of "survivors" of syphilitic infection living out their lives in Dickensian asylums. "Dad was absolutely stunned to learn," Kate later said, "that Hartford was the center of the white slave trade on the East Coast. There were endless houses of prostitution in tenements that turned out to be owned by some of Hartford's 'best' families."

Holding to the myth that syphilis and gonorrhea were diseases of the lower classes, doctors basically disregarded the problem. Sulfa drugs were still years away, but patients were not even told that the use of condoms could largely prevent sexually transmitted diseases. "Venereal disease was not exactly considered a polite topic," Kate said. "This was something you just did not talk about, period. The medical profession thought it was best ignored. Daddy felt otherwise."

Backed by only a few of his associates at the hospital, Hep launched a public information campaign, persuading the esteemed president emeritus of Harvard University, Charles Eliot, to head his newly formed (and blandly named) American Social Hygiene Association.

There were other reasons for Dr. Hepburn's passionate desire to warn the growing population of the venereal disease menace, reasons he shared with no one, not even his wife. In Virginia his own brothers Lloyd and Charles had contracted gonorrhea after visits to prostitutes; his other brother, Sewell, was to suffer his entire adult life from the effects of syphilis.

Not long after, Mrs. Hepburn reached a turning point of her own. "So there was Mother walking around the streets of Hartford holding on to my brother Tom with one hand and pushing me in my pram with the other, and suddenly it hit her: 'Yes, this is all very nice. But is this *it*? Is this what I am going to do with the rest of my life?'"

Practically overnight Katharine Houghton Hepburn transformed herself from proper matron to firebrand suffragette. Prodded by her activist sister Edith, who had set up a home for unwed mothers in Baltimore and was convinced a nation run by men would never address the problems of women, Katharine was elected president of the Connecticut Women's Suffrage Association. She led marches down New York's Fifth Avenue, wrote scathing letters to the editor, and organized rallies. The entire Hepburn clan joined in the cause. Hep sat on the floor and stenciled VOTES FOR WOMEN on posters. Tom, now five, and Kate, three, marched behind her, swathed in the white, purple and green colors of the movement, passing out leaflets and waving placards.

A third pregnancy scarcely interfered with Katharine's schedule. Richard Houghton Hepburn was born in 1911, and within six weeks Mother was back on the road with Tom, Kate, Dick, and the infant's nurse in tow. Robert Houghton Hepburn's arrival in 1913 did not interrupt his mother's plans to march on the White House. As President and Mrs. Wilson walked past, Katharine and six-year-old Kate waved their VOTES FOR WOMEN signs aloft. "Mrs. Wilson passed with a contemptuous sniff," recalled one of the demonstrators, "but the president lifted his hat and said, 'Good day, ladies.'" (Kate's sister Marion Houghton Hepburn was born in 1918, and Margaret ["Peggy"] Houghton Hepburn two years later).

At home in Hartford, Mother donned her "mandarin outfit"—a flowing silk Chinese tea robe embroidered with birds and flowers—and presided over a salon of freethinkers and radicals. The famous anarchist Emma Goldman was a frequent guest, and the rabble-rousing British suffragists Emmeline and Sylvia Pankhurst dropped by between prison stays. Katharine saw no contradiction in the fact that while she discussed ways to dismantle the established order, her family was tended to by a staff that included a maid, a cook, a housekeeper, and a nanny.

The majority of the Hepburns' neighbors were not amused. It was rumored that Tom and Kate were required to witness the births of their younger siblings. More accurately, when Kate was eight, her mother sat her down and described, with clinical precision, the sex act and its consequences. "Oh, then I don't need to be married to have a baby," Kate said. "Good!"

Over the years visitors to the Hepburn household commented on the family's casual attitude toward all bodily functions, including sex. Modesty was not the rule of the day. Guests were occasionally shocked to see Hepburn children of both sexes—as well as their parents—wandering about in various states of undress or completely nude. "Dad walked around naked. So did Mother," conceded Kate. "We all dressed together. We never thought anything about it."

But even as a young girl Kate was self-conscious about one thing: "I remembered listening to all the talk about nudity and false modesty and thinking to myself, Someday nobody is going to wear any clothes. I was totally freckled from head to foot, and nobody would want me." When she shared her concerns with Dr. Hepburn, he blurted, "Jesus Christ, Alexander the Great, and Leonardo da Vinci all had red hair and freckles, and they did all right!"

Hartford society hardly knew what to make of the raucous, uninhibited, decidedly nonconformist newcomers in their midst. "There was a group that thought Mother and Dad were great," Kate said, "and then there was a group that thought they were hotheads. They were both right."

Rocks were hurled through the Hepburns' windows late at night, and wherever Katharine went in Hartford she was treated like a pariah. Kate and her siblings grew up being shunned by the local children and picked on by neighborhood bullies. "Don't play with those Hepburn brats," their parents told them, and to a large extent they obeyed. As a result, Kate later conceded she "grew up with a little bit of a chip on my shoulder. What other people thought didn't concern us much anyway. Most people are raised to believe they are just as good as the next person. I was always told I was better."

Determined to maintain a united front against the onslaught of outside criticism, the Hepburns did not allow family infighting. Sibling rivalry was simply not tolerated, and whenever brothers and sisters fought they were punished—severely.

Indeed, despite their progressive leanings, the Hepburns were strict disciplinarians at home. Although corporal punishment was generally frowned upon among the upper classes following the turn of the century, it flourished at 133 Hawthorn. Kate boasted of having a "spanking dad. Were we spanked?" she asked. *"Beaten."*

Kate's parents set an example of civility, though there were infrequent lapses. They never argued about money or in-laws. Only politics. "You didn't cross Mother on that topic," Kate said. On several occasions she threw plates at the hapless Dr. Hepburn. Once during a particularly spirited debate, she tossed a pot of hot coffee at him. "She was in," Kate recalled of the incident, "a complete rage."

Kate grew up thinking the only things worth arguing about were the great issues of the day. "At the dinner table," she recalled, "every conceivable topic was discussed: venereal disease, prostitution, feminism, Marxism, Darwinism, Fabianism, even nudism. I really had a rather leftist upbringing. But no bunk was tolerated."

Nor were physical complaints of any kind. The Hepburns preached mind over matter at home. "Please, please just keep it to yourself," Kate was told whenever she felt under the weather. "Go to bed, go to sleep or something. Just go upstairs until you feel better. There's no need to make other people miserable now, is there?"

But there was no easy fix when, at the age of five, Tom was diagnosed as suffering from chorea, a nervous disorder more popularly known as St. Vitus' Dance. The ailment left Tom with a facial tic, making him the object of merciless teasing by his schoolmates. By virtue of the fact that they were born only eighteen months apart, Kate was understandably closest to Tom—and, among family members, the most sensitive to his plight.

Specialists treating Tom theorized that St. Vitus' Dance was aggravated by stress, and there was some suspicion that the condition might be inherited. In his mid-fifties the Reverend Sewell Stavely Hepburn, Tom's grandfather, had began to suffer hand tremors—"the shakes" he called them—which he controlled with a shot of whiskey. Later Parson Hep's head also began to tremble, an inherited disorder with which Kate would eventually have to cope. (Her grandfather's whiskey cure proved effective in stopping Kate's trembling. "The shakes stop if you drink enough," she said, "but then so does everything else.")

Rather than acknowledge some weakness in the family bloodline, Dr. Hepburn chalked up his son's twitching to a lack of willpower. The shaking would stop, he insisted, whenever Tom decided he really wanted it to.

At about the same time, the family was confronted with another medical crisis when four-year-old Kate was stricken with scarlet fever. Kate's temperature soared and her ears became painfully abscessed, but she pulled through. When a neighbor made the mistake of calling her "frail," Kate picked out an oak tree and ran straight into it to prove she was anything but.

Kate quickly proved herself the ultimate tomboy. "Being a girl was a torment for me," she remembered. Never quite sure how to handle his sensitive eldest son, Hep never had any such misgivings about Kate. To teach her how to ride a bicycle, he took her to the top of a hill and gave her a shove. "Paralyzed with fear" and "holding on to the handles for dear life," Kate careened toward an elderly man walking across the street at the base of the hill. "I was certain we'd crash. But he just smiled and caught me. I'd made it alive!"

At 133 Hawthorn Kate, not Tom, became the family's resident daredevil. She could, by her own account, "outdive, outswim, and outrun anybody." She would hang by her toes from a trapeze her father had rigged thirty feet above the gravel. An inveterate tree climber, the little girl spent entire afternoons perched in a hemlock tree on the front lawn. Neighbors called Katharine to warn her that Kate was sitting in the top of the tree. "Well, for heaven's sake," Mrs. Hepburn replied, "don't frighten her."

From the beginning it appeared there was little that could frighten her. When she was four, Kate got separated from her mother while Christmas shopping one afternoon in downtown Hartford. The little girl simply walked outside and asked a woman getting into her car for a lift. After hours of frantic searching, Katharine arrived home to find that Kate had put herself to bed.

When Kate was five, the Hepburns bought a summer house at Fenwick, a half-mile-wide sandspit where the Connecticut River flows into Long Island Sound. Hard by the Sound at Fenwick's northeastern tip, the Hepburns' chimneyed three-story shingled "cottage" stood on a sandbar and was separated from the rest of the tiny community by a grassy marsh. Like the

Hepburns themselves, it stood just a little bit apart.

It was at Fenwick that Kate made the conscious decision to deny her gender. From the age of nine until thirteen, she even shaved her head. "I told everyone it was to keep cool, but I really did it so the boys couldn't grab hold of my hair when we wrestled. I called myself Jimmy."

At Fenwick "Jimmy" sailed her own "sneak box," a tiny, unpredictable skiff she christened *Tiger.* One day she and Tom were swept three miles down the coast before *Tiger* capsized. Clinging to the overturned boat, they had started to drift out to the open sea when they were spotted and pulled to safety by Frank Ingham, a local fisherman. The incident led Kate to fantasize for the first time about being on the silent screen— as "Grace Darling," her own character based on damsel in distress Pearl White.

By setting an activist example, her parents gave Kate a strong sense of her place in the world. Yet it was Parson Hep, Grandpa, who stoked the fires of her imagination. "My grandfather used to come and tell us stories," Kate said. "He had this fantastic way of wrapping you up in this fantasy world."

Her parents found all their excitement from meeting real-life challenges. At Hartford Hospital Dr. Hepburn was making a name for himself not only as a venereal disease expert but as a pioneer in the lucrative new field of urology. Katharine meanwhile was spearheading the suffrage effort in Connecticut; on April 6, 1915 she won an important moral victory when the Connecticut legislature came within only a few votes of giving women the franchise.

Their euphoria was short-lived. Hep's handsome, successful brother Charles had been despondent for months, suffering a complete nervous breakdown that March. On April 16 he leaped from a front window of his New York town house and was impaled on a wrought-iron stake four stories below. He was forty-two.

Once again Katharine Houghton Hepburn found her family linked in the papers to depression and suicide. ATT'Y HEPBURN DIES AFTER SUICIDE LEAP, read the front-page headline in the *New York American*. Unlike the Houghtons, who did not deny that the gunshots that had killed Kate's maternal grandfather and uncle were self-inflicted, the Hepburns labeled Uncle Charlie's death an "accident resulting from a nervous breakdown." Denial would become a Hepburn family habit.

Even as a young child Kate coped with such unpleasantness in her own way: by escaping to a world of make-believe. In a ramshackle garden shed behind 133 Hawthorn, Kate built a miniature stage where she "used to do a lot of plays where I moved cardboard figures around and told them what to say." At Fenwick, Kate charged the neighbors fifty cents to see her backyard production of *Beauty and the Beast* ("I played the Beast"). Kate later conceded it was "a complete mystery why I had this urge to go out and display myself."

Tom, unlike his sister, was no exhibitionist. But when Dr. Hepburn enrolled him in West Hartford's Kingswood School in 1916, he set out to prove himself to his father. By this time the symptoms of St. Vitus' Dance had all but vanished. Handsome, popular, bright, and athletic, Tom appeared to thrive at Kingswood, which now occupied the old Mark Twain house at Nook Farm. He earned high marks and a spot on the football team. In his fourth year Tom was even nominated for the student body's highest honor, the Citizenship Medal.

If his parents were pleased with Tom's progress—or, for that matter, any of their children's accomplishments—only Mother let them know it. "Dad always told us when we did badly," Kate's sister Marion later said, "but never when we did well. One day I asked him why. And he said, 'I expect you to do well. That's the norm.' My mother, however, simply burst with enthusiasm when we did well, and mourned with us and encouraged us when we did badly." Katharine thought her husband was "too short on praise" and told him so. But, Marion recalled, her mother finally concluded Hep "just plain couldn't express that kind of thing."

Still, both Hep and Katharine were delighted with Tom's progress at Kingswood. So much so that in 1918 they enrolled Kate in the Oxford School, Kingswood's sister institution. Not surprisingly, she too proved to be a fierce competitor, excelling in figure skating, tennis, and golf. In the classroom she was no less formidable. When her parents read Kate's bright orange report card, they were delighted to see her getting high marks in English, French, art, geography, history, algebra, even "deportment."

It was in the eighth grade that Kate, then twelve, felt her first romantic stirrings—not for a boy but for her gym teacher, Cathy Watson. "Why Cathy, I don't know," Kate said. "She had a soft and gentle face, soft sandy hair; it was long, and she did it in a knot and a velvet ribbon she wore around her head. I just remember that I thought about her and watched her and waited for her and brought her presents. I can't even remember what she sounded like—just love, it was. First crush."

When local boys teased the freckled, ganglinglimbed Kate for being "goofy-looking," Tom sprang to her defense. She, in turn, simply "adored" him. "Tom was my big brother and my best friend and, next to my father, the most wonderful male person I ever knew," Kate said. Although Tom's best friend, like Tom one of Kingswood's bright stars, suffered several nervous breakdowns from the pressure to excel, Kate's brother showed few signs of stress. He was perhaps a bit high-strung and sensitive, given to periodic "nervous spells," but all that seemed to be subsiding.

The Hepburns decided to reward their two

oldest children that spring of 1921 by sending
them to spend five days in New York with Mary
Towle, Katharine's old Bryn Mawr friend and
Tom's godmother. "Auntie" Towle took a few
days off from her law practice to play host to
Tom and Kate at her quaint brick house at 26
Charlton Street.

They had already spent four full days sightseeing when, on Friday, April Fool's Day, Auntie
Towle took Tom and Kate to see a silent-film version of Mark Twain's *A Connecticut Yankee in
King Arthur's Court*. When a hanging scene suddenly flashed on the screen, Tom seemed trans-
fixed. Only a year before, Dr. Hepburn had told
his children about a stunt played during a college football game during his undergraduate
days at Randolph-Macon. To shock a visiting
northern football team, Hep and his buddies had
staged a mock lynching—a very convincing performance by one student who knew how to
tighten his neck muscles in such a way that his
windpipe would not be cut off. Despite warnings
that this was a very dangerous and potentially
lethal parlor trick, one day Kate and her father
found Tom "hanging" from a rope at 133 Hawthorn—a horrifying stunt for which the boy was
severely punished.

Saturday was devoted to exploring Central
Park, and that evening several neighborhood
youngsters—all girls, it turned out—dropped by
at Mary Towle's invitation to meet Kate and her
brother. "You're my girl, aren't you?" Tom

asked Kate when she seemed perturbed by the attention he was getting from the other young ladies. "You're my favorite girl in the whole world." Tom picked up Auntie's banjo and played a little before heading upstairs to bed at 10:00 P.M. He paused at the foot of the stairs to thank Auntie for "the most pleasant experience of my life."

In his tiny garret room with the exposed rafters, Tom put on his pajamas, then carefully placed his pants on the dresser with his suitcase on top of them to preserve the crease. Then he pulled down the covers, crawled into bed, and turned out the light.

The next morning, Kate and Auntie allowed Tom to sleep as they shared breakfast in the downstairs kitchen. But when they finished eating around 8:00 A.M. and he had still not appeared, Kate decided it was time to wake up her "sleepyhead" brother. From the bottom of the stairs, she called up to him. No response. So Kate climbed up the steps, past an open bathroom door at the head of the stairs, then a few feet down the hall toward the garret room.

Kate knocked on her brother's door. "Tom. Tom?" Still nothing. She turned the knob slowly and pushed open the door, but something was blocking it. From the doorway, she could see the bed—only one side of it had been slept in—and the trousers on top of the dresser. Kate took a few steps into the room. Her shoulder brushed against something. She turned to see Tom's body hanging from a rafter by a torn bedsheet he had fastened into a makeshift noose. His knees were buckled slightly, his toes touching the wooden floor. His face and hands were blue.

Kate gasped, but she did not scream. Auntie Towle was too prone to panic—"too emotional," as Kate later put it—to be of much help. So Kate dashed to a doctor's house across the street and pounded on the door. A maid opened it, just a crack. "Please help," Kate sobbed. "My brother's dead."

"If he's dead," the maid replied calmly, "the doctor can't help him." Then she slammed the door.

"Auntie" Bertha Rembaugh lived just a few doors away. She would know what to do. Within minutes Bertha, Mary Towle, and Kate were in the garret room, struggling to untie the tightly knotted noose. An ambulance was called. When Dr. Condy of St. Vincent's Hospital arrived seventeen minutes later, he found Kate, sobbing, still holding her brother's stiff body up clear of the floor so the noose no longer pulled at his neck.

Dr. Condy determined that Tom had been dead around five or six hours; that meant he had to have placed the noose around his neck at about 3:00 A.M. For the first time that Kate, or for that matter anyone, could remember, her mother wept openly. Katharine Houghton Hepburn had lost her parents suddenly, and now the life of her eldest child had been cut short cruelly and without warning. The apparent circumstances of Tom's death—unbearable melancholia triggering some suicidal impulse—once again raised the specter of inherited insanity.

At first Hep refused to believe that Tom might have taken his own life. The police had not adequately explained how his son could have died with his feet touching the floor. Speaking over the phone from Hartford, he told New York City police that his boy might have been murdered, then the crime scene clumsily staged to make it look like a hanging. But the fact remained that police could find no signs of any sort of struggle or forced entry into the house, and there had been no suspicious sounds throughout the night. When Hep visited the tiny attic room where his son had died, it was obvious that only one side of the bed had been slept on. On top of the dresser were the two parlor car tickets Tom and Kate were to use for the return train trip to Hartford. Nothing had been taken. Tom had no enemies. What would have been the motive?

After visiting the room where his son died and seeing the body, Hep abandoned his murder theory. "God only knows why he did it," Hepburn told reporters who gathered outside Mary Towle's house. "My son was normal in mind and body," he insisted, adding that the tragic act was one of "adolescent insanity. He was an athlete, bronzed with health and exercise. He won his color with the football team of his school last fall, and had expressed his ambition to finish his studies . . . enter Yale University, to study surgery and, as he said, 'follow in father's footsteps.' "

MYSTERY IN SUICIDE OF SURGEON'S SON, blared the headline in *The New York Times*. HARTFORD SCHOOLBOY, 15, VISITING HERE, IS FOUND HANGING IN HIS ROOM—WAS ATHLETIC AND HAPPY. MUST HAVE KILLED HIMSELF AS RESULT OF SUDDENLY DEVELOPED INSANITY, FATHER SAYS. Back home in Hartford, the front-page story in the *Courant* was equally sensational: DR. HEPBURN'S SON, 15, HANGS HIMSELF WHILE VISITING IN NEW YORK. DEAD BODY, SWINGING FROM CURTAIN, FOUND BY SISTER IN HOME OF AUNT—DESPONDENCY SUSPECTED.

The *Courant* quoted the medical examiner as saying Tom "was of a nervous disposition and had at one time been a sufferer of St. Vitus' Dance." The story went on to describe Tom as "bright, healthy, active—Thomas apparently had not a care in the world and was among the happiest of boys."

It was Kate who came up with a possible explanation for Tom's violent death—one that the family, so steeped in denial, might be able to accept. She reminded her father of the mock lynching during his Randolph-Macon days, and how they had caught Tom trying to reenact the stunt. It was the hanging scene in *A Connecticut Yankee in King Arthur's Court*, she suggested, that must have prompted him to try it again.

Dr. Hepburn jumped at the chance to portray

the events of April 3, 1921 as something other than suicide. In a new statement released to *The New York Times* on Monday afternoon, he tried to set the record straight. "I am convinced that I have done the boy an injustice," he told the *Times*. "In the first place, his whole life and temperament does [*sic*] not coincide with the suicide theory. While subject as a small boy to a few facial habits, he had outgrown them and was in the best mental condition that I have ever seen him. . . . I am now convinced that the boy was the victim of a foolish stunt."

Hep described Tom's previous attempts to perfect the hanging trick and then concluded that "this accident theory would explain all the findings. In view of the fact that I have given the world my opinion, that the boy committed suicide, and have thereby cast a blot upon his memory I feel anxious to repair this damage insofar as I am able."

Kate wanted to believe this version of events. All the Hepburns did. Just a few hours after making his revised statement, Hep called his surviving brothers, Lloyd and Sewell, to tell them it had all been a kid's parlor trick gone tragically awry. "I don't think they ever really knew what happened," Kate later conceded. "It was a terrible blow."

It was not the only blow the Hepburns suffered that week. That Tuesday, while Tom's body was being taken to Springfield, Massachusetts, for cremation, Hep's brother Sewell locked the door of his Annapolis, Maryland garage, climbed behind the wheel of his car, and turned on the ignition. The next morning Annie Hepburn found her husband dead from carbon monoxide poisoning. Battling the debilitating long-term effects of syphilis, Sewell had also been given to bouts of severe depression. His nephew's untimely death, it appeared, had pushed him over the edge. Tom's interment was postponed for several days so that Hep could attend his brother's funeral.

"Naturally my brother's death flattened me emotionally," Kate remembered. "It was a major tragedy." But even more than the painful loss of a single loved one, however, it was one in a series of devastating and bewildering blows. Kate's grandfather, great-uncle, two uncles, and her own brother—all suicides.

With Tom's death, the family dynamic changed dramatically. "It was as if, when Tom died, I sort of became two people instead of one—a boy *and* a girl. That's why I practically raised the other kids. I was a third parent. My younger brothers and sisters were more like my own children. . . . Oldest daughters are often called upon to do this. That's why there are so many oldest daughters who don't marry. By the time they've grown up, they feel as if they've already raised a family." By way of assuming her dead brother's persona, Kate took his birthday— November 8—as her own. She would not reveal her true May 12 birth date until she herself turned eighty-four, in 1991.

Inside the family she was a pillar of strength, even at age thirteen. She was drawn even more to her parents—particularly to her father, whose praise and approval she desperately craved. Knowing how much closer Kate had been to Tom than the younger siblings, the three seemed to share a special language. "When we would speak together," Kate recalled, "it was a very different conversation than they would have had with anyone else."

The family itself was an emotional fortress; Kate felt less "surefooted" when she ventured outside its walls. She admitted that Tom's death made her "a more moody, suspicious person. I tried school, but I felt isolated. I knew something that the other girls did not know: tragedy. And I would not, did not, want to talk about it." She stuck out the remaining two months, but when the school year was over later that May, Kate told her parents she would not return. She never attended high school but instead was tutored at home by a member of the Kingswood-Oxford faculty.

For her part, Katharine dealt with her son's death by plunging into a new and controversial cause. Convinced that "women would always be hopelessly handicapped if they did not have control of how many children they produced," she teamed up with birth control pioneer Margaret

Sanger to found the organization that eventually became Planned Parenthood.

That first summer Kate found some comfort in the unexpected friendship of a young man who arrived unannounced on the doorstep of the Hepburns' new house on Bloomfield Avenue in West Hartford. He was stooped, skinny, red-headed, and his face was pitted with acne scars. His name was Sinclair Lewis, and he and his wife, Gracie, had just moved into the neighborhood.

"Red" Lewis was intrigued by the brooding young girl who had endured so much, and she in turn felt she could talk to him. They went on long Sunday walks together. "We used to shinny up little trees," she said, "little willow trees that were very bendable, little birch trees, but he would look up at me in wonder."

Lewis was also a notorious drinker, and for that reason the Hepburns were at first reluctant to invite him to dinner. "Daddy would not purchase alcohol," Kate recalled. "He would drink it if it was given to him, but he would not purchase it." So Dr. Hepburn called Lewis up and said, "Listen, if you have to get drunk to stand me, you'd better bring your own, because we don't serve it." Respecting his host's wishes, Lewis, who in 1930 would become the first American to win the Nobel Prize for Literature, did not drink whenever he called on the Hepburns. Decades later, as Kate helped someone she loved deeply battle his addiction to alcohol, she looked back gratefully on Lewis's impressive act of self-control.

Kate retreated from the soul-crushing reality of Tom's death in other ways. "Did it push me further into make-believe? Who knows? I would think it must have. It must have." Like millions of others, she escaped into the world of silent movies. Entire afternoons were spent at the Empire or the Majestic, gazing up in wonder at the flickering images of cowboy stars William S. Hart (Kate's favorite) and Tom Mix, Rudolph Valentino, Lilian Gish, Gloria Swanson, and Mary Pickford. Kate's favorite female star was Leatrice Joy. "She was married to John Gilbert at the time, and I thought she was absolutely sensational." From the very beginning Kate Hepburn saw herself "as someday becoming a movie star. It seemed perfectly natural for me."

But Kate had other obligations. With Tom gone, she would now be the one to follow in Dad's footsteps and become a surgeon. She was fiercely proud of her mother's achievements, but by the time she was a teenager Kate had forged what became a lifelong identification with her father. He would be, simply, the defining force in her life—and the standard against which all men would be measured.

To satisfy Dad, Kate became a ferocious competitor. She was a medal-winning figure skater and diver and at fifteen was the second-ranked junior tennis player in the state. By this time she was also ranked as one of the most promising women golfers in the country.

Yet something was missing. In September 1922, after all the children had returned to school, leaving Kate and her childhood friend Allie Barbour at Fenwick with their respective tutors, they embarked on what Kate later called her "life of crime." Together they cooked up "the Plan"—a scheme to break into the summer homes of Fenwick's most prominent citizens after they had been closed up for the season.

By her own account, Kate "became a real expert on knowing whether a house was open or closed, whether anyone was in— spotting a window someone may have left unlocked...." Occasionally she would climb up a drainpipe or a trellis, then pry open an upstairs window. "I could get up on any roof," she would boast when she was well past eighty. "Still can today. Right up the gutter pipe, in and nothing could ever keep me out. I could break in, look over a place, and get in and out faster than any teenager in juvenile court."

Only once did they actually pilfer something: a crocodile-shaped nutcracker. "It fascinated me, so I stole it." Overcome with guilt, she broke back in the next day and put it back where she had found it.

For the most part Kate was content with "just casing the joint. I was a real second-story woman, climbing through windows and skylights. Why I lived, I don't know." It looked as if her luck had finally run out when, after climbing onto the roof of a house owned by Hartford's mayor, she lost her footing and fell headlong through an open skylight. She somehow managed to catch herself and dangled by her fingertips above the marble floor three stories below before summoning the strength to pull herself up. "*Terrifying*. I damned near dropped the whole three stories. It was just by the grace of God that I didn't."

That brush with death was not enough to convince the girls to stop. Allie's new boyfriend, Bob Post, joined them, and they suddenly turned to vandalism. They used a battering ram to smash through the back door of one Victorian mansion, then took talcum powder from a bathroom and spread it everywhere—over the paneled walls and furniture. They were caught—the cook next door witnessed the whole event—and Dr. Hepburn paid for the damage. Amazingly, Kate's disciplinarian dad did not punish her. "I think he understood the thrill," she concluded, "and that we were overcome with guilt." There were no more break-ins—for the moment. But Kate never outgrew her taste for excitement. "Danger," she explained, "intoxicates me."

The end of Kate's teenage crime spree coincided with an awakening interest in the opposite sex—and vice versa. The tomboy with a chip on her shoulder had evolved into a leggy, red-maned, blue-eyed beauty. The famous high cheekbones were just beginning to emerge.

"Jimmy" was gone. To please her parents after the vandalism episode, she even joined the staid Hartford Junior League and began bringing home Harvard men and Yalies for their approval. None passed muster. Without exception Hep found these rich college boys "excruciatingly boring. I'd have to sit with those goddamned men and I'd have to talk to them, and I'd think, If she marries any of them, it's going to be hell."

He needn't have worried. Kate was determined to become a doctor and enrolled at Bryn Mawr in the autumn of 1924. As her mother had done thirty years before, she crammed with a tutor to pass the entrance exam and squeaked by. "I got in by the skin of my teeth," she said, "and by the skin of my teeth I stayed."

The academic challenge was daunting, but not nearly as much as the prospect of having to interact with the other students. She had not, after all, shared a classroom with girls her age since she dropped out of Oxford, and she knew Bryn Mawr was the kind of place "where there are always people around to make you feel like an idiot."

To make the transition easier, the Hepburns arranged for Kate to have a large ground-floor room to herself in the western wing of Pembroke Hall, the turreted, medieval-looking dormitory where her mother had stayed. But as soon as she made her slow, "agonizing" grand entrance into the dining hall wearing an Iceland-knit sweater and a French blue skirt with buttons down the front ("I wore it all the time. That's all I had"), it was clear she could never be one of those "sophisticated, marvelously sure-of-herself girls." Kate was certain all eyes were on her when someone declared "Ah, self-conscious beauty!" Kate, who felt incredibly self-conscious and not remotely beautiful, sat down and ate quickly. For the next seven months she dined alone in local restaurants or had her one good friend, Alice Palache, bring meals up to her room.

More painfully shy than ever around strangers, Kate would get up at 4:00 A.M. to shower alone. In class things weren't much better. Scraping by in chemistry, she realized that a premed major was out. She toyed with the idea of studying to become a psychologist for a time but wound up majoring in world history.

"She was plenty smart," Palache said of her friend. "But she was badly trained. She hadn't gone to school for a long time, and she didn't ever learn how to study." She got by on an uncanny natural ability to quickly commit nearly everything she read to memory, a talent that ultimately proved useful in her chosen profession. "She memorized practically everything," Palache recalled. "Reams and reams and reams."

Retreating more and more into her fantasy world of movies and her books, Kate contemplated a very different career from the one originally envisioned for her. In one rare unguarded moment, she decided to confide in one classmate who had seemed particularly simpatico. "Know what I want to be when I get out of college?" Kate said. "An actress."

Kate's new friend could contain herself for only a few seconds. "You?" she asked, incredulous. "*You?*" Then she doubled over laughing.

Up until this point Kate was devoutly determined not to call attention to herself. She did not try out for any sports teams, or run for office, or go out of her way to socialize. "She didn't have too many friends," Palache said. Only four, in fact. They called themselves "The Tenement," though no one knew why, exactly. "We really were very exclusive. She wasn't known at all as anything, just as a pretty girl."

Before long, Kate returned to her old attention-grabbing ways. After hours studying in the library, she stripped off all her clothes and swam in the Cloister fountain "in a mad effort to stay awake." On a dare she stood naked on the dormitory roof in a snowstorm. She had a friend snap photographs of her nude in her dorm room, then laughed in the face of the pharmacist who refused to print them. After she moved to a second-story tower room in "Pem East," she routinely got around the 11:00 P.M. curfew by climbing up a trellis. Caught smoking in a stairwell, she was suspended for a week.

Yet it was Kate's disappointing academic performance, not her bizarre behavior, that nearly resulted in her being kicked out of Bryn Mawr altogether. By the end of her sophomore year

Kate had flunked Latin and was faring only slightly better in her other classes. Dean Helen Taft Manning wrote Kate's parents and suggested that it might be a good idea if she did not return.

That September of 1926 Kate was home mulling her fate when suddenly she doubled over with a stabbing pain in her abdomen. She was rushed to Hartford Hospital, where her father performed an emergency appendectomy—in defiance of rules against doctors operating on their own relatives. "To hell with the rules," Hep exploded. "Nobody operates on my daughter but me. Besides, I'm the best damned surgeon this hospital has got!"

Grateful to be alive, Kate was determined not to be an "embarrassment" to her family. She was allowed to return to Bryn Mawr and, pushing herself to the brink of a breakdown on two separate occasions, managed to bring her grades up to honors level.

Kate decided to participate more in college life and joined the swim and golf teams. She also joined the College Varsity Dramatics group, donning a navy blue blazer and chopping off her hair to play the lead role of Oliver in A. A. Milne's *The Truth About Blayds*. "I thought that I made a damned attractive young man," she said. She enjoyed cross-dressing so much, in fact, that one night she boarded a train for New York in her male getup, just to gauge the reaction of other passengers. At eighteen she had not yet gotten the hang of wearing men's pants. She reached in her pocket for change to pay the conductor, sat down, and then had to struggle to get her hand back out.

It was not difficult to see where Kate got her "histrionic bent," as her college friend Alice Palache called it. "She was emotional, not cold at all. Very affectionate, very warm. The Hepburns were always kissing somebody or hugging when you met. The Hepburns were very close, very intimate, and very affectionate. We'd all sit around, boys and girls together, without many clothes on, and nobody paid much attention . . . I never in my whole life saw my father naked, never. But Dr. Hepburn would be naked, coming out of his bath and saying something . . . We talked about current events and about birth control, about venereal disease. These things we never talked about at home."

In the summer of 1928 Kate and Alice Palache decided to embark on a European tour. Palache had saved up five hundred dollars, and after Kate threatened to hock her mother's furniture, Hep kicked in a matching five hundred dollars. In England they paid seventy-five dollars for a used Morris Cowley convertible, but only after Kate had convinced the owner—a Mr. Seymour—to buy it back for the same price when they were finished with it. "That was where I saw Kate's first very brilliant histrionic performance," Palache said. "Kate went into a song and dance . . . about these two young girls, alone, and what might happen to us if anything happened to the car. Well, you've never seen such a performance in your life. He was undone by it. It really was brilliant. So off we went."

Despite their finishing school wardrobe and expensive luggage, the girls were scraping by on five dollars a day. In Britain they stayed at cheap working-class pubs where the patrons were so rowdy the two American college girls propped a chair against their bedroom door to keep them out. Several times they resorted to sleeping in the car, "which was horrible because it was so damned small. My feet," Kate said, "would be sticking in her face, and hers would be sticking some place worse." When they thought it would be romantic to sleep on the shore of Loch Katrine in Scotland, they were warned by locals of marauding Gypsies and wound up arming themselves with a butcher knife. "I got up and lit a cigarette and started to walk up and down the shore," Palache remembered. "All Kate saw was this light, the cigarette, going back and forth. She was scared to death, and suddenly she appeared in front of me with the carving knife. It was really awfully funny."

In Paris they checked into a small Left Bank hotel, the Cayre, on the Boulevard Raspail, and encountered their first bidet. "We used it to put our Sterno on," Palache said, "because it seemed safer to heat water for tea." They were eating at a small café across the street when a young American family came in, "obviously not speaking a word of French. They wanted chicken," Palache recalled, "so he was flapping his arms up and down, pretending he was a chicken. I got up and went over and interpreted for them." The grateful family rewarded Kate and her friend with a carafe of wine for making their order understood to the waiter—a service they continued to provide each night in exchange for the free wine. Their table was next to a long wall mirror. "Palache had a fit," Kate said, "because I kept studying myself and my expression while we sat there."

Kate and Palache decided they would have to make the trip back to the United States in steerage, and for that they needed to be vaccinated. But Kate suffered a severe reaction to one of the shots. By the time they reached Mont-St.-Michel on the way to Cherbourg, her leg had become badly infected. "She couldn't really walk at all," Palache said. "It swelled up and was really terrifying."

After a week in bed, Kate recovered enough to make the voyage home. "I was limping badly and I guess the officers took pity on us," Kate said. "We only spent a few hours in steerage with all the immigrants before they insisted we move up to third class. Remember, it was the 1920s, and Europeans were just flooding into this country. That time in steerage with everybody singing and dancing and nobody speaking English—it was a real experience for a couple of spoiled college girls from Connecticut. Fascinating, just fascinating."

Nothing fascinated Palache more than her traveling companion. "She was a wonderful-looking creature. Wherever she'd be she'd be noticed." Kate was not without her annoying idiosyncrasies—habits that she would never get around to dropping: She never carried cash ("She always had someone with her who would") and always worried at the last minute that she'd left some thing behind. "Oh, my toothbrush! I must have left my toothbrush!" was a constant refrain. Said Palache: "She never had left anything but she always thought she had. . . . Fifty years later she was still pulling this same trick. Unbelievable."

Back at Bryn Mawr, Kate received her first review acting in the school's Christmas offering of *The Cradle Song* by G. Martínez Sierra. "Katherine [*sic*] Hepburn, as Theresa, was so extraordinarily lovely to look at," wrote the critic for the *College News*, "it was difficult to form any judgment on her acting."

Palache recalled that when it came to boyfriends, Kate "always had one or two around" to take her out. But she "wasn't boy crazy at all. Take 'em or leave 'em alone." She met her first serious boyfriend, graduate art student Bob McKnight, at a Yale dance. When he proclaimed his desire to become the greatest sculptor in the world, she answered with a prediction of her own: "I am going to be the greatest actress in the world." This time nobody laughed.

Kate was intrigued enough with McKnight to invite him to spend Easter with the Hepburns in Hartford. He slept on a cot in the room shared by Dick and Bob, and before dawn she crept in to steal a passionate kiss. A month later he took Kate on a picnic to his "secret spot" overlooking a pond, fully planning to propose marriage. But he never got the chance to pop the question. Instead Kate talked nonstop about the "thrilling" career possibilities before her—and how she would someday be a great star.

McKnight soon faced competition from Ludlow Ogden Smith, whose best friend, Jack Clarke, lived in a house adjacent to the Bryn Mawr campus lawn. Although Kate was initially attracted to the tall, rakishly handsome Clarke, it was the persistent "Luddy" who was determined to win her over. She was twenty, Luddy twenty-eight. "He was an odd-looking man," she later wrote of Luddy, who came from a prominent Main Line family. "Dark hair, dark eyes far apart. He was foreign-looking."

Luddy and Jack Clarke shared a ramshackle country house they derisively called the Hut, where Kate, Palache, and the other Tenement members occasionally came for the weekend. Both worldly, wealthy young men were "looking for trouble," as Kate put it. But in the spring of 1928 neither had succeeded in seducing the beguiling creature in their midst. They did, however, manage to persuade her to strip off her clothes and pose for dozens of nude photographs on the living-room couch. "I posed with total confidence, as I rather fancied myself," recalled Kate, who placed the nude pictures in a straw basket. She later misplaced the basket. (Kate was also a willing model for McKnight, who sculpted her in the nude.)

That spring Kate had her eye on someone else. H. Phelps Putnam was a popular poet of the time, and when Kate met him at a luncheon given by Dean Manning, she was "stricken with whatever it is that strickens one at once and for no reason when one looks at a member of the opposite sex. . . . I flew up onto a pink cloud. . . ." He was also married, a notorious womanizer, and an unrepentant alcoholic.

No matter. Kate would climb down her ivy-covered trellis and meet "Phelpie" for romantic moonlight walks on the grounds of Bryn Mawr. Over the course of their curious, short-lived, and ultimately unconsummated relationship, Kate tried and failed to seduce the poet, leaving deep fingernail marks on his back as a token of her frustration. She could not have known that Putnam's reticence was the result of a warning from her father. "If you lay hands on her," Hep told the poet calmly, "I shall shoot you."

Kate would, however, inspire him to write one of his most sensuous poems, "The Daughters of the Sun."

She was the living anarchy of love.
My lust, my liberty, my discipline. . . .
She was the very mask of my desire. . . .

Kate remained largely anonymous at school until Bryn Mawr's May Day, actually a two-day-long Elizabethan festival that included masques, maypoles, and revels. The climax was John Lyly's 1594 play *The Woman in the Moon*, with Kate in the lead role of Pandora. Rather than some delicate, will-o'-the-wisp, Kate's Pandora was feisty, sexy, and barefoot. The audience sat in stunned silence when she made her entrance, her red mane and diaphanous white gown blowing in the wind. At the end they gave her a thunderous ovation. "I didn't see it," she later said, "but I guess I was the brilliant feature."

Jack Clarke had watched Kate's performance from his porch and offered to introduce her to his friend, Baltimore theatrical producer Edwin Knopf—if she was interested. Just three weeks before graduation, Kate drove down to Baltimore and presented her letter of introduction to Knopf (whose older brother Alfred was in the book publishing business).

At the time Kate impressed Knopf as being "awkward, green, and freaky-looking." He politely told her to come back after graduation. "I was glad to see the last of her," he later recalled. When she returned four days before graduation, he inexplicably handed her a nonspeaking walk-on part, as one of Catherine the Great's six ladies-in-waiting in a comedy called *The Czarina*.

On June 7, 1928, Kate's parents took the train down to Bryn Mawr to see their eldest daughter graduate with honors. In the wake of all that had gone before—Katharine Houghton's deathbed promise to her mother, Tom's untimely death, the bizarre family history of depression and suicide—this was a singularly joyful event.

Kate borrowed a friend's car to drive her parents back to West Hartford. The last thing she wanted to do was spoil this day for them, but time was running out; she had to let them know that in forty-eight hours she would report for rehearsals in Baltimore. Hep detested actors, and she dreaded his reaction.

Kate had been driving for forty-five minutes when she finally got up the nerve to tell Dad she was now a professional actress. "Dad thought acting was sort of a cheesy way to make a living," she recalled. Predictably, Hep flew into a purple-veined rage. "Let me out!" he bellowed. "I'll take the train!" In the end Kate's mother ("She was all for it") calmed him down. He dug for his wallet and then, still muttering to himself, handed Kate fifty dollars—his bridge winnings—to cover two weeks' living expenses in Baltimore. "Enough to last," he told her, "until you recover from this madness. You'll be back. You just want to show off and get paid for it."

After her two weeks with the Knopf Stock Company in Baltimore were up, Kate went to study with noted voice and drama coach Frances Robinson-Duff in New York. When she wasn't learning to modulate her voice, which had a tendency to crack, Kate pursued the moody object of her desire, Phelps Putnam. She went so far as to move into the apartment where he was staying—forcing Putnam, who had already suffered one nervous breakdown, to decide if he would risk another (not to mention a bullet from Dr. Hepburn) or flee. He took off alone for Nova Scotia.

Luddy rushed to Kate's side and offered his shoulder to cry on. By this time Jack Clarke and Luddy both had moved to New York, and now they went out of their way to entertain their friend the aspiring actress. On weekends Luddy, who made no secret of his utter devotion to Kate, drove her to Fenwick, where he was instantly accepted by the rest of the family. It did not even matter that he was a Herbert Hoover Republican, although Mrs. Hepburn ("Mother leaned toward communism," Kate allowed) made a concerted effort to convert Kate's misguided young suitor.

At Fenwick and whenever they were together in New York, Luddy was openly affectionate toward Kate. Unlike Putnam, it was Luddy who did the pursuing—aggressively—and not the other way around.

One day in Manhattan Luddy's persistence paid off. He and twenty-one-year-old Kate were alone in Jack Clarke's apartment and, she recalled, "there was the bed, and there didn't seem to be any reason not to. . . . Luddy knew what he was doing and I didn't object. So we did it. And that was the end of my virtue."

Kate had more pressing concerns than the loss of her virginity that summer. Eddie Knopf decided to mount a production of *The Big Pond* in New York, with Kate as understudy to the leading lady. When Kate gave a particularly passionate reading, he fired the lead and gave the part to her instead. Before the opening on Broadway, there was to be a single out-of-town performance in Great Neck on Long Island. Kate's rapid-fire delivery was all but unintelligible to the audience. The next day she was fired.

Not everyone who saw the play thought Kate had been a disaster. One of the leading theatrical producers of the day, Arthur Hopkins, liked what he saw and offered her the part of a schoolgirl in a play called *These Days*. It closed after eight performances.

Then Hopkins assigned her—at the then princely salary of $125 a week—to understudy Hope Williams in Philip Barry's comedy *Holiday*. The play was a hit and catapulted newcomer Williams, a bona fide Park Avenue socialite, to stardom. Kate studied Williams's mannish stride, her patrician accent, and what she called Williams's "boy-woman" look carefully. Kate later confessed that she absorbed the Hope Williams image and mannerisms into her own persona.

While Kate waited in the wings ("I won't say I actually prayed for her to get sick, *but . . .*"),

Luddy's oft-repeated marriage proposal sounded
more and more appealing. He promised, among
other things, to buy her a Main Line mansion full
of servants. But one major obstacle remained. If
she married Ludlow Ogden Smith, she would
forever be known as Kate Smith, the name of a
talented young singer who was huge, both literally and figuratively.

To spare Kate any embarrassment, Luddy
agreed without hesitation to change his name to
Ogden Ludlow. After waiting around for two
weeks, hoping that Williams would miss at least
one performance, the impatient understudy
marched into Hopkins's office and announced
that she was quitting, leaving the theater for
good to become a housewife.

With her eighty-three-year-old grandfather
conducting the ceremony, Kate wed "Ogden
Ludlow" (still Luddy to all who knew him) in
the living room of the Hepburns' West Hartford
house on December 12, 1928. Unlike her mother,
Kate did not opt for the shock value of a black
wedding dress; she wore a white crushed velvet
Babani gown with gold-embroidered neck and
sleeves.

After a brief honeymoon in Bermuda the newlyweds went house hunting in Pennsylvania. But
after only two weeks as a married woman, Mrs.
Ogden Ludlow told her husband that she was
desperately unhappy. She wanted to act, *had* to
act. Luddy, as always, understood. Anything to
make Kate happy. They abandoned his plan to buy

a mansion in Pennsylvania and moved into his New York apartment at 146 East Thirty-ninth Street. She wasted no time asking for her old job back.

Hopkins did not look up when she walked into his office. "Yes, of course," he said without hesitation. "I've been expecting you."

"Really?" Kate said.

Hopkins looked at her for a moment and grinned. "Oh, yes."

Nobody drank or fought or caused more trouble than the young Spencer Tracy. Nobody.

—STANLEY KRAMER,
DIRECTOR AND FRIEND

I've been loved and I've been in love. There's a big difference.

—KATE

Him

Three

Between 1928 and 1932 *Spencer Bonaventure Tracy*
and Katharine Houghton Hepburn probably
crossed paths a hundred times and never knew
it as they struggled for Broadway stardom. During this time she gave a single poorly received
performance of *Holiday* (after understudying for
six months), was fired from Alberto Casella's
play *Death Takes a Holiday* while it was still in
previews, quit the Berkshire Playhouse after only
two weeks, and appeared only briefly in a forgettable comedy called *Art and Mrs. Bottle* ("One
good thing was that Noel Coward walked up
five flights to my dressing room just to tell me
that I was good and not to give up"). Even after
Barry wrote *The Animal Kingdom* expressly for
her, she was dismissed for being difficult. Kate's
leading man, British heartthrob Leslie Howard,
simply refused to work with "that irritating
girl." It was not until March 1932 that she finally
stood Broadway on its ear, playing a breast-

plated, spear-toting Amazon in Julian Thompson's comedy *The Warrior's Husband*.

By then Tracy had already moved to Hollywood and appeared in eleven films, but not before having paid his dues on the stage. Starting with the nonspeaking part of a robot in the 1922 science-fiction fantasy *R.U.R.*, Tracy appeared in such forgettable Broadway plays as *A Royal Fandango*, *Yellow*, *The Baby Cyclone*, and *Conflict* (not to mention countless stock productions) before getting his big break playing a doomed convict in the 1930 drama *The Last Mile*. When his moment in the sun finally arrived, Spencer was thirty, virtually penniless, the father of a deaf child, and a raging alcoholic with a temper to match.

Kate's nonconformist upbringing and history of family tragedy—especially Tom Hepburn's death by hanging—clearly fueled the desire for fame that was already burning inside her. Tracy too was driven, but by what? His family had not faced ostracism and derision, as Kate's had. He had no untimely deaths to contend with. And unlike Kate, whose own life hung in the balance when she was stricken with scarlet fever and then with acute appendicitis, in early life he was blessed with perfect health. Tracy's demons—the ones that propelled him to greatness but in many ways made his life unbearable—were entirely of his own making.

In stark contrast with Kate, Spencer did not grow up in a world of wealth and privilege. But he was raised, his mother would often remind him, "on the right side of the tracks" in Milwaukee, Wisconsin. Such distinctions were important to Tracy's mother, Caroline ("Carrie") Brown, who traced her roots back to seventeenth-century New England and numbered among her ancestors the philanthropist Nicholas Brown, after whom Rhode Island's prestigious Brown University was named.

John Tracy was not exactly what the Browns, rock-ribbed Protestant Republicans all, had in mind for Carrie. A staunch Roman Catholic whose parents fled Ireland at the height of the Great Potato Famine, Tracy had no social credentials. He was in many ways the quintessential hard-drinking Irishman, a strapping, darkly handsome charmer whom the quiet Carrie found irresistible.

Carrie, who later became a Christian Scientist, agreed to be married by a priest, and there was never any question that their children would be raised in the Catholic faith. The Tracys were living in Freeport, Illinois, when their first son, Carroll, was born in 1896. By the time Spencer arrived on April 5, 1900, the family had moved to Milwaukee, where John Tracy was general sales manager of the Sterling Motor Truck Company. While Carrie asked the hospital chaplain to join her in a prayer of thanks, John celebrated Spencer's birth by setting up rounds of drinks for his friends at every Irish bar in town.

Not long after, they moved out of their

cramped apartment and into a spacious slate-roofed house with a wraparound porch on Prospect Avenue just one block from Lake Michigan. Milwaukee at the beginning of the century was rigidly divided along ethnic lines. The Germans and Poles occupied the central parts of town. Middle-class Irish families like the Tracys were concentrated in the northeastern corner of Milwaukee, with the wealthiest in Shorewood even farther north. To the south and west were such shanty Irish neighborhoods as Tory Hill, arguably the toughest part of town.

Spencer was to make his presence felt in all parts of town, much to his parents' consternation. With his reddish hair and freckles, Spencer as a child bore a passing resemblance to young Tom Hepburn. And like Tom, he seemed troubled for no apparent reason and from a very early age.

Almost as soon as he could walk, Spencer fought, exchanging blows at the slightest provocation or with no provocation at all. He picked fights with all the boys on Prospect Avenue, and when he had beaten up everyone he knew, Spencer roamed the neighborhood searching for new victims.

It fell to the more even-tempered Carroll to correct his hotheaded younger brother's behavior and to protect Spencer when he got in over his head. It was generally accepted by the boys that Dad favored the dutiful Carroll while Carrie doted on the troubled Spencer. There was unquestionably a strong bond between Spencer and his mother, who forgave him his shortcomings, praised his smallest accomplishments, and tried desperately to understand what made him so angry.

But John, a two-fisted saloon habitué who took a grudging pride in Spencer's scrappy Irish temperament, could not countenance the boy's flagrant disobedience. He was a strict father—a "spanking dad," as Kate would put it—but the beatings were not so wounding as the look of disappointment on John Tracy's face. Just as Hep's praise became the most sought-after commodity in the Hepburn house because it was dispensed so sparingly, John Tracy's approval was something Spencer craved.

Tough spiritually and mentally as well as physically, John Tracy was described by Spencer as a "tower of strength." Certainly John, who loomed so large in Spencer's early life, exuded a kind of confident masculine power that his son would portray onscreen. "I think Spence carried a lot of guilt around about disappointing Dad," Carroll said. "Spence was more Mother's favorite, and I was Dad's, and I always figured Spence was in a constant battle with himself to win Dad over."

Yet the turmoil inside Spencer was so great that not even the beatings meted out by his father could make him toe the line. At the age of seven, claiming he had heard the second-grade teacher was a tough taskmaster, he expressly refused to appear for the first day of school. In the afternoons his father locked him in his room, but that didn't work: Spencer climbed out his second-story bedroom window, shinnied down the drainpipe, and ran off to the hardscrabble South Side. There he bumped into the aptly nick-named Ratty and Mousie Donovan, who were not compelled by their saloonkeeper father to attend school at all. Spencer handled the encounter the only way he knew how: He slugged it out with the bigger of the boys, Ratty, until they respected one another. "They were tough eggs—as pugnacious a pair of toughies as the Dead End Kids ever portrayed," Spencer recalled. "But we became darned good friends."

John and Carrie Tracy, meanwhile, combed the city in search of their missing boy. It was almost nightfall when they were finally notified by the police that a curiously well-dressed lad of about seven was playing with two dirty-faced street urchins in an alleyway behind Donovan's Bar. "I remember how my mother grabbed me and wept," Tracy said. "That should have cured me, but it didn't."

Spencer tried for a time to please his parents. At school he became a star baseball player and boxer. He joined the Boy Scouts, and along with Carroll became an altar boy. John had hoped that one of his sons would become a priest. The other, he fantasized, would join in a family trucking firm, "Tracy and Son."

But Spencer's ways did not stay mended for

long. A favorite pastime was to build forts with his new friends Ratty and Mousie at the Kinnickinnic River mudflats, a notoriously dangerous spot frequented by vagrants and derelicts. Another favorite hangout was Donovan's, where the boys hid behind the bar and listened to the patrons' graphic, obscenity-laced conversations. It was also behind the bar at Donovan's that, at the age of ten, Spencer licked the drippings from a leaky draft beer keg. It was his first taste of alcohol.

In 1912 John's investments took a nosedive and the family was forced to relocate to more modest accommodations, a significantly smaller house at the corner of St. Paul Avenue and Thirtieth Street on the more downscale West Side. For the most part the Tracys' new neighbors were blue-collar workers who labored either in the slaughterhouse or the casket company in the Menominee River valley below.

Spencer's violently antisocial behavior, which at another time would almost certainly have landed him in reform school (and today on a psychiatrist's couch), escalated. He continued to pick fights, to bully and terrorize other pupils for no apparent reason. Over the course of just a few years his uncontrollable temper and disruptive behavior would result in his being asked to leave no fewer than fifteen schools. Spencer, already a silent-film buff, later insisted he "wouldn't have gone to school at all if there had been any other way of learning to read the subtitles."

The most chilling incident, however, happened not in a classroom but at home. One Sunday after the Tracy family had attended mass, fourteen-year-old Spencer and his father got into a furious "screaming and yelling fight," as one neighbor called it. The boy fled to the cellar and, moments later, came dashing out, smoke billowing up behind him. Apparently furious that he had not gotten his way and unable to control his rage, he had deliberately set fire to newspapers and wood shavings on the basement floor.

As flames shot out the basement windows, fire trucks came roaring up the street. The entire neighborhood gathered outside on the street to watch the firemen battle the blaze for twenty minutes before finally bringing it under control. John was rigid with rage, but Carrie placed her hand on the trembling boy's shoulder while she explained to the fire captain that Spencer had been experimenting with cigarettes in the basement. It was all an innocent accident, she insisted. The fire captain stared for a moment, not entirely convinced. "OK," he said, shaking his head. "If you can vouch for it." There would be no charges.

Ironically, the basement where Spencer's life almost ended in a ball of fire that Sunday morning soon was the birthplace of his phenomenal talent. Inspired, as Kate was half a continent away, by the derring-do of William S. Hart and the antics of Charlie Chaplin, Buster Keaton, and the Keystone Kops, Spencer staged his own versions in the cellar and charged the local kids a penny for admission. Ratty, Mousie, and other local toughs were enlisted to play supporting roles while Spencer always cast himself in the lead—a situation that, not surprisingly, led to more pitched battles between Tracy and his feisty friends.

At St. Rose's parochial school, however, Spencer was making a concerted attempt to behave himself. At age fifteen, the nuns at St. Rosa's finally handed him his eighth-grade diploma. "Boy," he later said, "that was a gala day."

Spencer's progress was derailed the following year, when John Tracy decided to quit his job in Milwaukee and cast his lot with a new company in Kansas City, Missouri. Unable to adjust to his new surroundings, Spencer wasted no time making enemies among students *and* teachers at St. Mary's High School. After only a couple of months he was kicked out for unruly behavior. He was then admitted to a school in another part of town, Rockhurst High, but his reputation as an incorrigible preceded him. Before school officials could expel Spencer, John Tracy quit his new job and returned to Milwaukee.

This time the Tracys tried an alternative to the Milwaukee public school system. They enrolled their troubled young son in the Jesuit-run Marquette Academy, an affiliate of Marquette University. It was in fact Spencer's idea. He had bumped into William J. O'Brien, one of the "tough eggs" he had palled around with in Tory

Hill, and discovered he was attending Marquette Academy on a scholarship.

Bill O'Brien shared Spencer's love of silent pictures, but his interest in playacting went even farther than Tracy's. The darkly handsome hooligan was stagestruck and rhapsodized about what it would be like to be a famous actor on the stage—a song and dance legend like George M. Cohan, perhaps, or another Al Jolson. Wisconsin would, in fact, produce more than its share of legendary actors, from Orson Welles and Alfred Lunt to Fredric March.

But Broadway was worlds away, and Spencer had been indoctrinated with the popular belief that there was something distinctly effeminate about the acting profession. O'Brien's chatter made him vaguely uncomfortable. Still, at Marquette Academy Tracy and O'Brien—who went on to achieve screen stardom in his own right as Pat O'Brien—became fast friends.

"Intoxicated," as he would later put it, by the religious atmosphere, Spencer stunned his family by announcing his decision to become a priest. "The priests are all such superior men—heroes," he recalled. "You want to be like them—we all did. . . . You lie in the dark and see yourself as Monsignor Tracy, Cardinal Tracy, Bishop Tracy, Archbishop—I'm getting gooseflesh!" (Decades later Tracy told his friend Garson Kanin that when he donned a habit to play priests in *Boys Town*, *San Francisco*, and *The Devil at Four o'Clock*, he would "feel right, right away. Like they were mine, like I belonged in them.")

Instead, soon realizing that he was probably not temperamentally suited to the priesthood, Spencer opted for a uniform of a different sort. He enlisted in the Navy with his brother Carroll ("Someone has to keep Spencer out of the brig") and best friend Bill O'Brien just as the United States entered World War I. After basic training at the Great Lakes Naval Training Center near Chicago, Tracy was shipped off to the Norfolk, Virginia Navy Yard. Carroll and O'Brien remained behind. For seven months, Spencer scoured latrines and swabbed down decks but never ventured more than a few miles offshore. Considered a loner, he did, nevertheless, get drunk in the company of the other sailors—too drunk to accompany them to the local whorehouses. Without ever seeing duty overseas, he was mustered out of the service immediately after the war ended on November 11, 1918.

Spencer returned to Milwaukee with a newfound appreciation for his parents and all that he had put them through. The military had taught him to appreciate the value of self-discipline, and while he would always have a fearsome temper, for the first time in his life he could control it.

As if to atone for all the pain he had caused, young Tracy completed his junior year at Marquette Academy without incident and in the fall of 1919 enrolled in the Northwestern Military and Naval Academy. He paid the tuition himself, using the thirty-dollar monthly stipend paid veterans who wished to continue their educations.

Over the course of his senior year at the military school Spencer was profoundly influenced by his roommate, seventeen-year-old Kenneth Edgers. The son of a wealthy Seattle businessman, Edgers was already sophisticated beyond his years but without a trace of snobbishness. Easygoing, witty, and kind, he seemed to Spencer to be the very model of a young gentleman. Spencer copied his roommate's mannerisms, his style, and after they graduated followed Edgers to Ripon College, about a hundred miles northwest of Milwaukee near the Wisconsin town of Fond du Lac.

Spencer Tracy was twenty years old when he finally graduated from the twelfth grade, and by the time he reached the Ripon campus in January 1921 the beefy, square-jawed freshman looked and acted older than some faculty members. Spencer's sometimes sullen demeanor and deceptively mature appearance at first intimidated female students. His dating life was, by all accounts, virtually nonexistent.

Yet for Spence, who had long been self-conscious about his age, being older had unexpected advantages. When he left for Ripon, Tracy told his father that he intended to go on to medical school and become a doctor. In truth, the future Pat O'Brien had already convinced him that there was a lot of money to be made in the acting game.

As they had at the Northwestern Military and Naval Academy, Edgers and Tracy shared a dormitory room at Ripon. Their next-door neighbor at the West Hall dorm happened to be John Davies, a junior who appeared in most of the plays put on at the college. Davies introduced Spencer to drama Professor J. Clark Graham, who suggested he audition for Ripon's spring production of Clyde Fitch's *The Truth*.

Pacing outside the rehearsal hall as he waited his turn, the congenitally anxious Tracy bolted toward the stage when his name was finally called. In the process he tripped over a pile of band instruments. "Gosh," he said, scratching his head, "I think I busted the drum." The tension broken, he then shifted gears and read the lead role of Warder. Unlike the other actors, he did not need a script. Like Kate, he had a phenomenal ability to commit reams of material to memory, seemingly effortlessly.

Competing against seventeen- and eighteen-year-old classmates who were still dealing with acne and cracking voices, Tracy handily won the part. At the time Kate found her brother Tom's body hanging from a rafter—a pivotal event from which the only escape was acting—Spencer was rehearsing the college play that would seal his destiny.

Professor Graham had been impressed from the beginning with the quiet strength, the instinctive poise underlying Spencer's performance. The critic for the campus paper agreed. "Mr.

Tracy proved himself a consistent and unusually strong actor in this most difficult straight part," read the June 23, 1921, review in *College Days*. The piece went on to praise his "steadiness, his reserved strength and suppressed emotion."

Overnight, Tracy was a campus celebrity. And for the first time he was attracting the interest of the opposite sex. But now his mind was on other things. At Professor Graham's urging he learned all he could about the theater. He read everything he could but had yet to see a professional production. When the great Laurette Taylor came to Milwaukee in a touring production of her Broadway hit *Peg o' My Heart*, Spencer sat on the edge of his balcony seat, studying her every gesture. He was impressed by the *natural* quality of Taylor's performance—how she made it appear as if she weren't acting the part at all, but living it.

Later in Chicago he felt the same way when he saw the mesmerizing Lionel Barrymore in *The Claw*. "He wasn't acting at all, in the usual way," Tracy remembered. "He coughed right in the middle of a speech, and it was part of the characterization. He was doing what Laurette Taylor did—just being."

Tracy took every opportunity to hone his own, instinctively naturalistic style—at the expense of his studies. His public speaking instructor, H. P. Boody, despaired over Tracy's sloppy schoolwork. But when it came time for Spencer to be called upon to give a speech with "emotional content," he brought the entire class to the verge of tears when he spoke of his sister's tragic death. Professor Boody later asked John Davies to convey his heartfelt condolences, but Tracy only scowled at his friend in disbelief. "Are you kidding?" Spencer said. "Hell, I don't have a sister, not even a dead one."

That fall Spencer scored another hit at Ripon in *The Valiant*. His parents had driven up from Milwaukee to see him in *The Truth*, but it was not until this second triumph in *The Valiant* that he felt confident to tell them of his true intentions: He wanted desperately to become a professional actor.

Like Kate's mother, Carrie Brown Tracy was supportive, happy that her troubled son had at last found a calling. Carrie, who had recently embraced the teachings of Christian Science founder Mary Baker Eddy, had not been particularly enthusiastic about his purported plans to become a doctor anyway.

Like Dr. Hepburn, to whom he bore more than a passing physical resemblance, John Tracy reacted with rage. His son Spencer an *actor*? When Spencer's friends pointed out that he had already proved himself to be a promising talent, John Tracy pointed to his son. "Can you imagine," he demanded with a smirk, "*that face* ever becoming a matinee idol?"

Undaunted, Tracy starred in another college play, *The Great Divide*, to more acclaim. Then he put together a company of his own, the Campus

Players. During the 1921 Christmas holidays the troupe took *The Truth* to dilapidated playhouses in a half dozen small Wisconsin towns.

Professor Boody, still unaware that he had been duped by Spencer into thinking he had a dead sister, invited Tracy to go on tour with the Ripon debating team. Tracy accepted, but only because the tour itinerary included a three-day stop in New York. Convinced of Tracy's talent, Professor Graham wrote ahead asking Franklin Haven Sargent, the founder of New York's prestigious American Academy of Dramatic Arts, to give his promising young student an audition.

Sargent himself was waiting when Spence arrived at the academy's offices in the Carnegie Hall building. That morning Sargent, who had established the academy thirty-eight years earlier, had been fretting over the "pretty boy" mentality that had come to dominate the theatrical community. When Spencer gave a forceful reading of *Sintram of Sgagerrak*, Sargent nodded his approval. "You're a good masculine type," he told the stunned college freshman, "and there are never enough of those." He invited Tracy to start in June or even earlier if he wished. Later Sargent remembered that Tracy "was manly and capable of a strong, dominating presence. . . . he certainly wasn't pretty. . . ." (History was to show that Sargent and his successors at the academy were remarkably successful at turning out stars. Ultimately the academy numbered among its alumni Edward G. Robinson, Rosalind Russell, Lauren Bacall, Jason Robards Jr., Grace Kelly, Anne Bancroft, and Robert Redford.)

From a state of euphoria Tracy was soon plunged into a deep depression. He became, recalled one of his fellow debate team members, "more withdrawn than usual, and he *always* was a difficult guy to know." Spencer, as the women in his life were to find out, dreaded making the hard choices in life. Now he was faced with turning his back on Ripon and the teachers—particularly J. Clark Graham—who had nurtured his talent.

Spencer also dreaded his father's reaction, but that proved unwarranted. John Tracy still dismissed his son's dream of becoming an actor as silly, but he nevertheless agreed to pay his tuition at the academy—as long as Spencer used his thirty dollars a month from the government to pay all his own living expenses. "And son," he added, still worried that Spencer was not handsome enough to succeed on the stage, "always be sure you keep a fine wardrobe!"

That spring, shortly after his twenty-second birthday, Spencer quietly dropped out of college and headed for his new life in New York. He had been in Manhattan only two weeks when Spencer literally bumped into his old friend "Pat" O'Brien at a neighborhood cigar store. O'Brien, it turned out, was also set to start classes at the academy. Together the two street toughs from Milwaukee rented a dank, dark twelve-by-twelve-foot room in a run-down rooming house at West End Avenue and Ninety-eighth Street.

Subsisting largely on a diet of water, rice, and pretzels, the two "were frozen in winter," O'Brien recalled. In summer "the heat was out of Egypt. But somehow we really didn't mind. Actually we were often very happy." Tracy, who claimed he and O'Brien went for nearly three days with no food at all, nonetheless shared O'Brien's fondness for those early hardships and even credited them with making him a better actor. "It was lots of fun," he said, "and there's something about going hungry that makes you discover the utmost of your resources."

Pounding the pavement in search of work, Tracy landed his first Broadway part—the ten-dollar-a-week nonspeaking role of a robot in the Theatre Guild's production of *R.U.R.* (which stood for "Rossum's Universal Robots") at the Garrick—in October 1922. After a month he was given one line of dialogue—and a five-dollar raise.

R.U.R. had closed by the time Tracy graduated from the American Academy of Dramatic Art in March 1923, and he soon discovered that parts—even nonspeaking walk-ons—were hard to come by. He refused to give up. To pay the bills, he worked a variety of jobs: door-to-door salesman, piano mover, bellhop, sparring partner at a gym.

Threatened with eviction, his phone cut off, Spencer faced the very real prospect of returning home to Milwaukee in disgrace when he read about a new stock company being started by Leonard Wood, Jr., in White Plains, New York. There was only an opening for an actor willing to do bit parts, but Tracy jumped at the chance to earn twenty dollars a week.

On the train to White Plains Spencer noticed a slim brunette with perfect posture and a warm smile. She was wearing a green dress. They exchanged furtive glances but said nothing until they both got off at the same station. Tracy introduced himself, and was delighted to discover that the attractive young woman was also a member of the Wood Stock Company. In fact she was the company's leading lady. Her name was Louise Treadwell.

Four years older than Spencer, Louise was also in many ways worldlier. Born in New Castle, Pennsylvania, as a teenager she had gone through the emotional turmoil of her parents' divorce. (Contrary to the popular assumption years later that she would never end her marriage to Spencer because of their devout Catholic beliefs, Louise was raised an Episcopalian and remained an Episcopalian throughout her life. She also had no strong moral opposition to divorce, having experienced it firsthand.)

Alliene Treadwell was the classic stage mother, a frustrated singer and dancer who sought to live out her dreams through her talented daughter. Alliene pushed Louise relentlessly, and when Louise started landing ingenue roles in Chicago and New York, Mom insisted on going along to coach her from the wings.

Louise did not crave stardom with the same intensity as did Alliene and convinced her mother to let her take a break from her show business career to attend college. Louise enrolled at Lake Erie College, but as soon as she graduated with honors in 1917, her mother forced her back onto the stage, this time as a chorus girl.

Just as Spencer resisted his father's attempts to bar him from a theatrical career, so Louise resented being forced onto the stage by her mother. Finally fed up with Alliene's constant interference, Louise returned to live a "normal" life back home in Pennsylvania. That changed in 1919, when Alliene died suddenly, sending her daughter into a downward spiral of remorse.

Guilt, which was to play such an overwhelming part in the Tracy Saga, propelled Louise back onto the stage. By the time she met Spencer, she had already appeared in stock in *Nothing but the Truth* and on Broadway in *The Pigeon*. She was not a star, but she was considered a solid professional with a promising future.

The first Wood production was *The Man Who Came Back*, with Louise in the starring role and Spencer given a single line to deliver. But when he gave that single line—"To hell with him!"— the audience always erupted in applause. "I loved him," Louise later said, "because he was so earnest, so attentive, and such a good actor.

With a single line, boomed out in that strong voice of his, he could instantly command the attention of the audience."

The Wood company folded after only three months, and Louise was promptly asked to join Stuart Walker's Repertory Theater of Cincinnati. She agreed to sign, on one condition: that Walker also hire Spencer as her leading man. "By then," she later conceded, "I also knew that I wanted Spencer Tracy as my husband." Spencer now had his foot in the door. It was only one of many debts to Louise he would, without any pressure from her, spend a lifetime repaying.

Spencer proposed to Louise in a Cincinnati restaurant. They were married in a civil ceremony on September 12, 1923, between the matinee and evening performance of a play called *Buddies.* They had talked over the differences in religion, and neither felt this constituted any sort of obstacle. The dignified, ladylike Louise reminded Spencer of his mother ("a *lot*"), and Carrie Brown Tracy was also a Protestant. Ecumenism aside, he professed to be astonished that she would marry him under any circumstances.

There would be no honeymoon. As soon as they finished their run in *Buddies,* the couple returned to New York, where Spencer had landed a supporting role in a new play starring Ethel Barrymore, *A Royal Fandango.* Producer Arthur Hopkins, who would also figure rather large in

Kate's early career, had cast Tracy along with another newcomer, Edward G. Robinson.

A Royal Fandango was a royal flop, and the *New York World* critic went out of his way to write that Tracy and Robinson were so wooden they "looked as though they had been picked up by the property man." With no prospects in New York, Spencer would again have to hit the road—this time without Louise, who was already expecting their first child.

John Tracy seized the opportunity to suggest that his son seek gainful employment in another, less fickle line of work—the trucking business, perhaps. But Carrie and Louise Tracy, who had grown fond of each other, had complete faith that Spencer would ultimately prevail as an actor. At Carrie's insistence, her daughter-in-law would come to Milwaukee to have her baby while Spencer acted in stock companies from Elizabeth, New Jersey, to Grand Rapids, Michigan to pay the bills.

The months on the road, spent in rocking, smoke-filled railway cars and in vermin-infested hotel rooms, pushed Tracy to the brink. The only bright spot during this period was the birth, just ten months after their wedding day, of their first child on June 26, 1924. Despite John Tracy's attempts to undermine Spencer's acting career, the little boy was named after his grandfather.

Johnny was, to all outward appearances, a perfectly healthy, robust child. But when he was nearly ten months old, Louise slammed a screen door inadvertently and noticed that the sound did not rouse the baby from his nap. "Then I called to him, and he didn't awaken," she said. But when she touched Johnny, "his eyes flew open, and he was looking at me, and I knew he was deaf."

Rather than bother Spencer on the road with her concerns, she went to a physician who confirmed her fears: Johnny had been born totally and irreversibly deaf. Then, still not sharing the news with her husband, Louise went from one doctor to another in search of a different, less devastating opinion. She did not find it.

Incredibly, no one—not Louise, not his parents or his brother, Carroll, or his closest friends in the theater—was brave enough to break the news to Spencer. All feared that it might send the moody, mercurial Tracy over the edge. They were right to be concerned.

As a result, Spencer Tracy was the last to learn of his own son's deafness. In a scene that might have come from one of his later movies, Spencer was playing with Johnny on the floor when it occurred to him for the first time that the toddler was not reacting to his father's words. "Hey, what's the matter with this kid?" Tracy asked his wife. "He acts like he doesn't hear me."

Finally Louise confessed what she had known for months. He refused to accept the diagnosis at first, but he could no longer deny the truth about their son's condition after throwing a small party to celebrate his first birthday. They sat Johnny on a sofa with his back to the kitchen, put a single candle in the middle of a cake, and marched out loudly singing "Happy Birthday." The baby did not turn around or respond to the racket at all. "It was only then," said a friend, "that it really hit Spence. Hard. He was forced to admit to himself that the boy was totally deaf."

Predictably, Tracy blamed his son's disability on himself. "He felt it was all his fault, absolutely," confirmed Pat O'Brien. "Spence always felt Johnny's deafness was God's way of punishing him—the father—for being such a terrible sinner. There was no other explanation for it, as far as he was concerned. Young, healthy Irish guys just didn't have defective children. . . . He felt that just didn't happen, unless God *wanted* it to happen. It was completely out of left field. Spence just didn't know how to handle it."

Louise was no less shattered, but unlike her husband, she was not given to black moods or self-flagellation. She sprang into action, seeking out the specialists who might one day cure their son or at least help him to cope as a nonhearing person in a hearing world. She was told that Johnny would never learn to speak and that it was best he be institutionalized as quickly as possible. She rejected that advice and decided to devote her entire life, if need be, to teaching the boy how to read lips and eventually to speak.

Typically, Spencer crumbled under the strain. He reacted to the news of his son's deafness by embarking, in the words of Pat O'Brien, "on the first *big* drunk of his life, as far as I know." He disappeared for four days, holed up at Brooklyn's Hotel St. George with a case of bootleg whiskey.

It is questionable whether this was in fact Tracy's "first big drunk." It was undeniably not his last. Over the decades Spencer went on marathon binges, disappearing for days or even weeks at a time without warning—sometimes alone, often in the company of other women. Then, just as suddenly and unexpectedly, he would resurface and not touch a drink for months, even years.

In more sober moments Spencer reasoned that the best contribution he could make to Johnny's welfare was financial. He wanted the best specialists in the field for his son, and that would cost money. So, in the summer of 1925, he resumed his work in the theater with a new sense of purpose.

After another frustrating year bouncing around in stock ("I had done more than fifty plays, and a lot of guys without my talent were making it on Broadway while I was still stuck in the sticks"), Tracy auditioned for the great George M. Cohan and Cohan's Broadway play *Yellow*. During rehearsals the famously irascible Cohan stopped Tracy mid-speech and said, "Kid, you are the best actor I have ever seen."

"Wha-t?" Tracy stammered.

"I said, 'Kid, you are the best goddamned actor I've ever seen.' Now, go ahead!"

Over the five-month run of *Yellow* Cohan served as Tracy's mentor ("Spencer, I have one bit of important advice: Act *less*") and verbal sparring partner. Tracy had already established a reputation as being tactless, rude, even mean at times. "He's the most difficult son of a bitch I've ever known," said another struggling actor of the period, James Cagney. "And the best. Certainly the best actor. [But] he's too demanding. . . . A hard man."

Tracy reminded Cohan of himself as a brash, cocky young man, and Spencer's orneriness actually appealed to him. "He always stood up to me and took my guff. We needled each other back and forth all the time," Cohan recalled, "and instead of getting mad, I'd break up when he told me to go fuck myself."

Appropriately, Cohan next cast Tracy in a farce about a Pekingese dog called *The Baby Cyclone*. It proved to be a modest hit, and for the first time Spencer's parents—who had moved to New York after John Tracy took a job with General Motors—were able to see their son on Broadway. During this period father and son grew closer together than they had ever been; while Carrie and Louise took care of Johnny, the two men often met for lunch near the senior Tracy's office or dinner in the theater district.

Then, in early 1928, Carrie told her son that his father was dying of cancer. "My father was a powerful man," Tracy recalled. "In every way. Body and mind." But as he wasted away from the disease, John Tracy would look at Spencer "beggingly—as though I could help if I wanted to. Once, visiting, I heard him crying out. Nothing to do but wait and suffer and wait . . ."

Spencer had just finished the second act in Cohan's *Whispering Friends* when he returned to his dressing room and found Cohan waiting to tell him the news. Tracy went back onstage and finished the show, then went to the funeral home. "I looked at what was left—just practically nothing . . ." Tracy recalled. From that point on Spencer Tracy harbored a crippling fear of cancer, and even told his friend Garson Kanin that he planned to commit suicide if he was ever stricken with the disease. Tracy paid less attention to the fact that his father had also suffered from heart disease—the genetic predisposition that would have a large impact on the future state of Spencer's health.

His father's death plunged Spencer into another canyon of despair. At the small West Side apartment he shared with his wife and son, Tracy would brood for hours, then explode over some trivial matter. He even wound up unintentionally venting his rage at Johnny. "I wanted to help with the boy, but I was no damn good at it," Spencer admitted. "I would come in after Louise had been working with him for hours and start undoing the good she had done. Maybe she had been working with him all day on a word like 'shoe,' showing it to him and saying the word over and over, trying to get him to read her lips. So I would pick up the damn shoe and throw it across the room and scare the poor kid half to death. I had no patience, and it's amazing how much he had—and has."

Gradually Spencer, all too aware of his impatient streak, left Johnny's education and therapy in Louise's capable hands. "I loved the boy, and it was painful and frustrating not to be able to help."

More and more Tracy sought solace in the company of his drinking buddies at the Lambs, the famous show business watering hole on West Fifty-first Street. He needed to surround himself with people, though he was careful never to let anyone get too close. "Even then," a fellow club member said, "the walls were up. He was witty, charming, very entertaining. Those of us who knew Spencer could see he was not a happy man, but there was nothing we could do about it—nothing he would *let* us do about it."

New York during the Roaring Twenties offered a thousand ways for a man to forget his troubles, and for a time Spencer Tracy seemed determined to try them all. With the high-living Jimmy Walker ensconced as mayor, corruption and organized crime flourished. Mobster-run speakeasies and brothels proliferated throughout the city. Tracy was a regular at Sally's, one of midtown Manhattan's more popular houses of ill repute, and at the decidedly more downscale Lu's. At both institutions he made known his preference for oral sex, an act from which obviously there would be no risk of an unwanted pregnancy. In the spring of 1929, however, he was barred from Lu's after causing an ugly scene. Tracy had flown into a drunken rage, beaten up one of Lu's girls, and, in the Runyon-esque vernacular of one eyewitness, "busted up the joint."

"Weeze," as Spencer affectionately called Louise, was always on hand to guide his friends to the bedroom when they carried him home in the predawn hours. She never criticized her husband, nor did she interrogate him about the trips to the speakeasies and the bordellos. But when it came to his profession, she did not equivocate: Mrs. Tracy was in that regard one of Spencer's toughest critics. She was convinced that so long as he confined himself to the kind of fluff for which Cohan was so famous, Tracy would continue to feel creatively stifled. It was Louise who reminded Spencer that he was above all else a dramatic actor and that his future lay in serious roles.

Spencer, who rightly confessed to being "a lousy judge of material," trusted Louise's judgment and decided to concentrate only on heavy drama. When a neophyte actor named Clark Gable bowed out of a new play called *Conflict*, Tracy jumped at the chance. But *Conflict* fizzled. So did his next play, *Nigger Rich*, the aptly named *Dread*, and *Veneer*, which Spencer took to calling *Venereal*.

More discouraged than he had ever been,

Tracy told friends at the Lambs Club that he would quit acting completely if his next role did not pan out. The play was *The Last Mile*, and by the time it opened on Broadway on February 13, 1930 with Tracy in the lead role of Killer Mears, he was convinced it was going to be another disaster. "Boys, I'm in one hell of a flop," he told his buddies. "Don't see the show. I've got no confidence in it."

Audiences and critics disagreed. *The Last Mile* was hailed as a taut prison drama, and Tracy was singled out for special praise. *The New York Times*'s Brooks Atkinson lauded Spencer for his "muscular determination," while Tracy's old friend Pat O'Brien, who could afford only a balcony seat, claimed he had seen "a one-man performance of amazing power, of near greatness. . . . Spence was an overnight sensation!"

As O'Brien well knew, at age thirty and with dozens of plays behind him, Tracy could hardly be called an "overnight sensation." But *The Last Mile* did finally make him a full-fledged Broadway star. It also brought him to the attention of a young Hollywood director who was scouring New York theaters in search of two actors to star in the Fox studio's upcoming prison film *Up the River*. Within a week John Ford—who went on to direct such classics as *The Informer*, *Stagecoach*, *The Grapes of Wrath*, *How Green Was My Valley*, and *The Quiet Man*—had found the two men he wanted. One was Spencer; the other was a lean thirty-one-year-old with a slight stoop and a pro-

nounced yet oddly appealing speech impediment. His name was Humphrey Bogart.

Tracy and Ford, two hard-drinking, no-
nonsense Irishmen (Ford's real name was Sean
Aloysius O'Fearna), clicked immediately. "I'm
not handsome," Tracy said when Ford offered
him the part in his movie, "and I can prove it!"
Rather than use the tickets he had been given to
seven different Broadway shows, Ford preferred
to spend every night marveling at his new
friend's riveting performance in *The Last Mile*.
(Ironically, that year Clark Gable also got his
start in films as a result of playing Killer Mears
in the play's Los Angeles production. Tracy and
Gable, both heavy drinkers, went on to become
lifelong friends.)

To hire Tracy for his film, however, Ford had
to battle the Fox casting department. When talking pictures arrived three years earlier, all the
studios had raided Broadway for actors who
sounded as good as they looked. Cagney, Edward G. Robinson, Claudette Colbert, Ginger
Rogers, Bette Davis, Fredric March, Irene Dunne,
William Powell, Paul Muni, and Barbara Stanwyck were among those snapped up almost immediately by studio talent scouts. At that time
Spencer Tracy was, in fact, screen-tested in the
role of a buccaneer. The verdict then was that he
was just "too ugly" for the movies. Beneath the
pirate makeup, Ford assured studio executives,
Tracy looked just fine. They reluctantly agreed to

sign him to a one-picture contract, at the impressive salary of one thousand dollars per week.

Taking a six-week leave of absence from *The Last Mile,* Tracy boarded the Super Chief for California alone. Just one year after the stock market crash and the start of the Great Depression, the American people flocked to the darkened theaters by the millions to escape the dreary reality of their daily lives. The movie business was booming, and Tracy was poised to be a part of it.

While he waited to start shooting *Up the River*, Spencer struck up a friendship with a fellow George M. Cohan crony, Will Rogers. A power in the movie industry and at the time arguably the most beloved man in America, Rogers proved an invaluable ally. He lunched with Tracy at the studio commissary and introduced the newcomer to the hottest producers, directors, and stars on the Fox lot. Tracy also accepted an invitation to watch Rogers and his friends play polo at the exclusive Riviera Country Club. Tracy had never seen a polo match, yet in the months to come he would, with Rogers's help, master the difficult and dangerous sport.

His confidence bolstered, Spencer rented a bungalow on Franklin Avenue in L.A. and sent for Louise and Johnny to join him. On the set of *Up the River*, which had now been retooled as a comedy, Tracy always made good his promise to "get it right the first time"; he never needed a second take. He also clicked with his gritty costar and even bestowed him with a nickname that caught on instantly with cast and crew: Bogie.

Up the River was a hit, and as soon as his run in *The Last Mile* was up, Tracy signed a five-year $350,000 contract with Fox, the rough equivalent in purchasing power of $4 million in 1997 dollars. Tracy's old Broadway buddies Cagney and Edward G. Robinson had been signed by Warner's and exploded on the scene as movie gangsters: Cagney in *The Public Enemy* and Robinson in *Little Caesar*. Fox needed its own psychotic criminal type, and on the basis of *The Last Mile* and *Up the River*, Tracy fit the bill nicely.

Tracy's spirits were quickly dashed by news that autumn of 1931 that his son had suffered a setback. A polio epidemic had swept through Los Angeles during the brief time the Tracy family was there. On the train trip back East Johnny had fallen ill, and in New York doctors confirmed that the boy had contracted the sometimes fatal, often crippling disease. After several weeks it became clear that Johnny would survive with only some damage to his leg muscles. This time the Tracys meant it when they celebrated Thanksgiving aboard the L.A.-bound Twentieth Century Ltd.

Between 1931 and 1933 Tracy churned out sixteen mostly forgettable films with titles like *Quick Millions*, *Six Cylinder Love*, *Sky Devils*, *Disorderly Conduct*, *Society Girl*, and *The Painted Woman*. Frustrated with the quality of the scripts being offered, he stormed into Fox's front office and demanded to be released from his contract. When studio executives refused, Tracy reverted to his rebellious, tantrum-filled childhood.

Although he spent every available weekend playing polo at the Riviera Country Club with the likes of Rogers, Darryl Zanuck, Leslie Howard (who a few years earlier had refused to share the Broadway stage with "beanpole" Katharine Hepburn), and Douglas Fairbanks Sr., Tracy was becoming better known for the sports he engaged in after hours. Some of these pursuits were innocent enough. Every Thursday night, in hotel rooms or at restaurants like Romanoff's and the Brown Derby, Tracy got together with six of his brethren from the New York stage: Pat O'Brien, Frank McHugh, Lynne Overman, Frank Morgan, Ralph Bellamy, and Cagney. Errol Flynn later joined the group, which was variously known as the Irishmen's Club, the Irish Mafia, and the Boys Club.

Ironically, although prodigious quantities of alcohol were consumed at these weekly meetings, Tracy never touched a drop. "Tracy went on binges," said journalist James Bacon, a longtime friend and periodic drinking buddy. "Once he got started, he drank a lot. And he wasn't always such a nice person when he drank. For whatever reason, he did not drink when they all got together. Maybe he valued their friendship so much he didn't want to lose control and wind up punching one of them. Or all of them."

Tracy more than made up for his one night a

week of abstinence. He had been in Hollywood less than a year, but his drinking bouts were already legendary. He also made little attempt to conceal his visits to a pricey Sunset Boulevard brothel frequented by studio executives and their out-of-town guests. After one of these visits, he was behind the wheel of a friend's car and weaving onto Sunset when he was stopped by police. A pitched battle ensued, and after being slapped into handcuffs and leg straps, Spencer was unceremoniously hauled off to jail and tossed into the drunk tank. Fox's troubleshooters, accustomed to bailing unruly stars out of trouble, managed to talk the police into not pressing charges.

Far from chastened, Tracy did not behave much better during daylight hours. Often he did not go home at all. Instead he showed up on the set wearing his wrinkled evening clothes from the previous night's revelries, reeking of alcohol, cigarette smoke, and cheap perfume. Yet when the cameras rolled, he always knew his lines and nearly always delivered them flawlessly.

At this stage in his life Tracy had little respect for women in general but even less for those in the movie business, and he showed it by cornering every female on the set. His twenty-year-old costar in 1931's *Goldie*, Jean Harlow, watched Tracy lure script girls and starlets alike into his dressing room and then listened to the sounds of their lovemaking. Spencer believed, Harlow cracked, "that his movie contract gave him a license to feel."

Harlow resisted his advances but took his advice. It was Tracy who bluntly told her to cut out some of her more pretentious mannerisms and "stop trying to act like the goddamn queen of England." Within two years the brassy, wisecracking, gum-snapping "platinum blonde" was Hollywood's biggest sex symbol.

During the filming of Tracy's next picture, *She Wanted a Millionaire*, *The Hollywood Reporter* claimed that he was involved in a classic love triangle with his leading lady, Joan Bennett, and the movie's producer, John Considine. (Years later Bennett, who also starred with Tracy in the original *Father of the Bride*, was involved in another triangle that came to a violent end when her husband, producer Walter Wanger, shot her lover, Jennings Lang, in the groin. Lang survived, and Wanger went to prison for the shooting.)

From then on Tracy's antics, which included punching a Fox employee who had taken his parking space, were fodder for the scandal sheets. Louise did not confront Spencer, instead choosing to ignore all the stories and concentrate on their son's welfare. Home was now a twelve-acre ranch in Encino, and on those increasingly rare occasions when Spencer was there they behaved, according to their friends, like any happily married couple.

In late 1931 Louise told Spencer she was expecting another child. The ostensibly happy news hit Spencer hard. According to Cagney, Tracy "went through hell." "He was terrified," Cagney said, "that the second child would be born deaf too." Everyone was relieved when, on July 1, 1932, Louise gave birth to a perfectly healthy girl. She was christened Louise but would always be known as Susie.

At the studio, Spencer continued to press for better pictures. When he was loaned out to Warner Brothers to make another prison film, this one called *20,000 Years in Sing Sing*, Tracy was delighted. Produced by Hal Wallis and directed by Michael Curtiz, *20,000 Years in Sing Sing* would be Tracy's first major box-office hit. It was also the first big break for his equally headstrong leading lady, Bette Davis. "We were an awful lot alike," she recalled. "We even had the same birthday. We weren't the best-looking people on the lot, but we knew we *were* talented and we weren't getting the parts we deserved. We also weren't just going to sit back and take it."

There were two more flops—*Face in the Sky* and *Shanghai Madness*—before Tracy got his next shot at a solid role. Film pioneer Jesse Lasky had just arrived at Fox and wanted to cast its most brash young star in his first Fox film, *Helldorado*. But only days before production was scheduled to begin, Tracy vanished.

While the studio publicity department kept the press at bay, Fox's private investigators scoured every bar and brothel in a hundred-mile radius of Los Angeles. Louise was not concerned; she had been through these disappearances countless times during their marriage, and she knew he would turn up eventually. But Fox was locked into a tight shooting schedule and could not postpone *Helldorado*. With Tracy still missing and no other options, Lasky replaced him with Richard Arlen. The movie bombed at the box office.

Tracy, in fact, carefully choreographed many of his disappearances. Most lasted about two weeks, and began when Tracy, lugging a suitcase packed with whiskey bottles, boarded a train in Los Angeles for the four-day trip to New York.

Once there he checked into the same hotel he used for his Broadway binges, Brooklyn's St. George. Using any one of several aliases (his favorite was Ivan Catchanozoff), Tracy paid off the hotel management to keep quiet. Spencer later told Cagney that once he got in the room, he went through the same ritual: He stripped nude, climbed into the bathtub with the open suitcase full of whiskey on the floor beside him, and began polishing off each bottle. He stayed there, alternately drinking and passing out for a solid week, not bothering to leave the tub even to relieve himself. It usually took Tracy a week to finish off his whiskey supply. When it was over, he bathed, shaved, put on a change of fresh clothes, and returned to Los Angeles.

When Tracy finally surfaced after the *Helldorado* fiasco, he expected a tongue-lashing or worse from Lasky. Instead the producer forgave him.

"I sent word to him that I would never ask him what happened but that it might have happened to me instead of him and I was glad it didn't so I was willing to forget it," Lasky recalled. "I added that there were plenty more good parts and I wanted to see him, but not till he had taken a little vacation and pulled himself together. He went to Honolulu and then reported back to the studio scared stiff, but not stiff."

Inexplicably, Lasky rewarded Tracy for his bizarre behavior by handing him the plum role of Tom Garner, the doomed railroad tycoon in Preston Sturges's *The Power and the Glory*. "I don't know to this day whether it was exuberance, lack of confidence, or personal problems that caused his lapse, because I never asked him," Lasky said. "But I knew somehow in a way I can't explain that if I overlooked it, it wouldn't happen again." Yet it did happen again and again—not to Lasky, who had earned Tracy's loyalty, but to other producers and directors assigned to work with him at Fox.

In 1933 Tracy was loaned out to Columbia to make *Man's Castle*, a Frank Borzage–directed romance about unrequited love on the wrong side of the tracks. Tracy's costar was a lithe, elegant, high-cheekboned beauty who exuded so much intelligence and class that she was far from convincing as the down-on-her-luck resident of a Depression shantytown.

Tracy was famous for the laserlike intensity with which his eyes bored into the souls of his fellow actors, male or female. This time, however, everyone on the set from Borzage to the grips recognized that Tracy and his leading lady were making more than just eye contact. They lingered in the love scenes and playfully teased each other between takes.

The first week of filming Tracy asked her out to dinner. Like everyone else in Hollywood, she knew all about Tracy's reputation as a womanizing drunk and all-around troublemaker. But she instantly recognized him as a tortured genius, a deeply spiritual artist whose cocky exterior belied "an ocean of pain."

By this time Tracy had become a staple for *The Hollywood Reporter* and the other trade dailies. "What makes people read this stuff?" someone on the set of Tracy's latest picture supposedly asked. A crew member pointed to Tracy, sitting slumped and slightly hung over. "He does," said the crew member.

Again the gossip columns were filled with accounts of Spencer's latest indiscretion. Only this time the stories were not about his drunken escapades with nameless women but about his serious involvement with a specific young actress. For her part Louise was once again willing to remain silent. But she also realized that this woman was not like the others and that for the first time Spencer seemed hopelessly smitten. To make matters worse, the Other Woman was even more famous than Tracy. Her name was Loretta Young.

Confronted with the rumors of his affair with Young, Spencer issued a limp denial. "One night I asked Loretta to have dinner with me," he told a reporter. "I was tired of eating alone. It was just one of those things, offhand, unpremeditated." After he told another writer that "it was all platonic," one of his costars in 1934's *Now I'll Tell*, the actress Helen Twelvetrees, cracked, "When was Spence sober enough to say a thing like that?"

In August 1933 Spencer moved out of the family ranch in Encino and into rooms at the Riviera Country Club. The next day Louise issued a terse statement formally announcing the couple's separation after a decade of marriage on grounds of incompatability. Officially, they both hoped for a reconciliation. But that seemed only the dimmest of possibilities. Louise had immersed herself in her family and the raising of money for research aimed at finding new ways to open up the world to deaf children.

For all his denials Spencer openly pursued his affair with Loretta Young over the next year. They were photographed driving in an open Duesenberg, dining at Ciro's and Chasen's, and dancing into the early-morning hours at the Mocambo. To squire the elegant Miss Young to parties and premieres, he had even acquired a new Fred Astaire wardrobe of top hat and tails.

It was a tempestuous affair from the start, and the tabloids faithfully reported every drama-filled twist and turn, from tearful spat to passionate embrace. At one point Tracy received a note threatening to kidnap him, his children, or Loretta if he didn't drop eight thousand dollars at a specified location. The threat turned out to be a hoax, but Tracy was so shaken he could not report for work on the set of his first and only musical, *Bottoms Up*.

Tracy responded to the mounting pressures with violence. Reporters were an easy and convenient target. At various times he knocked them to the ground, kicked them, and smashed their cameras. Polo provided another much-needed outlet for Tracy's oceanic reservoirs of pent-up aggression. He had abandoned the game for a time after a spectacular collision with two other players in June 1933 had left him with a wrenched back and badly sprained arm. That accident had, in fact, led Fox to prohibit Tracy from competing while in the process of making a film. To get back in shape—he had put on twenty pounds since leaving Louise for Loretta Young— Tracy resumed competition, this time registering with bemused club officials under his Ivan Catchanazoff pseudonym. Fox executives were not amused when while filming *Marie Galante*, "Ivan" took another spill in the summer of 1934 and wound up in the emergency room.

Tracy's daredevil antics notwithstanding, the powers-that-be at Fox were most concerned about his scandalous private life. But Spencer was clearly besotted with Young—so much so that he was now willing to divorce Louise even if it meant excommunication.

Ironically, Loretta, who had been drawn to Spencer in part because of their shared Catholic faith, turned down Tracy's marriage proposal rather than violate the church's strict ban on divorce and remarriage. She convinced Spencer that marriage was impossible for them, though religious considerations did not matter to him as much as the impact a divorce might have on the children. Johnny had grown into a bright, well-adjusted, athletic ten-year-old, and Spencer did not want to put him through the emotional trauma of seeing his parents divorce.

In October 1934 Young issued a statement that left little room for misinterpretation. "Since Spencer Tracy and I are both Catholic and can never be married," she said flatly, "we have agreed not to see each other again." Spencer reacted by going on another one of his benders at the St. George Hotel. Young later described their decision not to marry "a lesson in self-denial."

For Tracy the decision was a turning point. If he would not divorce "Weeze" to marry Loretta Young—whom he then described as "the love of my life"—he vowed that he would never divorce, period. After their fourteen month separation Tracy returned home to his wife and children. "Weeze knew I was going to come home eventually," he said. "The wonder was that she would take me back at all." Tracy added that when he walked back into the Encino house, "a door closed ... and neither of us will ever open it again. She has never mentioned the affair from that day."

But Tracy's all-consuming pursuit of Young had taken a toll on his health. For his entire adult life Spencer had battled chronic insomnia, seldom managing to sleep more than two or three hours in any twenty-four hour period. On the set he was running on adrenaline, cigarettes (two packs a day), and gallons of sugar-laden coffee—a volatile mixture that led to more blowups.

Except for loaning Tracy to MGM to do the critically acclaimed satire *The Show-Off,* Fox continued to squander his talents. During the filming of another loser, *It's a Small World,* an unhappy Spencer disappeared again—this time to a hotel room in Yuma, Arizona. On March 11, 1935, he got into a fight with Louise over the telephone that quickly escalated into a full-fledged tantrum. By the time police arrived, Tracy, still shrieking at Louise, had smashed all his room service plates and glasses against the wall and was starting in on the furniture. Again he had to be physically restrained by three officers and hauled off in handcuffs. The charges this time: drunkenness, resisting arrest, and vandalism. As soon as he was released on bail, Tracy and a friend took off across the border to the bars and brothels in Nogales, Mexico.

A few weeks later Tracy showed up drunk on the set of *Dante's Inferno* and demanded major changes in the script. He then attacked the film's director, Harry Lachman. While cast and crew scurried for cover, Spencer suddenly passed out. Studio chief Winfield Sheehan ordered everyone out and padlocked the set so that Tracy would have time to sleep it off. Instead Tracy woke up and began demolishing the scenery, lights, and props. A crowd gathered outside and listened to the hourlong rampage. When it was over, uniformed studio guards wrestled Tracy into a straitjacket and drove him home to Louise.

Tracy was well aware of his behavior under the influence of alcohol, and it scared him. Even during his binges he tried to phone Louise at home just to make contact. Occasionally he called his brother, Carroll, who served as his accountant, advisor, and one-man entourage. The message was invariably the same, but Louise and Carroll knew what it meant. "I'm gone," Spencer would mumble into the phone. "I'm gone. I'm gone. . . ."

The *Dante's Inferno* tantrum was to be Spencer Tracy's last at Fox. In April of 1935, after five years and twenty-four mostly dreadful films, he was called into the head office and told to behave. He nodded in agreement, then strolled to the corner bar. Four hours later he stumbled back to the head office to show the executives just how seriously he had taken their scolding. They responded by firing him on the spot, one of the biggest mistakes, it turned out, the studio ever made.

Being unceremoniously dumped by Fox, he

soon came to realize, was one of the best things that ever happened to Spencer Tracy. Irving Thalberg, the brilliant young producer whose reputation was to grow to near-mythic proportions, had been eyeing Tracy for years. But his straitlaced boss, the all-powerful Louis B. Mayer, was less sanguine about adding Spencer to the MGM roster. Mayer had his hands full with the perpetually soused Wallace Beery and was reluctant to take on another troublemaker. Thalberg insisted that the violence and drinking stemmed from the lousy roles Tracy had been given at Fox and that MGM "didn't make too many terrible movies." Thalberg recalled, "I talked him into it." Within two hours of his dismissal by Fox, Tracy signed a new contract with MGM on April 2, 1935.

Unfortunately, Tracy's first three pictures at MGM—*The Murder Man, Riffraff,* with his old friend Jean Harlow, and *Whipsaw,* with Myrna Loy—were not much better than what he had been assigned at Fox. On August 15, 1935, while Tracy was working on *Riffraff,* Will Rogers and aviator Wiley Post were killed in a plane crash at Point Barrow, Alaska. The world was stunned, but no one took the news harder than Rogers's friend Tracy. He went on the expected bender but pulled himself together in time for the memorial service at Forest Lawn. From that point on, he told friends, it was never the same when he played polo. "The fun just went out of it," he said.

That autumn he shot *Whipsaw,* a cops-and-robbers movie originally intended for the urbane Miss Loy and her *Thin Man* partner, William Powell. A creature of habit, once again Tracy clashed with his director—and slept with his leading lady. Already a major star, Loy had been in the business a full decade and had made more than fifty films. On the screen she personified cool sophistication—the perfect foil for the no-nonsense, unflappable Tracy. Offscreen he was so different from the Hollywood matinee idols Loy had known socially that she could not help being intrigued. "Spence loved all kinds of women, but the women that really got to him were the ones with that extra something called *class,*" Cagney said. "And for some reason he really got to them." The Tracy-Loy Affair, which they miraculously managed to keep under wraps, fizzled after shooting on *Whipsaw* had ended, only to be revived on the set of a later film.

By the time he began shooting the dark psychodrama *Fury* with the expatriate Austrian director Fritz Lang, Spencer was again in a scrappy mood. The two men raged at each other but never allowed their disputes to escalate into violence. Punches were thrown, however, during the making of Tracy's next film, *San Francisco.* The movie chronicles the intersecting lives of a saloon owner (Gable), a singer (Jeanette MacDonald), and a priest (Tracy) in the months before the Great Earthquake of 1906. Gable, the biggest box-office draw in the MGM stable, was the undisputed star. But it was clear to everyone working on the film that even in a supporting role Tracy was somehow managing to dominate the picture.

Halfway through the shooting, Tracy was dining at Hollywood's Trocadero nightclub when director William ("Wild Bill") Wellman (*Wings, Public Enemy*, the original *A Star Is Born*) made a taunting remark about Loretta Young. Spencer took a swing, but it was Wellman who connected, sending Tracy sprawling to the floor. The next morning makeup was used to conceal a black eye.

(Tracy's impassioned defense of Loretta Young's honor seemed above and beyond the call: She was now in the throes of an affair with Tracy's *San Francisco* costar Clark Gable. Young had fallen for Clark Gable in 1934, during the filming of Jack London's *Call of the Wild*. Sixty-one years later it would be revealed that Young had secretly given birth to Gable's child. Just as he had christened Humphrey Bogart Bogie, so it was Spencer who first called Gable the King.)

Mayer, who kept a close watch on the behavior of the stars who made up the MGM "family," reacted like an angry father to the inevitable headlines surrounding Tracy's Trocadero fistfight. L. B. also wondered if, after being reminded of his penchant for violence, audiences would accept Tracy as Father Mike, the chaplain of a Barbary Coast mission in *San Francisco*.

Tracy had doubts even before accepting the role, worrying that it was sacrilegious for someone with his sinful ways even to think of portraying a man of the cloth.

Their fears proved unfounded. Only weeks after Tracy had been hailed by critics for his portrayal of a wrongly accused man in *Fury*, MGM released *San Francisco*. The picture was a huge hit, establishing Spencer as Clark Gable's equal. "Personal reviews marvelous," Tracy wrote in his diary. "Got away with murder."

Tracy now plunged into the comedy *Libeled Lady*, with Jean Harlow, William Powell, and Myrna Loy. There was enough publicity surrounding the romance between Harlow and Powell—they announced their engagement at a party on the set—to ensure that *Libeled Lady* would be a smash. But the fact remained that of the movie's four big stars, Tracy ranked at the bottom.

When the Academy Award nominations for Best Actor were announced, however, it was Tracy, not Gable, whose performance in *San Francisco* was recognized. He lost to Paul Muni in *The Story of Louis Pasteur*, but the nomination alone was enough to get his salary bumped from a thousand dollars a week to the princely sum of five thousand dollars a week. (Katharine Hepburn, nominated for *Alice Adams*, also lost that year—to Bette Davis for *Dangerous*.)

While the cast of *Libeled Lady* toasted Powell and Harlow, Thalberg called Tracy away from

the party and told him that he was leaving MGM
to start his own company. He would be taking a
number of MGM's top stars with him, and he
promised to make Tracy first among equals if
Tracy joined the mutiny. Spencer agreed, but
three weeks later Thalberg died of pneumonia.
He was thirty-seven.

Thalberg still had a posthumous hand in lift-
ing Spencer to the summit of the Hollywood
heap, having offered him the role of Manuel, the
Portuguese fisherman, in the Victor Fleming–
directed film version of Rudyard Kipling's *Captains Courageous*. Tracy was not supposed to be
the star of the film; the story of a rich brat transformed by the kindness of a Portuguese-
American fisherman was originally intended as
a vehicle for Shirley Temple's male counterpart,
thirteen-year-old Freddie Bartholomew. But before Thalberg's untimely death, he did all that he
could to make the role irresistible to Tracy. Thalberg ordered the screenwriters to expand Tracy's
character, so that Manuel's drowning was the
film's pivotal scene. To sweeten the pot, Lionel
Barrymore, whom Tracy had long idolized, was
hired to play the supporting role of a crusty
Gloucester salt.

Nonetheless Spencer agonized over the part.
He had always resisted wearing makeup as unmanly, but the part required that his skin be
darkened and his hair curled. As he walked
across the MGM lot one day, Joan Crawford

leaned out of her car and yelled, "Hey, look who's here. It's Harpo Marx!"

He also worried about mastering Manuel's Portuguese accent. When the director, Victor Fleming, brought in a Portuguese-American fisherman as a technical advisor, Tracy cornered the man. "I have to sing this song about Little Fish," he told the Portuguese fisherman. "Now, how would you say that? 'Leetle feesh'?"

The man looked at him quizzically before answering. "I would say," he replied very succinctly, " 'little fish.' "

Tracy settled on an accent he was confident he could do convincingly, something he had picked up during his theater days in New York: Yiddish. "In the film," he later said, "I probably had the most un-Portuguese accent in history."

His accent was only one of the things that concerned Tracy. He was hopelessly tone-deaf. "He has no voice, and his singing was terrible," Fleming said, "but it was just right because Manuel's singing would have been terrible too."

"I was positive I was doing the worst job of my life," Tracy said. "I just felt sure I wouldn't surmount the singing, the dialect, and the curled hair." He was also impressed by Freddie Bartholomew's innate naturalistic style ("Freddie is the only child star I ever saw who tries to be real instead of cute"), and he worried that the boy would upstage him. Tracy was so convinced that *Captains Courageous* would be a major disaster that he distanced himself from it as much as humanly possible. "This is Freddie's picture," he told reporters, "as it should be."

A sufferer from what was later called the Impostor Syndrome, Tracy doubted his talent and lived in constant fear of being "found out." Tracy's close friend the producer-director Joseph Mankiewicz remembered that "Spence was really torn up at the time. He looked and acted like a bull—sometimes a raging bull—but like many great artists, he had troubles living up to his own expectations. He was really very fragile emotionally. And then Harlow died. . . ."

Jean Harlow's death that year at twenty-six stunned the nation in much the same way Marilyn Monroe's did a quarter century later. When Harlow, who had not yet finished *Saratoga*, fell ill from uremic poisoning, her mother, a devout Christian Scientist like Spencer's mother Carrie, delayed getting her the medical attention that might have saved Harlow's life.

In his diary under the date June 7, 1937, Spencer scrawled, "Harlow died. Grand girl . . ." Mankiewicz said that Tracy "was very fond of Harlow. They saw one another as two regular people in a sea of phonies. Her death upset him almost as much as Will Rogers's had." Studio executives wasted little time mourning the loss, shooting a blond stand-in from behind and at a distance so that *Saratoga* could be released on schedule.

Spencer reacted to the sad news of Harlow's needless death by alternately brooding at home with Louise, hitting the bottle, and squiring a variety of beautiful women around town. At one point he moved into a sixth-floor room at the Beverly Wilshire Hotel and, during a drunken rampage, tried to toss Carroll out the window. Had MGM's security chief Whitey Hendry not forced his way into the room in time to pull the star off his brother, Tracy probably would have succeeded. The official line: Shooting on *Captains Courageous* was suspended while Tracy recuperated from a case of pneumonia. A reporter who tried to corner him in a public rest room found out that despite his studio-concocted illness, Tracy was strong enough to shove him into a urinal.

After shooting was completed in January 1937, Tracy began escorting fifteen-year-old Judy Garland to various nightspots in and around Los Angeles. Jimmy Cagney warned his friend the inevitable gossip could ruin his career. Tracy continued to see Garland privately, and after their romance ended, they remained close, a friendship that endured another thirty years.

Judging by the number of times studio publicity departments said he was ill instead of drunk, the general public could easily have assumed Tracy was one of the most sickly stars in Hollywood. In 1937, however, he actually did suffer a number of health problems. He was diagnosed with a thyroid condition and after weeks of persistent throat pain wound up undergoing a tonsillectomy on his thirty-seventh birthday.

"Sometimes," quipped a friend, "the guy actually is sick!"

When *Captains Courageous* was released, Spencer was not prepared for the response of the critics and the moviegoing public. "So magnificent are its sweep and excitement," rhapsodized *Time*, "that *Captains Courageous* . . . offers its credentials for admission to the thin company of cinema immortals."

Sitting in the back row of a darkened theater was a slender young woman, one leg slung over the arm of her chair, dabbing at her eyes with a handkerchief. "Whenever I think of that Portuguese fisherman going down with his boat, I weep like a baby," she later said. "I think it is just the best goddamned performance I've ever seen."

She was so enthralled by Tracy that she dashed out to see *Fury*. "His performance, an abstraction—a manifestation of character—" she later said, "is so remarkable that it is as total as birth or death." Even then she detected something different about the actor, whom she was years away from meeting. It seemed to her that unlike other actors who applied a character's traits and mannerisms to the outside, this Tracy fellow was "just reaching down and pulling it all up from inside. He is sort of a closed box, with all these emotions crashing around inside."

Had he known her then, Katharine Hepburn's opinion would have meant something to Spencer. She had already won an Academy Award for her role as an aspiring actress in 1933's *Morning Glory*, caused a sensation that same year as Jo March in *Little Women*, and after a series of flops was about to make a major comeback heading up an all-star cast in *Stage Door*. Her much-ballyhooed romance with Howard Hughes, followed as closely by the press as the Tracy–Loretta Young Affair, had just ended.

She would, of course, eventually become the world's greatest expert on Spencer Tracy. Yet in all that time nothing would match that moment when she first saw him on the screen. Over the years she would see *Captains Courageous* again and again and again, breaking down each time Manuel, the fisherman, sank smiling beneath the waves. It would forever remain Katharine Hepburn's favorite Spencer Tracy picture. "I feel like a complete fool every time I cry," she said, "but I just can't help myself. Damn!"

At lunchtime they'd just meet and sit on a bench on the lot. They'd hold hands and talk—and everybody left them alone in their little private world.

—GENE KELLY

KATE: *My God, I'm* famished.
SPENCER: *I don't see how. You've been eating* people *all day.*

Them

Four

Hepburn and Tracy had somehow managed to cross paths without ever meeting in New York, and in Hollywood, a decade and nearly sixty films would pass before their first fateful encounter. Meantime, Tracy continued his pursuit of some of the town's most glamorous women.

"Nobody at MGM gets more sex than Joan Crawford and Spencer Tracy—and that includes the times they get it together," Joseph Mankiewicz said. Indeed, when Tracy and Crawford met on the set of Mankiewicz's *Mannequin*, their reputations preceded them. Crawford's appetite for men was, if the rumors were to be believed, even more insatiable than Tracy's for women and booze. Nor was the fact that she was married to one of MGM's biggest matinee idols, Franchot Tone, any impediment to Crawford's extracurricular fun.

The first day of shooting Crawford flirted openly with Tracy, and after he pretended to spar with her, she even concocted a pet name for him: Slug. Tracy, who had apparently recovered from Crawford's caustic remark about his "Harpo Marx" hairdo in *Captains Courageous*, responded by teaching her some of the finer points of polo.

The columns were filled with stories about Tracy and Crawford feuding on the set, but there was never any friction between them. "We worked together as a unit as if we'd worked together for years," she said. "In the most serious scene Slug could break me up. . . . Take after take. But I learned. From Slug I learned to keep my own identity in a scene, not to be distracted by anything, including Tracy."

Their first dinner date went the way Crawford planned all her dates. She picked the time, the restaurant, and which nightclub they would go to afterward for dancing. Had it not been for Tracy's famous withering glare, she would have ordered for him as well. When they got back to her Beverly Hills mansion, she disrobed as soon as they got in the door and slunk naked to the floor. Tracy obliged, and they made love on the rug in the foyer. "Professional, clinical, lacking in warmth" is the way one of her later conquests, Kirk Douglas, described Crawford's lovemaking technique. "I got out fast."

Tracy did not get out quite as fast as Douglas, but he did end the affair not long after they had completed *Mannequin*. Crawford had only kind words for him professionally, but she never forgave him for breaking off their romance. "Joan hated Spence for it," Mankiewicz said. "Not so much because the affair was over, but because he was the one to break it off. She liked to do the dumping."

On March 10, 1938, Spencer lay in his hospital bed recovering from a hernia operation. Meanwhile all Hollywood gathered at the Biltmore Bowl for the tenth annual Academy Awards ceremony. When C. Aubrey Smith announced Spencer Tracy as the winner of the Best Actor Oscar for *Captains Courageous*, Louise Tracy, who had come unescorted, rose and strode briskly toward the podium. The film community had been reading for years about Tracy's extramarital exploits and about the long-suffering wife who had devoted her life to working with the deaf. Few, however, had ever actually seen Mrs. Spencer Tracy, the woman who had managed to hold on to her famous husband despite his well-publicized dalliances with such women as Myrna Loy, Loretta Young, and Joan Crawford.

Louise, wearing an off-the-shoulder gown and a flower behind her left ear, grasped the statue firmly in one hand and shook Smith's with the other. A hush fell over the throng. Clearly Louise's presence was intended to send a message that despite everything, the Tracys remained a family. "I accept this award," she said confidently, "on behalf of Spencer, Susie, Johnny, and myself." There was a pause, and then the audience gave Louise a thunderous ovation.

Unexpectedly L. B. now stood up. "I'd like to praise Spencer Tracy's sense of discipline," Mayer said. "Tracy is a fine actor, but he is most important because he understands why it is necessary to take orders from the front office, because he understands why it is important to obey directors, because he understands that when the publicity department asks him to cater to certain visitors, it is a necessary inconvenience." The thinly veiled warning was not lost on academy members—or on Tracy himself.

Louise made her way past well-wishers to a phone. "Darling," she told Spencer as he sat in his hospital room, "you won it." Overwhelmed by a sense of vindication tinged with his ever-present sense of guilt, Tracy wept.

The next day the Tracys posed for photographers in the hospital garden, one of those "necessary inconveniences" L. B. had referred to in his speech. While cameras clicked and shutters whirred, Louise handed the Oscar to a seated Spencer. For just the right touch of drama, he clutched a cane in his right hand. It was not until they got home that they read the inscription on the base of the statuette. For his performance in *Captains Courageous*, the Academy Award for Best Actor was presented to *Dick* Tracy.

The Tracys spent part of that summer of 1938 vacationing in New York, as they had the previous year. Spencer, ducking fans and photographers, occasionally sneaked into a Broadway show. But most nights were spent drinking at the

Lambs. "Mr. Tracy had a hollow leg," recalled a former staff member of the club, "and could drink anybody under the table. But after he had a few, he became a completely different person, the classic mean drunk, and everybody sort of backed off. It was rare that he passed out—only twice that I know of—but everybody was kind of relieved when he did. They just let him sleep it off upstairs." As she had a decade earlier, Louise never uttered a word of complaint when he stumbled home drunk or not at all.

Tracy teamed with his former *San Francisco* buddy Clark Gable and his ex-lover Myrna Loy to make Victor Fleming's *Test Pilot*. Tracy was no match for Gable in a flight suit, and as always, Gable got the girl. "Everyone was rooting for Tracy to get the girl," Stanley Kramer said. "He was Everyman. He wasn't that handsome, he had flaws, but he was one helluva guy. People were asking Myrna Loy why the hell she wouldn't go for him instead of Gable."

Still, Tracy's down-to-earth mechanic managed to upstage the King with one of the most drawn-out death scenes in screen history. Predictably, *Test Pilot* was a box-office hit, with Tracy garnering most of the critical praise. Spencer, *Time* declared, was nothing less than "cinema's No. 1 actor's actor."

Certainly Humphrey Bogart shared that opinion. "As far as actors go . . . I'd say Spence is the best by far," said Bogie, who over the years was exposed to all sides of the multifaceted Tracy.

"He and I have our ups and downs personally—he's a moody son of a bitch—but professionally I rate him tops. The thing about his acting is there's no bullshit in it. . . . Spencer *does* it, that's all. Feels it. Says it. Talks. Listens. He means what he says when he says it, and if you think that's easy, try it."

"The guy's good and there's nobody in this business who can touch him, so you're a fool to try," Gable said of his friendly rival. "And don't fall for that humble stuff, either—the bastard knows how good he is. . . . Any actor or actress who's ever played a scene with Spencer will tell you—there's nothing like it. He mesmerizes you. Those eyes of his—and what goes on behind them."

What Tracy didn't know was whether he should tackle the role of another priest so soon after *San Francisco*. Adding to the dilemma was the fact that the character he was being asked to portray was not only a living person, but someone he knew and revered: Father Edward J. Flanagan, founder of the Nebraska home for wayward youths known to the world as Boys Town.

Spencer doubted he could convey Father Flanagan's "warmth, inspiration, and humanness of feeling in a picture. But I became so absorbed in the characterization that by the end of the first week I had stopped worrying." It helped that Father Flanagan, whose "There are no bad boys" motto spoke directly to Spencer's own troubled childhood, visited him often on the set.

Despite his vaunted "actor's actor" status, Tracy was still not the biggest star in *Boys Town*. That distinction fell to seventeen-year-old Mickey Rooney, then Hollywood's top box-office draw. Rooney was cast as one Father Flanagan's success stories, Whitey Marsh. The movie's up-beat, inspirational message as delivered by Spencer and Mickey proved irresistible to Depression audiences. *The New York Times* hailed Tracy's performance as "perfection itself." *Boys Town* was a blockbuster and earned Tracy his second Academy Award.

This time he showed up to accept the Oscar in person and to share the spotlight with his old *20,000 Years in Sing-Sing* costar Bette Davis, picking up her second Academy Award for *Jezebel*. "Well, I guess they finally came to their senses," Tracy told Davis after the award ceremonies.

"That night we became members of a very exclusive club," Bette recalled. "On the surface, Spence was so calm, so charming and self-assured—nothing like the wild man I had worked with. He could be devastatingly sarcastic, but at the Oscars he refused to touch a drop—wisely, I think—and it seemed almost as if he was *finally* at peace with himself. It wasn't until later that I realized that it was all just another marvelous Spencer Tracy performance. He was still a very deeply troubled, unhappy man. Full of doubt and rage. He just decided that if he was going to get through the evening, he would just have to play Father Flanagan!"

Like the rest of Hollywood, Davis knew that Tracy had taken up residence in a suite at the Beverly Wilshire Hotel. She also speculated about "what kind of woman Spence would eventually end up with. It would have to be someone with an ego as enormous as his but someone also willing to be the world's biggest martyr. I had no idea if any woman like that existed—in or out of Hollywood."

In 1938 Tracy worked in fits and starts on three major film projects: *Northwest Passage, I Take This Woman,* and *Stanley and Livingstone.* But it was almost a year following the release of *Boys Town* before the first of these, Darryl Zanuck's *Stanley and Livingstone,* was released.

The true story of intrepid journalist Henry Stanley and his search in Africa for the lost missionary Dr. David Livingstone was originally intended as a vehicle for the resident Fox heartthrob Tyrone Power. But in a curious swap Power was loaned to MGM for *Marie Antoinette,* and in return MGM got Tracy for *Stanley and Livingstone.*

Spencer was intrigued by the story of Stanley and was eager to work with his old polo-playing pal Zanuck. He also looked forward to asking one of the most famous rhetorical questions in history: "Dr. Livingstone, I presume?"

After he finished shooting *Stanley and Livingstone* in April 1939, Spencer and Louise sailed for

Europe. If there was any doubt about the magnitude of his stardom, it was dispelled by his reception in London. Warned that a mob of eight thousand fans was waiting for him at Waterloo Station, Spencer and Louise switched trains at the last minute. Unfortunately no one had told the celebrated conductor Arturo Toscanini to do the same. When he got off the train that was supposed to be carrying Tracy, the maestro was knocked to the ground by frenzied fans. "This scared Spencer so," Louise said, "he started talking immediately about coming home."

Stanley and Livingstone was enough of a hit to make audiences overlook Spencer's next movie, the disastrous *I Take This Woman*, showcasing an exotically beautiful newcomer named Hedy Lamarr. Plagued from the start by script and production problems, the shooting schedule dragged on interminably. Tracy began calling it *I Retake This Woman*. But L. B. Mayer, who had discovered Lamarr and changed her name from the less than mellifluous-sounding Hedwig Kiesler, pressed on. The film, skewered by the critics, nonetheless turned a profit—testimony to the public's growing fascination with the sultry Lamarr and Tracy's star power. However, Tracy resented the lengths to which Mayer had gone to build up his protégée. Relations between the two men would never be the same.

Northwest Passage was more to Tracy's liking. Based on Kenneth Roberts's best-selling novel, *Northwest Passage* was an epic saga of survival in the wilderness set in colonial America. After countless script changes and other delays, four of the original stars—Robert Taylor, Franchot Tone, Wallace Beery, and Greer Garson—had dropped out. Tracy was now joined by Robert Young (who became best known for his television series *Father Knows Best* and *Marcus Welby, M.D.*) and veteran character actor Walter Brennan.

On location in Oregon, director King Vidor drove cast and crew hard. In one scene Tracy and his men form a human chain to cross a raging river—a perilous sequence Vidor insisted be done without stunt doubles. Tracy admired Vidor's tenacity and came to his defense when local Indians working as extras demanded that their pay be raised from five dollars a day to ten dollars a day. "You tell them they're only playing half-breeds," Tracy said, "so five dollars is all they deserve." The argument, however offensive, worked.

Tracy got along well with Young, Brennan, and the other members of the all-male cast and crew. But as the weeks of location shooting dragged on, he became more and more weary of the isolation. He needed human interaction and, despite his oft-professed distaste for intrusive fans, craved the adulation to which he had now become accustomed.

As he watched Tracy grow more and more testy, Vidor worried that his name-over-the-title star might start hitting the bottle to take his mind off things. Spencer's mood brightened after an attractive young woman inexplicably began showing up on the periphery of the set to do nothing but gaze adoringly at him. He was never told that the "fan" was actually a local girl who had been hired by the studio to boost his sagging ego.

Released on February 23, 1940, just three weeks after the problematic *I Take This Woman,* *Northwest Passage* proved to be a major hit with audiences. Over the next six months two more Spencer Tracy formula pictures were released: *Edison the Man* and *Boom Town,* which reunited him with Gable and Lamarr. Both gave audiences the Tracy they had come to expect. While the respected *New York Times* critic Bosley Crowther described *Boom Town*'s Gable as "brassy, direct and tough," he wrote that Tracy, as always, "flows deep and sure."

Yet the public persona was never more at odds with the real-life Tracy than during 1940 and early 1941. He remained a fixture at Romanoff's, the Trocadero, and Ciro's, sometimes with Louise but usually escorting the likes of Olivia De Havilland and Judy Garland, now a more respectable eighteen.

It was not until the early months of 1941 that Spencer fell deeply and seriously in love—once again with one of his costars. John Barrymore had triumphed in a silent version of *Dr. Jekyll and Mr. Hyde,* and in 1932 Fredric March had won an Academy Award for his portrayal of the tortured Dr. Henry Jekyll. Now MGM wanted to remake the Robert Louis Stevenson classic with its most distinguished actor in the title roles.

Spencer declined at first but ultimately gave in to the personal entreaties of L. B. Mayer himself. The parallels with his own schizophrenic personality were not lost on Tracy. He went so far as to suggest to the director, his old friend Victor Fleming, that Jekyll be portrayed as the ultimate mean drunk. Instead of being transformed by some mysterious potion, Tracy wanted Jekyll to turn into the evil Mr. Hyde after one too many drinks. "Every once and a while," Tracy explained, "Jekyll would go on a trip. Disappear. And either because of drink or dope or who knows what, he would become—or should I say turn into?—Mr. Hyde. Then in a town or neighborhood where he was totally unknown, he would perform incredible acts of cruelty and vulgarity. The emotional side of Jekyll was obviously extremely disturbed."

He had another innovative idea: to have one actress play both principal female characters in the play: Ivy, the prostitute, and Beatrix, Dr. Jekyll's virtuous fiancée. He even had a specific actress in mind, someone he had never met: Katharine Hepburn. Fleming listened politely, then turned down both suggestions.

Tracy did convince Fleming to make a crucial casting change, however. Sexy "Sweater Girl" Lana Turner had been slated for the role of the prostitute murdered by Hyde. Ingrid Bergman, who had burst onto the scene opposite Leslie Howard in *Intermezzo*, had been typecast as the virginal fiancée.

Bergman wanted the juicier, lustier part of Ivy. Badly. Fleming refused, until Tracy threatened to walk off the picture if he didn't screen-test her for the role. Bergman was so convincing on the set that Fleming did not even bother developing the film; Turner, who was just as tired of being typecast as a sexpot, gladly switched.

Like everyone else in the profession, Bergman, who at twenty-five was sixteen years younger than Tracy, stood in awe of her costar. "I was thrilled to be working with Spencer Tracy," she said, "because he was respected in my own country and at the Royal Academy in Stockholm, where I had been." Each day at lunchtime they disappeared to Simon's, a Beverly Hills drive-in, to compare notes over milk shakes and hamburgers.

Bergman, still very much married to Swedish physician Petter Lindstrom and the mother of a little girl named Pia, had begun an affair with Fleming even before shooting started. But in a matter of weeks she had left Fleming for Tracy, a move that shattered the director and strained relations between the two old friends.

Barrymore and March had relied heavily on makeup to create the monstrous-looking Hyde—everything from false noses and teeth to wigs, fake fingernails and in the case of Barrymore, even a sort of fake cranium to make his head appear elongated. At first Tracy, who had always thought makeup was somehow emasculating, would have none of it and angrily demanded that he be left alone by the MGM makeup department. "I just can't do that sort of thing," he said. "It's like constructing a dummy and then trying to breathe life into it. I like to make people—force people—to believe that I'm whatever I want them to believe. Inside out—instead of outside in. No makeup."

But Fleming eventually convinced him to follow in his predecessors' footsteps, and soon Tracy was sporting false teeth, a fright wig, and pounds of strategically applied putty. Mortified, after each take he was whisked from the set to his dressing room hunched down in the back of a limousine with blacked-out windows.

Vibrant, worshipful Ingrid Bergman seemed the perfect antidote for the ongoing assault on Tracy's manhood. As filming progressed, his confidence in the project waned, but his relationship with Bergman grew stronger. "Ingrid Bergman was very beautiful in that fresh-scrubbed, wide-eyed-but-not-quite-so-innocent way," director Joseph Mankiewicz said. "She was *different*, a breath of Arctic air. There was nothing phony about her. She was *bright*, and she wanted to learn at the foot of the master. Did Spence love her? Who wouldn't, if given the chance?"

The torrid Spencer Tracy–Ingrid Bergman Affair lasted months after they had finished shooting *Dr. Jekyll and Mr. Hyde*. When Tracy invited her to join him in San Francisco, ostensibly to discuss future film projects, she had to decline. Word of the affair had filtered back to Dr. Lindstrom, and Ingrid's husband was livid.

Dr. Jekyll and Mr. Hyde marked a first for Tracy. Even in his worst films Tracy had always been singled out for special praise. Again, reviewers singled him out—only this time their remarks were withering. "Mr. Tracy's role is not so much evil incarnate," wrote *The New York Times'* Theodore Strauss, "as it is the ham rampant. When his eyes roll in a fine frenzy, like loose marbles in his head, he is more ludicrous than dreadful."

Even before its release Tracy had proclaimed *Dr. Jekyll and Mr. Hyde* "rotten" and set out to find a project worthy of his talent. He was lucky enough to be offered two. He chose a screen version of Marjorie Kinnan Rawlings's Pulitzer Prizewinning novel *The Yearling* and in May 1941 left to start filming on location in the Florida Everglades.

Amazingly, Tracy had apparently not considered the very real possibility that shooting in the sweltering, mosquito-infested swamp might be less than pleasant. His chronic insomnia was aggravated by insect bites and the stifling heat, but somehow Tracy managed to stay sober. No one had figured out how to prevent mosquitoes from swarming over the camera lens, making the cinematographer's job virtually impossible. Tracy stuck it out for six weeks, but after Victor Fleming had been brought in to replace King Vidor as director, MGM decided to cancel the picture.

Fortunately for Spencer he had that other film project to fall back on. The movie was called *Woman of the Year*, and the woman who had brought it to Metro and hired everyone from the director to the cast was also to be his leading lady. Her name was Katharine Hepburn.

"I don't know the man," Kate Hepburn told her friend Garson Kanin after *Captains Courageous* was released, "but gosh, I would love to do a picture with him!" Her interest was purely professional. In 1938 Kate was riding out the latest in a series of career crises that had plagued her since she became an overnight sensation on Broadway seven years earlier as an Amazon named Antiope in *The Warrior's Husband*. From the moment Kate, clad in a breastplate, helmet, and tunic, bounded onto the stage with a dead stag draped over her shoulder, audiences were enthralled. "Not very ladylike, I suppose," Kate said of the role, which required her to strut around like a man while showing lots of leg, "but it got the job done."

Fox bought the rights to *The Warrior's Husband* and passed on Hepburn just as it had initially passed on Spencer Tracy four years earlier. But a talent scout for RKO-Radio Pictures named Lillie Messenger spotted Kate's performance and wired producer David O. Selznick that she had found the star for his new film, *A Bill of Divorcement*.

"The RKO executives," Hepburn recalled of her first screen test for the studio, "said I looked 'like a cross between a monkey and a horse.' " But George Cukor, hired to direct *A Bill of Divorcement*, was intrigued by one small gesture. "At one moment in a very emotional scene, she picked up a glass. The camera focused on her back. There was an enormous feeling, a weight about the manner in which she picked up the glass. . . . She was," he allowed, "quite unlike anybody I had ever seen." (When she saw the test years later, she realized "there was something awfully heartbreaking about the girl I was in those days. I was trying so hard—too hard. I was so eager—too eager.")

Even though her father would always handle Kate's finances, going so far as to issue her a monthly allowance on which to live, she already knew how to drive a hard bargain. Reluctantly RKO acceded to Kate's salary demand of fifteen hundred dollars a week, three times its original offer.

On July 1, 1932, Luddy Smith waved good-bye from the platform as his wife boarded the Super Chief for Los Angeles. She did not want him to accompany her. Instead Kate's handpicked traveling companion was to be the one person who had helped her navigate the social waters of Manhattan, American Express heiress Laura Harding.

Three and a half years after their wedding, Luddy knew full well that when it came to Kate's list of priorities, their marriage ranked a poor second (if that) to her career. But he clung to the hope that once she achieved the recognition she so desperately craved, Kate might find more time for their relationship and even add the role of working mother to her repertoire. He reminded Kate that her mother had managed to be a social crusader and raise six children—albeit with the help of housekeepers and nannies.

For the moment the obligingly good-natured Luddy, whom the rambunctious Hepburns embraced as one of their own, would have to be content knowing that he was married to a phenomenal, unique woman who might someday actually behave more like a wife. "Luddy is such a dear," Kate often said when asked what her husband thought about her unconventional lifestyle. "He's just been swell about everything."

Luddy was confident that no man was a match for Kate's ambition. What Luddy had not counted on was that Kate would be so strongly drawn to a member of her own sex. Athletic and broad-shouldered, her hair cut short in a bob, Laura Harding had flirted briefly with the thought of pursing a career in the theater and had actually met Kate before she married Luddy—when both young women were taking voice lessons from the formidable Frances Robinson-Duff. "I thought, She's not my type," Harding recalled of the moment she first set eyes on Kate. "She had long hair pulled back in a knot, a man's sweater pinned at the back with a big safety pin—what we called a Brooks sweater—and a tweed skirt." Before long Kate and Laura—"The first real friend I had in New York," Hepburn later said—were inseparable.

Kate made another memorable, if not altogether positive, impression when she arrived at RKO. "As long as I live I will never forget the first day she appeared on the lot," said Adela Rogers St. John, then working as an RKO screenwriter. "Everybody was in the commissary at lunch when she walked in with Mr. Cukor. Several executives nearly fainted. . . . We beheld a tall, skinny girl entirely covered with freckles and wearing the most appalling and incredible clothes I have ever seen in my life. . . . George Cukor looked across at us. He was a little pale but still in the ring."

Selznick was so distraught by the sight of this "boa constrictor on a fast," as Cukor described her (Selznick's brother Myron called her "the cadaver"), that he nearly sent Hepburn packing. Selznick's wife Irene, who also happened to be Louis B. Mayer's daughter, recalled that Kate's "behavior was not only unconventional, it was slightly wacky. . . . We had a wave of misgivings, but the girl had class and plenty of spunk."

Oblivious to the way others perceived her, Kate assumed the imperious demeanor of an established star. When her *A Bill of Divorcement* costars John Barrymore and Billie Burke (perhaps best known to today's audiences as Glinda, the Good Witch of the North, in *The Wizard of Oz*) autographed photographs for some visiting distributors, Kate refused. "If you study for twenty-five years," Cukor shouted at his upstart discovery, "maybe your signature will be worthy to go with theirs!" Her second day in Hollywood a sweet middle-aged woman invited Kate and Laura to dine with her and her husband at their home—an invitation Kate rudely brushed aside until someone told her the woman was Mary Pickford, the husband was Douglas Fairbanks, and their house was Pickfair.

Barrymore, then fifty and ravaged by a lifetime of debauchery, played Kate's father in *A Bill of Divorcement*. Behind the scenes, the Great Man cornered the ingenue in his dressing room and let his food-stained dressing gown fall to the floor, revealing that he wore nothing underneath. Stunned, Kate pushed Barrymore away. "My first thought was to get out, but I simply couldn't move," she later remembered. "I was petrified—couldn't speak."

"Well, come on, what are you waiting for?" Barrymore replied. "We don't have all day." He moved toward her until she "practically plastered herself against the wall."

"No, no, please, I cahnt," she protested. "I simply *cahnt*. My father doesn't want me to have any babies!" With that she dashed out of the room.

Kate's reply, blurted out under duress, may have been disingenuous, but it spoke volumes about the hold Dr. Hepburn had over his daughter's subconscious.

Barrymore determined that Hepburn was "a creature most strange. A nut." It was an image Kate worked hard to project. She boasted about the seven or eight showers she took daily and claimed to follow her grandfather's habit of brushing her teeth with soap. She insisted on wearing a threadbare pair of men's work pants when the cameras weren't rolling, and when the wardrobe department snatched them from her dressing room, she strolled through the lot in her underwear. The wardrobe department promptly returned her pants.

No one could deny, however, that she was one of the most dedicated workers anyone had ever seen. Up each day at 6:00 A.M., she was always the first to report for work—a habit she shared with Spencer Tracy—and the last to leave, often twelve or thirteen hours later. She worked six days a week, and although she clashed with Cukor repeatedly, Kate was willing, even eager, to repeat a scene again and again in pursuit of the perfect take.

"*A Bill of Divorcement* is an event, a milestone in motion picture history," declared *The Hollywood Reporter*. "After last night, there is a new star on the cinema horizon, and her name is Katharine Hepburn." The film, the article went on, "is only a forerunner of the way she will capture followers by the millions." The *New York Post* agreed that Kate "has the makings of a star," and the New York *Herald Tribune* predicted "an important cinema career" for Hepburn.

No one was more surprised than David O. Selznick, who referred to her as "that horse face" and had no intention of picking up Hepburn's option until preview audiences registered their overwhelming approval.

Her generous new deal with RKO, like the first, was hammered out by her agent, Leland Hayward. The Princeton dropout with the Savile Row wardrobe and the perpetual tan eventually counted among his 150 clients the biggest names in Hollywood. Among them: Greta Garbo, Fred Astaire, James Stewart, and Henry Fonda. "Just charmed the birds off the trees," said Cukor, "the money out of the coffers and ladies into their beds."

Nothing clicked between Hayward and Hepburn when he greeted her at the train station that first day in Hollywood. But after her success in *A Bill of Divorcement*, he started paying closer attention. "I was a big flash," Kate said. "Just the kind of flash that fascinated Leland."

It was impossible not to be intrigued. Kate had been vacationing with Luddy in Europe when the film was released, and on her return to New York was besieged by photographers. With Luddy obligingly out of sight, she denied being married but told reporters that she nevertheless had five children—"three of them colored."

During the filming of the forgettable *Christopher Strong*, in which she played an aviatrix who becomes pregnant by a married man, the married Miss Hepburn began an affair with the equally married Hayward. Lanky, debonair, independently wealthy Hayward had in fact wed, divorced, and then remarried the strikingly beautiful Texas-bred aviatrix-debutante Lola Gibbs. Remarriage had been his idea; when she left him the first time, Hayward was so devastated that he threatened to kill himself.

With Gibbs ensconced a safe distance away in New York, Hayward felt perfectly free to pursue some of Hollywood's most desirable women, from *King Kong*'s Fay Wray to the mysterious Garbo herself. He would soon divorce Gibbs a second time, and go on to marry the mentally unstable Margaret Sullavan, Hollywood glamour girl Slim Hawks, and Pamela Churchill (later Pamela Harriman, U.S. ambassador to France).

"What made Leland irresistible," his third wife, Slim Hawks, later recalled, "was his boyish attentiveness. He didn't play golf or tennis, he thought all that was a lot of crap. His sport was women, and I adored him for that." Kate did not mind Hayward's overt distaste for two of her favorite sports; they were opposites in many other ways as well, and that only strengthened the magnetic field that drew them together.

Kate often repeated her father's fashion philosophy that any man who owned more than two suits was "a fop." Leland owned dozens, not to mention more than three hundred pair of custom-made shoes. The Hepburns drove their cars into the ground; Hayward kept a Rolls in his garage in Manhattan and tooled around Hollywood behind the wheel of a Hispano-Suiza.

She was the proverbial early bird, and he made the late-night rounds of restaurants and parties that were the lifeblood of his business. Each evening Leland would sit at Kate's table and sip a cocktail while she ate dinner, then leave for a night on the town, returning to join her in bed around midnight. Kate did not begrudge Leland his need to know; they shared a passion for gossip. Kate recalled that Hayward was her source "for the most luscious information about the world we seemed both to be living in. . . . All the gossip. Lovely." (Even at this early stage in her career Kate intimidated most of the men with whom she came in contact. When asked why Kate was "so terrifying," *Christopher Strong* author Gilbert Frankau answered, "Because she's a tornado.")

Laura, who had known Leland in New York, was an important part of their tight little "family." She shared their evenings of delicious gossip and woke up each morning to find Hayward dozing in bed while Kate wolfed down her breakfast in the kitchen.

This cozy arrangement also made it possible for them to conceal their relationship from the outside world and, most important, from their respective spouses. As far as anyone knew, Kate lived with Laura Harding in Quinta Nirvana, a tile-roofed ranch house in Coldwater Canyon.

Kate and Laura were such constant, devoted, and openly affectionate companions that soon both coasts were abuzz with the rumor that they were a lesbian couple. It did not help that at the RKO cafeteria Laura once loudly referred to herself as Kate's "husband." Or that Kate giggled naughtily when Laura called her by a pet name, "Max," drawn from the cartoon character Max Hare. Apparently the animated rabbit was speedy enough to return his own shots on the tennis courts—a feat the frenetic Kate often seemed on the verge of accomplishing.

Kate's real husband was back in New York, driving up to West Hartford or out to Fenwick every available weekend to visit his in-laws. Blissfully unaware of his wife's affair with Hayward, Luddy played with Kate's brothers and sisters and made plans for her eventual return.

Christopher Strong was a dismal flop, but her next role—that of stagestruck Eva Lovelace in *Morning Glory*—was a huge hit and earned Kate her first Academy Award. That summer of 1933 she assayed an even more memorable part: the headstrong, irrepressible Jo March in *Little Women*.

The making of *Little Women* was far from pleasurable. George Cukor, who was gay, was an unparalleled master at eliciting powerhouse performances from actresses—so much so that he became known as Hollywood's premier "woman's director." He and Kate were in fact just embarking on a profound professional and personal partnership that was to last a lifetime. But on the set of *Little Women* they butted heads frequently.

Once, Cukor slapped Kate across the face when she botched a scene. "She had to run up a flight of steps carrying some ice cream, and I told her to be very careful because we didn't have a spare of the dress she was wearing, so she *mustn't* spill that ice cream. But she did and ruined the dress, and then she laughed—and I hit her and called her an amateur."

"You can think what you want," she replied haughtily. Later shooting had to be postponed when, as a result of the pressure, she began vomiting and couldn't stop.

But fewer parts suited her better. Drawing on her own upper-middle-class New England girlhood, Kate had never felt more comfortable in a character's skin. "It was to me my youth!" Kate later said, and confessed that she had based much of the character on her high-strung, brilliant Aunt Edith.

Conversely, Kate could not have been more woefully miscast than she was for her next RKO picture. Audiences would not buy Kate as a barefoot Ozark faith healer in *Spitfire*, and she couldn't blame them. "Shame on you, Kathy," Hepburn later scolded herself.

Still, Hepburn was a bona fide movie star now, and she was confident her career could withstand such periodic setbacks. So confident, in fact, that she was determined to return to Broadway in triumph, starring in Jed Harris's production of *The Lake*.

In the 1920s Harris had been one of Broadway's most successful producers, the man behind such hits as *The Royal Family, The Front Page,* and *Serena Blandish* (and later *Our Town* and *The Crucible*). He was also widely detested. Actors called him "The Vampire." Laurence Olivier patterned his leering, sinister Richard III after Jed Harris, and Walt Disney used Harris as his model for the Big Bad Wolf. After a string of flops in the early 1930s Harris was now in desperate need of a smash to restore his standing. Only Kate stepped forward to help, agreeing to do *The Lake* for a paltry five hundred dollars a week.

Actresses found Harris's studied, Svengali-like malevolence oddly seductive, and Kate was no exception. "He had a way of treating you as if you were an inferior creature," Kate later confessed, and for whatever reason, she found herself drawn to him. Their affair—she had not bothered to tell Harris she was married—was mercifully brief.

Just a few days into rehearsals for *The Lake*, Harris fired the director and took over the job himself. From the outset he seemed determined to destroy his star's confidence by ridiculing her every gesture and humiliating her before the rest of the cast. "If I turned left, he said turn right," she remembered. "I sat. He said stand." Hepburn knew that Harris was "no fool" and wondered what he hoped to gain by "tormenting" her.

The Lake opened on December 26, 1933, and was an unqualified disaster. It did, however, spawn Dorothy Parker's classic comment in the *New Yorker* that Hepburn ran "the gamut of emotion from A to B." It eventually became clear why Harris had tried to derail his star: He had sunk every penny he had into the play, and when it became clear even to him that *The Lake* was dry, Harris tried to recoup at least some of his losses by forcing Kate to buy her way out of her run-of-the-play contract. The ploy worked. When he threatened to take *The Lake* on the road—audiences would pay to see a movie star in anything—Kate emptied her bank account to pay Harris off.

Meanwhile Kate and Luddy—who still clung to the dream that she and he would someday live together like any other married couple—picked out a four-story brownstone in the elite East Side enclave of Turtle Bay and moved in.

Leland Hayward, now divorced from Lola Gibbs a second time, pressed Kate to divorce Luddy and marry him. But "dear, sweet" Luddy had worked hard to win over Kate's family, and they stood squarely in his corner. Kate's sister Marion was now fifteen, and the entries in her diary reveal how the drama was unfolding from the perspective of the Hepburns:

Jan. 1, 1934—Lud and I left for New York today. . . . Katy's personal maid helped me pack my trunks. . . . Lud and I had dinner on the train and we talked about boys and falling for people. He asked me if i had fallen for anybody and I said no, which was the truth and he said he thought I was wise not to. . . . I was glad that I went down with him because I sort of got to know him a little better, and he is a very nice sort of person. I certainly hope that he and Katy don't get divorced.

January 7
At 10:30 at night Katy did Romeo and Juliet over the radio. I just loved it. She made $5000.

Two weeks later Kate asked Luddy to move out of the brownstone. Just so that he would be on hand to watch over her and do the occasional odd job—Luddy was a talented do-it-yourselfer—Kate's erstwhile husband moved into the town house directly behind hers. All he had to do was stroll across their communal garden and knock on the back door.

From Marion's journal:

January 21
Katy, Lud and Mother came home last night. . . . Katy and Lud don't live together anymore. Oh dear, I guess they are really going to get a divorce. Lord knows why. Oh, I hope I never get married. What's the use. You only get messed up in the end and one of you has to suffer for it.

April 4
Katy came home and left just after supper. She really is going to devorse [*sic*] Lud. She says she's going to marry Leland. Gosh, I hope not. I don't see why she does it because Lud is so much nicer than Leland.

Luddy pledged his undying love to Kate but, true to his nature, agreed not to stand in the way of her marriage to Hayward. In April 1934, under the pretext of touring the ancient Mayan ruins of the Yucatán, Kate and Laura Harding flew to the Mexican town of Mérida. There she appeared before a judge who granted her a Mexican divorce.

Once back in California, Kate and Leland settled into their routine, she later said, like "an old married couple." An old married couple with a permanent houseguest. Suddenly Quinta Nirvana seemed a little cramped for Kate, Leland, *and* Laura. Late that summer they moved to a large house on Angelo Drive high above Benedict Canyon. Once owned by Fred Niblo, who had directed the silent-screen version of *Ben-Hur*, the house boasted tennis courts, a pool, and a breathtaking view of Los Angeles.

Life with Hayward during their four years together, according to Kate, "was so easy. Joy was the constant mood." Hepburn confided to her friends the Selznicks that she and Leland would indeed soon be married. Then Laura, who never felt at home in California, returned to work for Leland out of his New York office. With Laura gone, the homosexual rumors subsided, and Kate's relationship to Leland was exposed.

Strangely, Laura's departure threw off the delicate balance between Kate and Leland. Kate's constant and ever-present friend had been a stabilizing influence—the one person she could turn to for advice and encouragement on the set or at home. Leland, who had his own far-flung business interests to attend to, could not replace her. But others could.

Kate leaned on her worldly costar Charles Boyer during the filming of the ill-fated *Break of Hearts*. Their brief romance ended even before she began making her next film, *Alice Adams*. Again, Kate became infatuated with one of her coworkers—this time her director, the coolly intractable George Stevens.

The sexual tension between Kate and Stevens, who had no qualms about shooting a scene thirty or more times, sometimes erupted into namecalling on the set. The poignant story of a smalltown girl with social pretensions, *Alice Adams* required Kate to express a degree of vulnerability on the screen she never had before. When Stevens decided he wanted Kate to walk to a window, place her fingertips on the glass, and break down in tears, she insisted that the scene be done as it had been rehearsed—with Kate flinging herself on the bed and sobbing.

"It's ridiculous!" she shouted. "There's a limit to stupidity. I've put up with all of it I can. You dumb bastard, I'm going to cry on the bed!"

Stevens, biting down hard on his ever-present pipe, threatened to walk off the picture rather than surrender the point.

"A quitter!" Kate laughed. "If I ever had any respect for you, it's gone now! You're yellow!"

Stevens stood his ground, and eventually Kate did the scene at the window. "It was painful," Stevens said, "and perfectly what I wanted." Hepburn was uncharacteristically restrained in *Alice Adams,* and audiences were moved. She received her second Academy Award nomination for the film but lost to Bette Davis in *Dangerous.*

Hepburn was jolted back to reality in December 1934, when Leland was suddenly stricken with a painful prostate problem. Despite Dr. Hepburn's obvious fondness for Luddy, Kate wanted her father to perform the necessary surgery. The couple flew to New York's Idlewild Airport, where in her haste to escape reporters, she was nearly decapitated by a propeller. HEPBURN DARES DEATH TO ELUDE THE PRESS, read the *New York World-Telegram* headline.

Kate did manage to elude the press stakeout at the hospital for several days. But when photographers surprised her outside the Hepburn house in West Hartford, she flew into what she called "a blind, towering rage." She grabbed one photographer's camera and smashed it to the ground, then ran inside, shouting at her sister Peggy, "Where's a shotgun? Get it! Get it!" No firearms were used, but Kate's mother did grab a wire basket and begin swinging it wildly at the invading newsmen, who wisely backed off.

The incident was just one of many that set the fractious tone of Kate's relationship with the press. She no longer made up lies about her marital status or the five children she supposedly had. Instead she declared her private life to be her own and affected a Garbo-like disdain for reporters in general. On the rare occasions when she agreed to do an interview to promote a picture, Kate placed a timber-size chip on her shoulder and dared her interrogator to knock it off. "Now that's a damn silly question," she would say point-blank. "Unless you've got something more intelligent than that to say we can end this right now."

In 1935 Kate was reunited with Cukor to make *Sylvia Scarlet*, based on the Compton Mackenzie novel about a petty thief's daughter who escapes from England dressed as a man. It was her first film with a onetime Cockney stilt walker who had appeared in his first film under his real name, Archibald Leach. Archie was now being sold to the filmgoing public as Cary Grant.

It was Grant who arranged for his close friend Howard Hughes to drop in on Kate—literally— during the making of *Sylvia Scarlet*. Much of the film was shot on the bluffs above Southern California's rugged Trancas Beach, and each day Kate and Cukor took turns having their respective servants set up an elaborate picnic lunch.

On one of these idyllic afternoons a Boeing

Scout circled overhead, its silver nose glistening in the sun, then landed on a meadow above the picnickers—"close," Hepburn recalled. "Too close." Out of the cockpit climbed the rangy, boyishly handsome Hughes, resplendent in leather flight jacket, jodhpurs, and riding boots. Only two years older than Kate, he had already made a name for himself as a movie mogul, a record-smashing aviator, and a world-class playboy.

Kate had read that the mysterious and fabulously wealthy Hughes wanted to meet her, and now she was furious with Cary for making that possible. She treated their drop-in guest with thinly veiled contempt, chatting away animatedly with Cukor and Grant while Hughes sat silently nearby. "I never looked at Howard," she said. "What a nerve."

As they got up to leave, Kate pulled Cary aside and whispered, "I thought we had an agreement to bring only interesting people for lunch." She needn't have worried about Hughes overhearing. Kate later discovered that he was practically deaf. "He was apparently incapable of saying, 'Please speak up, I'm deaf,' " Kate said. As a result, he missed most of what people were saying, "and this was tragic." It contributed, Kate suggested, to "ruining his life and making him into an oddball."

Once *Sylvia Scarlet* was finished, Kate was sure she had a hit on her hands. But both she and Cukor failed to anticipate the public's reaction to a film about gender bending. In one key scene a maid who believes Kate to be a man kisses Hepburn full on the lips. The effect on audiences of the day was predictable. Scandalized, they fled the theater in droves.

In his typical, comforting fashion, Cukor wired Kate in Hartford:

PREVIEWED OUR LITTLE LOVE CHILD LAST NIGHT AUDIENCE GENERALLY INTERESTED THROUGHOUT STOP A BIT CONFUSED ABOUT THE STYLE OF THE PICTURE APPLAUDED FOR FULLY A MINUTE AFTER IT WAS OVER STOP REVIEW IN REPORTER NOT FAVORABLE STOP DAILY VARIETY QUITE FAVORABLE AND EXTREMELY NICE ABOUT YOU STOP LA TIMES RESPECTFUL AND ENTHUSIASTIC SAYING IT IS A MOST EXTRAORDINARY PICTURE STOP WE ALL DID OUR BEST AND I THINK NONE OF US HAVE BEEN DONE IN BY IT AT ALL STOP I THINK YOU ARE ABSOLUTELY LOVELY IN IT. MY LOVE TO YOU

GEORGE

Kate had weathered similar setbacks and was confident that her next project—*Mary of Scotland*, with Spencer Tracy's old friend John Ford in the director's chair—would put her back on top. Twelve years older than Kate, married and the father of two, "Pappy" Ford had already racked up such credits as *Arrowsmith, The Lost Patrol,* and *The Informer*. He was widely regarded as the most gifted director of his generation. Neither bubbly like Cukor nor taciturn like Stevens, Ford was a forceful, consummately charming storyteller in the Irish-American tradition. What's more, he resembled Kate's father. She warmed to him instantly, and he to her. They clearly cared for each other; he was visibly shaken when, doing her own stunts on horseback against his advice, she was nearly beheaded by a tree branch.

After they finished *Mary of Scotland* that May, Ford accompanied Kate to Fenwick, where they walked the rocky shoreline, played golf, and sailed back and forth across Long Island Sound. She called him by his real name, Sean, in deference to his Irish roots and he seemed content just to absorb the sights and sounds of her private world.

Speculation to the contrary, Hepburn and Ford were never lovers. While skirting the issue of marriage with Hayward, she had nonetheless remained faithful to him. But the playful bantering with Ford led to a genuine affection between the two.

Unfortunately Ford was a profoundly troubled man, and he afforded Hepburn her first frightening glimpse into the emotionally turbulent world of the chronic binge drinker. At one point, in an attempt to sober Ford up, Kate gave him a mixture of whiskey and castor oil that made him violently ill. "It was terrifying," she recalled. "He fell asleep and I thought he was dead. . . . I really nearly killed him." It was a preview, in a sense, of the life she would someday have with another Hollywood legend.

Kate could not overcome *Mary of Scotland*'s uninspired script, but that did not dissuade her from plunging into two more back-to-back costume dramas: *A Woman Rebels*, about an unwed mother in Victorian times, and J. M. Barrie's quaintly arch period piece *Quality Street*.

Throughout the two years since she unceremoniously dumped Luddy, Leland had pressed Kate to set their wedding date. By mid-1936 he had stopped trying. That fall Hayward went to New York for the opening of *Stage Door*, written by one of his clients, Edna Ferber, and starring another, Virginia-born Margaret Sullavan.

The lead role in Ferber's play had originally been tailor-made for Kate, and in the past Leland would have made certain that she among all his clients would have been offered the part. But now he was feeling slighted, and he turned to Sullavan for solace.

A trousers-wearing renegade who flouted convention and treated the press with haughty disdain, Maggie Sullavan was regarded as a sort of southern belle version of the renegade Miss Hepburn. Her previous marriage had been to the up-and-coming Henry Fonda—a union that ended when Hank discovered she was having an affair with the loathsome Jed Harris ("I couldn't believe that my wife and that son of a bitch were in bed together. But I knew they were"). Sullavan, famous in acting circles for her wildly er-

ratic behavior, was already romantically
involved with Hayward when she abruptly married director William Wyler. She had known Wyler, who went on to direct such classics as
Wuthering Heights, *The Little Foxes*, and *The Best
Years of Our Lives*, less than a month. Stunned by
the sudden turn of events, Leland then put even
more pressure on Kate to marry. But Sullavan
and Wyler split after one year, and in the absence
of any interest from Kate, Hayward welcomed
Maggie back.

On November 15, 1936, midway through the
shooting of *Quality Street*, news crackled over the
radio that Leland had married Margaret Sullavan. Kate was devastated—"thunderstruck," she
later confessed. Sobbing uncontrollably, she
phoned her mother in Connecticut.

"But you didn't want him, Kath," Mrs. Hepburn replied, and her friend Cukor agreed.
"Kate, what's wrong with you? You could have
married him if you wanted him. You didn't."

"Oh, stop saying that!" she protested. "What
am I going to do?" Kate sent a congratulatory
telegram, but it had been an unexpected blow. It
took her months to recover.

Hepburn had help in this endeavor from Howard Hughes, who was now in hot pursuit.
Hughes's reputation as a ladies' man was even
more formidable than Leland's. Silent-screen
beauty Billie Dove, Jean Harlow, and Ginger
Rogers were just a few of his conquests, which
would grow to include Bette Davis, Lana Turner,

Olivia De Havilland, Rita Hayworth, Jane Russell, Ava Gardner, Susan Hayward, Gene Tierney, and Marilyn Monroe.

Hughes swamped Kate with flowers and phone calls. In a reprise of their first meeting he swooped down in his plane and landed on a sloping strip of fairway at the Bel Air Country Club, dangerously close to the spot where Kate was taking a golf lesson from the club pro. Hughes hauled his clubs out of the plane and joined them. Enraged club officials refused to let him take off, so Hughes got a lift from Kate to the Beverly Hills Hotel. His Boeing Scout meanwhile had to be dismantled and removed from the course in a truck at the then-staggering cost of ten thousand dollars. "The man," Kate said, "is pushy."

After her humbling experience in *The Lake*, Kate was eager to prove herself to theater audiences. When Theresa Helburn and Lawrence Langner, her good friends from New York's Theatre Guild, offered Kate the title role in a new Broadway-bound production of Charlotte Brontë's *Jane Eyre*, she jumped at the chance.

Remembering how Jed Harris had forced her to open prematurely in *The Lake*, Kate insisted this time that the play tour extensively before it was performed before a New York audience. She also asked that her name be listed below the title with the other actors, a gesture Langner described as "generous."

"Generous!" she replied with a laugh. "I just don't want to stick my neck out."

Jane Eyre opened in New Haven the day after Christmas 1936 and began a fourteen-week trek across America. The wounds from Hayward's betrayal were still fresh, and Kate tended to them herself rather than socialize with cast members. "For the first time in my life," Kate said, "I was terribly, terribly . . . lonely."

When *Jane Eyre* reached Boston, Kate checked into her suite at the Ritz—only to find flowers from Howard Hughes and a note saying he had just checked into the same hotel. They shared romantic room service suppers after each night's performance, and when the play moved on to Chicago, Hughes followed. This time, as Kate put it, "persistence paid off." They consummated their affair in her ninth-floor suite at the Ambassador East Hotel.

The night of Kate's Chicago opening, Hughes vanished as suddenly as he had appeared. Under a veil of secrecy, he flew back to the Hughes Aircraft hangar in California. At 2:14 A.M. on January 19, 1936, Hughes took off from Burbank's Union Airfield in his silver and blue racer, the *Winged Bullet*. Hughes's mission: to break his own transcontinental air record of nine hours, twenty-seven minutes, and ten seconds.

As he crossed over the Grand Canyon, Hughes started to feel light-headed. Then he began slipping in and out of consciousness, his arms too heavy to lift and his hands too numb to grasp the controls. At the last minute he realized his oxygen mask was malfunctioning. He ripped off the mask and began sucking the oxygen straight from the tube. And he kept the tube clenched in his teeth until he reached Newark 7 hours, 28 minutes, and 25 seconds after taking off. Amazingly, he had managed to shave 119 minutes off his own record.

AM DOWN AND SAFE AT NEWARK, LOVE HOWARD, read the telegram Hughes sent Kate in Chicago. He need not have bothered. Kate had already whooped for joy when she read the front-page headline in the *Chicago Daily News:* HUGHES SPANS THE U.S. BY AIR IN 7½ HOURS.

Hughes told the mob of reporters that greeted him in Newark that he was going to rest up in New York, then promptly flew off to rendezvous "secretly" with Kate. In the excitement of the moment he proposed, and she impulsively accepted.

It seemed only logical at the time, since they clearly had so much in common. Both were children of privilege. Kate and Howard even shared a similar physiognomy: Each was tall, lean, angular, and possessed seemingly inexhaustible reservoirs of energy. They were narcissistic, unapologetically self-centered, and could be ruthless in pursuit of their own interests. They defied convention and shared an abiding hatred of the press. Both, Kate conceded, had "a wild desire to be famous." Yet they clung to the incongruous belief that they could be famous without giving

up their right to a private life. The similarities
that drew them together were precisely the
things that would ultimately drive them apart.

That January in Chicago, however, they were
blinded by love. While Hughes was still winging
his way west, he had someone from his office in
Los Angeles call the Cook County clerk's office
to inquire about the requirements for obtaining
a marriage license. Meanwhile the concierge at
the Ambassador Hotel made the same inquiry on
Kate's behalf.

The result, predictably, was bedlam. The Chicago papers were filled with stories proclaiming:
HUGHES AND HEPBURN WILL MARRY TODAY. At
2:00 P.M. on January 21 three thousand fans stood
outside the theater, waiting for Kate to appear
for a rehearsal. Kate felt "like a hunted animal."
To avoid walking through her hotel lobby, she
climbed down a fire escape and then had to
make the long climb back up again when the lad-
der from the first floor to the ground became
stuck.

Later that day Cook County Clerk Michael J.
Flynn held a press conference and said that he
expected to marry the world's most talked-about
couple any minute. But through the hotel concierge Kate issued a formal statement at 5:00 P.M.
"Miss Hepburn wishes to announce," the dour-
faced concierge told reporters, "that Miss Hepburn and Mr. Hughes will not marry today."

Still, from St. Louis to Toledo to Columbus to
Pittsburgh and beyond, Kate and Howard were

inseparable for the rest of the tour. They even seemed to enjoy what came to be known as the "Kate and Howard Chase," darting in and out of hotels and stage doors, collars turned up against the assault of popping flashbulbs.

Artistically Kate had not found *Jane Eyre* satisfying, and she did not have enough confidence in the property to take it to Broadway—certainly not after *The Lake*. After the show closed in Baltimore, she and Hughes cruised the Caribbean aboard his spectacularly appointed 320-foot yacht *Southern Cross*.

When they got back to California, Kate moved into Muirfield, Hughes's estate in the tony Hancock Park section of Los Angeles. Although Hughes already employed a housekeeper Beatrice Dowler, Kate brought along her own cook, the cook's handyman husband, and her personal maid. Soon their staff swelled to eight, including two chauffeurs, a laundress, and a butler.

As the chatelaine of Muirfield, Kate sought to exert a civilizing influence on Hughes, who still numbered among his friends wildcat roughnecks from the oil fields of Texas, hard-living test pilots, and several members of organized crime. When the likes of Lucky Luciano and Bugsy Siegel came to dinner, Mrs. Dowler was instructed to serve them on the cheap china and then throw the plates away after they had left. "It would be more economical, don't you think, Howard," Kate suggested, "if you just invited a better class of friends?"

Hughes clearly gloried in having a partner who was glamorous and accomplished in her own right but also in every sense his intellectual equal. Hollywood was their common ground; as mavericks in the business who had not only survived but flourished, they could talk for hours about the art of filmmaking. But unlike other stars Hughes had known, Kate was equally passionate about his far-flung business interests and his accomplishments in the field of aviation.

Kate's friends realized that she had been deeply hurt by the betrayals of Jed Harris and Leland Hayward, but most were not aware that she still harbored unresolved feelings toward John Ford. The director's reluctance to make clear his intentions—was he interested in her romantically or not?—confused and infuriated Kate. Ford's vacillation had made Hughes's ardent pursuit all the more appealing.

Still, to some it seemed an odd coupling. "I don't know what she was doing with Howard Hughes," said her friend Anita Loos. "He had a whole stable of girls, and Kate simply wasn't the type to have anything to do with that kind of thing." But Cary Grant, who had pushed the relationship from the outset, saw them as eminently compatible. "They were like two wild horses," he said. "Nobody was about to tame either one of them—or at least I didn't think so at the time. There was a real electricity between them. . . ."

There was a spontaneity to the relationship

that neither had ever experienced before. Muirfield was situated next to the Wilshire Country Club, so that whenever they felt like squeezing in a few holes, they hopped the fence and played through. Or they would simply stroll the fairways hand in hand, taking in the California sunsets without being pursued by hordes of photographers and screaming fans.

Much of their affair took place in the sky. The couple crisscrossed the country more than twenty times, often with the inexhaustible Hughes at the controls for twenty-four hours at a stretch while Kate dozed in a sleeping bag behind the cockpit. Once New Yorkers gasped when Hughes's seaplane, piloted by Kate, took off from the East River and then swooped beneath the Queensboro Bridge. At other times they skinny-dipped off the seaplane's wings as it bobbed in Long Island Sound.

Kate's carefree life with Hughes contrasted sharply with her career, which in 1937 was once again at a crossroads. "There is probably no one in pictures who needs a real money film as much as this actress," lamented *Variety*. Kate, who had just paid $27,500 for her New York town house, could not have agreed more.

She had lost the play *Stage Door* when Leland Hayward championed Margaret Sullavan for the lead, but RKO had paid $130,000 to secure the movie rights for Kate. After the abysmal failure of *Quality Street*, however, the studio decided to hedge its bets. Ginger Rogers was hired for *Stage*

Door on the pretext of being groomed for more serious dramatic roles. It was the first time Kate shared top billing with another actress, and Hepburn felt this was a sure sign that RKO no longer had faith in her ability to carry a film—not even with a supporting cast that included Eve Arden, Lucille Ball, and Ann Miller.

In the bitchily comic *Stage Door* Kate plays a debutante turned actress who checks into the Barbizon-like "Footlights Club" and promptly alienates everyone. Her wealthy father uses connections to get her the role promised to a more gifted actress, and when that actress kills herself, Kate's character goes onstage and gives the most moving performance of her life. The play within a play, *Enchanted April,* actually parodies *The Lake,* with Kate delivering *The Lake*'s overwrought "the calla lillies are in bloom again" speech at the film's three-handkerchief climax.

Stage Door opened at Radio City Music Hall in October 1937 and was instantly hailed as the greatest backstage movie of all time. (It remained so until the release of *All About Eve* in 1950.) It also turned a respectable profit. But Kate realized that *Stage Door* was an ensemble effort and therefore not a true test of her drawing power.

While searching for a new project, she met a young writer-director named Garson Kanin. A fan of Kate's since her days on Broadway, he quickly became one of her most trusted friends. Early on he witnessed firsthand one of Kate's many eccentricities: a paralyzing fear of restaurants. "I sit down," Kate explained, "and suddenly become terribly self-conscious. All eyes are on me, I'm absolutely convinced. What fork do I pick up? Are they watching me chew? Do I have spinach on my chin? Then I become panicky. When things get really out of hand, I faint in restaurants." But Kanin did manage to coax her to Chasen's early one evening, and as they became more engrossed in the food and the conversation, they failed to notice the restaurant gradually filling up. Once she did, Kate leaped to her feet and dashed out of the restaurant with a bewildered Kanin trailing far behind.

Even before *Stage Door* was released, Kate embarked that fall of 1937 on her next film, Howard Hawks's quintessential screwball comedy *Bringing Up Baby*. In this film Hepburn is typecast as a Connecticut heiress in hot pursuit of a stuffed-shirt paleontologist played by Cary Grant. Along the way the couple encounters a batch of Connecticut Yankee oddballs, a terrier named George, and a pet leopard that purrs like a kitten when it hears the song "I Can't Give You Anything but Love, Baby." Professor and heiress end up swinging perilously atop a collapsing Brontosaurus skeleton at the American Museum of Natural History.

"Kate has an amazing body—like a boxer," marveled Hawks, who was soon to discover a nineteen-year-old phenomenon named Lauren Bacall. "It's hard for her to make a wrong turn. She's always in perfect balance. . . . I've never

seen a girl that had that odd rhythm and con-
trol." Not everyone shared Hawks's high opinion of his controversial star. Just as they wound
up the principal photography on *Bringing Up
Baby*, Harry Brandt, president of the Independent
Theatre Owners of America, released his list of
stars who were "Box Office Poison." Heading
the list was Kate, followed by, among others,
Marlene Dietrich, Joan Crawford, Fred Astaire,
Mae West, and Greta Garbo. In this era of all-
American escapist fare, Shirley Temple, Mickey
Rooney, Deanna Durbin, Clark Gable, and Spen-
cer Tracy reigned supreme at the box office.

"They say I'm a has-been," Kate replied. "If I
weren't laughing so much, I might cry." Behind
closed doors she *was* crying—frantic that
Brandt's little publicity stunt might just finish her
off. RKO executives took the box-office poison
label to heart, deciding to shelve *Bringing Up
Baby* rather than spend any more money on dis-
tribution and advertising.

At a time when she desperately needed a
shoulder to lean on, Hughes, deep in preparation
for his planned round-the-world flight, was darting from London to Paris to Washington nego-
tiating the requisite flight clearances. There was
time in his schedule, however, for dalliances
with other women—most notably a tryst with
Woolworth heiress Barbara Hutton at London's
Savoy Hotel. Later, Hutton would marry
Hughes's loyal friend Cary Grant.

To anyone who knew about Kate's tragic family history, what happened next might have seemed not altogether illogical. While in makeup at RKO, an agitated Kate suddenly bolted for an open window and, according to makeup artist Layne Britton, climbed onto a second-story ledge. Cary Grant spent the rest of the morning "talking Kate out of her taking her own life."

A tower of strength to the outside world, Kate still defined herself in terms of her career. By her own admission, ambition superseded all else. She now felt more vulnerable professionally than ever, and the notion of exiting the planet on one's own terms had some appeal. It was not the first time she had thought about what it meant to take one's own life, and it would not be the last.

As soon as Hughes surfaced, he came to Kate's rescue, buying *Bringing Up Baby* from RKO and distributing it through the Loew's chain. The film ultimately came to be regarded as the best of the genre, but at the time of its release it fizzled. Moviegoers who could barely scrape up the price of admission had, at least for the moment, grown tired of spoiled heiresses and their impeccably tailored suitors. Their taste now ran to Little Orphan Annie and Spencer Tracy's salt-of-the-earth Father Flanagan.

RKO executives had no intention of sticking by their embattled star. In an obvious attempt to force her to break her contract, they made Kate a take-it-or-leave proposition to do a barely-B picture called *Mother Carey's Chickens*. It was at this juncture that Kate's old friend George Cukor, assigned the job of directing the film version of *Holiday* for Columbia, convinced Columbia chief Harry Cohn to offer Hepburn the lead. For Kate, who had understudied the part on Broadway, "there was no question at all—I had to do it." She had been warned about the notoriously libidinous Cohn, but when they met for the first time, she could not possibly have been prepared for his opening line. "Leland Hayward tells me"—Cohn grinned—"you're great in the hay." Kate kept right on talking as if she hadn't heard a thing. So he repeated the crude remark. Again Kate chattered away, unfazed by the mogul's persistent boorishness. No one had ever simply ignored Cohn before, and he had no idea how to respond. By the time they were finished Cohn, who had always intended to hire Irene Dunne, was completely disarmed. He offered Kate the part and a hefty $150,000.

With her business manager–father's blessing, she gave half the money to RKO in exchange for loaning her out to Columbia. In *Holiday* Kate played the archetypical Park Avenue society girl—this time the black sheep of the family, who falls in love with her snobby sister's self-made fiancé (again played by Cary Grant). The fiancé's working-class roots are what most appeal to Kate's character, and much of the dialogue in *Holiday* is devoted to skewering the manners and mores of the very rich. But it was above all else a stylish drawing-room comedy, and despite good reviews ("vibrant, moving—first class screen acting," wrote the New York *Herald Tribune* critic of Kate's performance) audiences stayed away. (Forty years later Hepburn watched the movie for the first time on television. "All I could think of was, who is that delightful creature?" she said. "It was really damn good.")

As she did with all her "beaus," as she called them, Kate paraded Hughes in front of the entire Hepburn clan at Fenwick that May. Luddy, as always, was on hand to make Kate's current love interest feel uncomfortable (as he had done so artfully with Jed Harris, Leland Hayward, and John Ford) and to curry favor with his former in-laws. Hughes did not make it easy for the Hepburns to know him. He would not actually share meals with the family—preferring to eat alone in his room late at night—but he would sit with them as they dined, a sullen figure whose deafness made it impossible for him to participate in the Hepburns' customary debates.

Even on the golf course, where the talented Hughes might have impressed Dr. Hepburn, Luddy managed to steal the show, whirling about with a camera, taking shots of the game while Kate mugged outlandishly for the camera.

"Stop, dammit," Hughes finally exploded. "I can't concentrate." Luddy just kept right on clicking away, and Hughes blew up again.

"Look, Howard," Dr. Hepburn said, "Luddy has been taking pictures of all of us years before you joined us, and he will be taking them long after you have left. He's part of this family. Now. Go ahead. Drive. You need a seven iron, by the way."

Kate recalled that "in a fury, Howard drove and landed six feet from the pin. Sank a two. Not bad in a pinch."

Regardless of her parents' obvious lack of enthusiasm for the peculiar Mr. Hughes, Kate had already made up her mind. On May 28 the Los Angeles *Herald* ran the headline KATHARINE HEP-BURN TO WED HUGHES. Indeed Hughes had ordered his principal lieutenant, Noah Dietrich, to call the crew of the *Southern Cross* back from vacation, to see to it that the Art Deco master suite was completely refurbished and that the galley was stocked with ample supplies of caviar and Dom Pérignon.

But less than two weeks later the wedding hit yet another snag. Kate, who had bought up the remainder of her RKO contract and was now a free agent, had received only one offer. Paramount approached her to do a film for an astonishingly low ten thousand dollars. Kate declined—not because of the money but because she did not like the script. Hughes, however, was "very upset" that she would turn down the only offer to come her way. "He felt that I was embarrassed by my failure," she said, "but somehow I wasn't. Well, obviously it mattered, but not enough to govern my actions."

The part she (along with every other actress) was angling for was that of Scarlett O'Hara in David O. Selznick's production of *Gone with the Wind*. Cukor had been hired to direct, and he pleaded for the producer to hire Hepburn. But when pressed to give a reason why he wouldn't cast Kate in the role, Selznick blurted, "Because I just can't imagine Clark Gable chasing you for ten years!"

"I may not appeal to you, David," she replied. "But there are men with different tastes!"

Although Hepburn remained on the Scarlett O'Hara short list for months, Paulette Goddard had the inside track until December 10, 1938, when Selznick was introduced to a breathtakingly beautiful unknown. Her name was Vivien Leigh. (Laurence Olivier's future wife went on to win the Academy Award for her portrayal of Scarlett which, ironically, was presented to her by Spencer Tracy.)

Hughes's insistence that Kate knuckle under and accept the paltry ten-thousand-dollar Paramount offer now before her revealed two important things to Kate: that the opinion of others mattered far more to Howard than it did to her, and that he lacked faith in the woman he supposedly loved. She, however, had complete faith in his ability to beat Wiley Post's existing solo record when Hughes flew his new Lockheed Lodestar around the world. There was no way to overestimate the danger; it had been less than a year since Howard's good friend Amelia Earhart had vanished over the South Pacific. Knowing it might be their last time together, Kate and Howard moved into a secret hideaway on Manhattan's East Fifty-second Street.

In the early-morning hours of July 10 Howard and Kate drove in her chauffeured Lincoln to Long Island's Floyd Bennett Field. "Keep me posted," she said before kissing him good-bye.

Hughes smiled and said, "You'll hear from me, kiddo."

The world held its breath as Hughes's Lodestar pushed on to Paris, Moscow, Siberia, and beyond. Cheering crowds mobbed him at each stop, and back in New York reporters kept a noisy vigil outside Kate's East Forty-ninth Street town house. The world was in the grip of what was being called "Hughesmania." For the first time Kate realized that she no longer had the upper hand in the relationship. If they were to be married, he would not be Mr. Katharine Hepburn; she would most definitely be Mrs. Howard Hughes.

Hughes touched down at Floyd Bennett Field at 2:37 on the afternoon of July 14, 1938. He had cut Wiley Post's record nearly in half. Mayor Fiorello La Guardia was among those on hand to greet him, but during a reception Hughes managed to sneak out a back door to rendezvous with Kate. The next day more than a million people turned out for a ticker tape parade honoring the man *Life* described as "the rich young Texan with a poet's face."

After similar parades in Washington, Houston, and Los Angeles, Hughes settled in at Muirfield and awaited Kate's response to yet another marriage proposal. She did not answer but did invite him to join her at Fenwick. By the time he left a week later, she had still not firmly made up her mind.

On September 21, 1938, ominous black clouds rolled in, and winds began to whip up along the Connecticut shoreline. Within hours a hurricane had demolished Fenwick, and Kate, her mother, and the family maid had narrowly escaped with their lives. Power and phone lines were down everywhere, but Kate started for the center of town. "My God," she remembered, "it was something *devastating*—and unreal—like the beginning of the world—or the end of it—and I slogged and sloshed, crawled through ditches and hung on to keep going somehow—got drenched and bruised and scratched—*completely* bedraggled—finally got to where there was a working phone and called Dad."

When he heard that nearly three hundred people had been killed by the storm in Connecticut and Rhode Island, Hughes dispatched a rescue plane to Fenwick. The pilot reported back that he had found Kate merrily "sifting sand with an army of small boys, hunting for the family silver." Amazingly, she dug up eighty-five pieces of flatware and the entire tea service.

Modern Screen magazine posed the question on millions of lips. The cover of the popular fan magazine showed a dashing Hughes gazing covetously beneath aviator goggles at the lushly beautiful Miss Hepburn. WILL AMERICA'S HERO, HOWARD HUGHES, the headline asked, MARRY KATHARINE HEPBURN?

Hughes could no longer tolerate Kate's stalling. He gave her three days to answer his latest marriage proposal. "I have to know where I stand," he told her. Certainly he knew that Kate had a way of ignoring ultimatums. After two and a half days of silence their mutual friend Cary Grant intervened. First he tried to persuade Hughes to call Kate. When that failed, he went to Kate and pleaded with her to break down and make the first move. But it was too late. Kate had made up her mind. "I felt I was madly in love with him. I think he felt the same way about me," she conceded. But in the end both desired fame more. "Ambition beat love, or was it LIKE?"

"Kate was about fifty years ahead of the feminist movement," said veteran Hollywood reporter James Bacon. "She simply wasn't interested in being married. Howard Hughes told me he asked Kate to marry him and that she turned him down flat. He said she was unlike any woman he had ever known—and believe me, he had known plenty! He was desperate to have her and tried every trick in the book to get her to say yes. But in the end Kate told Hughes she did not want to marry him or, for that matter, anybody. Ever."

In truth, fame had been the glue that held them together. Kate admitted that he was "sort of the top of the available men and I of the women"—that in effect they were the only single man and single woman worthy of each other. They had made "a strange pair, a colorful pair," but somehow over their three years together, Kate observed wistfully, "love had turned to water."

Hughes was shattered by Kate's decision not to marry him. Although he went on to propose to Ginger Rogers and to marry the actress Jean Peters, Kate was the love of Howard Hughes's life.

They were no longer lovers, but even after she had rendered her verdict, Hughes played a large part in Hepburn's personal and professional lives. He would, in fact, be instrumental in reviving her career.

Not long before the hurricane reduced stately Fenwick to a pile of splinters, the playwright Philip Barry had visited there to talk with Kate about his idea for a new play. It centered on an aloof, arrogant Philadelphia society girl named Tracy Lord and her impending marriage to a boring blueblood. On the eve of the wedding her fatally charming ex-husband, C. K. Dexter Haven, shows up along with a reporter and a photographer from a scandal magazine. Tracy suddenly finds herself falling for not only her former spouse but also for the reporter. Along the way she is transformed from smug "ice goddess" to compassionate, tolerant human being. Barry already had a title picked out: *The Philadelphia Story*.

Eager to return to the stage, Kate literally looked over the playwright's shoulder as he crafted *The Philadelphia Story* to reflect her voice pattern and mannerisms. The parallels between Tracy Lord and Katharine Hepburn were many and obvious, from her love of swimming to her desire for privacy and passionate distrust of the press. The most revealing similarity centered on the dilemma confronted by both Tracy Lord and Kate: To marry or not to marry?

Katharine was still pondering the question when Hughes offered to finance the play sight unseen. Even after she turned down his marriage proposal, he wound up financing half the cost of mounting the play, with Kate and the Theatre Guild splitting the other half. With Hughes's help she also wisely bought the movie rights to the play for herself.

While Barry polished the script, Kate dropped in at F.A.O. Schwarz, the New York toy store, and purchased a set of children's building blocks. She emptied the box on the floor of the Hepburn family's West Hartford home and, with her parents and brothers and sisters, pieced together a model of the new Fenwick.

With a cast that included Van Heflin, Joseph Cotton, and Shirley Booth, *The Philadelphia Story* opened on March 28, 1939, at the Shubert Theater. It was the megahit for which Kate and the financially strapped Theatre Guild had been devoutly praying. The critics used words like "sparkling" and "radiant" to describe both play and actress, but they also praised Kate for her courage in the face of adversity. *The New York Times'* Brooks Atkinson wrote that Kate was "a woman who has at last found the joy she has always been seeking in the theater." Richard Watts of the *New York Herald Tribune* added, "Few actresses have been so relentlessly assailed by critics' wit, columnists, magazine editors and other professional assailers over so long a period of time . . . and faced it gamely and unflinchingly and fought back with courage and gallantry."

Kate sold the movie rights to L. B. Mayer for $175,000 and was paid another $75,000 to star in the film. Mayer, whom Kate praised as the most honest man she had ever dealt with in the movie industry, gave her final approval of the director, the screenwriter, and the cast. George Cukor, who had been fired from *Gone with the Wind* after three weeks and replaced by Victor Fleming because the macho Gable was allegedly uncomfortable working with a gay director, was available to direct *The Philadelphia Story*.

Although it augured well for her, Kate was outraged at the way Cukor had been dismissed from *Gone with the Wind*. In early 1939 she wrote him in longhand on her white stationary with "KATHARINE HOUGHTON HEPBURN" emblazoned across the top in red letters. Ostensibly she was thanking him for the gift of a potted plant, presumably one that had been well fertilized. Featuring Hepburn's famous lack of punctuation, the affectionate tone and stream-of-consciousness style were typical of their correspondence:

When you write give me your phone number—I've lost it—you were an angel to try to get to me.

Dearest George—

My whole house now reeks of [manure] at nite and so do I—I expect to be known as the smelliest actress on B'Way—(Yes, I know what you're saying) but not this time Thank God—in their own idiotic way they have gone overboard.

I shall never know but we stand them up and I found no reason to try to analyze so pleasant a state of affairs . . .

What in the world happened about G.W.T.W. It disgusted me! . . . That I simply can't imagine the picture not directed by you—but then it has been a pain in the neck—and I should think that you are probably relieved of an interesting but very problematical venture—Certainly I should think it would be very difficult to recreate your original enthusiasm anyway I am still revolted by the whole thing.

I haven't seen Tallulah [Bankhead]'s play [The Little Foxes] yet but everyone says that she and it are really something—As we have different matinees I shall see it soon. Your girls seem to have redeemed themselves finally. . . .

We are rebuilding our Fenwick House—on the hurricane site but of brick with steel supports—and at least this time we won't float away.

What goes on with you—How are all your house changes—the garden—my tree—who is still invited to Sunday lunch. . . . Please write me—with Sincere thanks for my present.

All my love, Kate

After a year on Broadway in *The Philadelphia Story*, Kate returned to Los Angeles to ponder her choices. She moved, together with her companion Laura Harding, into a hilltop house that had once belonged to silent-screen star John Gilbert. Signifying her final exit from Howard Hughes's Muirfield, Kate brought along her cherished collection of stuffed animals and arranged them carefully on her bed. Not surprisingly, the few fortunate visitors to Kate's room found it odd, to say the least, that this symbol of sophistication and liberated womanhood still surrounded herself with dolls—another quirk in a life chockablock with bewitching, often contradictory idiosyncrasies.

At this turning point in her career, Kate was

determined that *The Philadelphia Story* be as big a triumph on screen as it was on the stage. Gable was the top box-office draw in the country in 1940, and the way he had treated Cukor did not stop Kate from offering him the part of the magazine reporter. For the role of C. K. Dexter Haven, she wanted America's No. 2–ranked star, Spencer Tracy.

She was not surprised when Gable turned her down, but when Tracy declined, she was greatly disappointed. Even before she gave Philip Barry the green light to finish the play, she had envisioned Tracy playing her ex-husband. She told Cukor that one of the reasons she found Tracy Lord so appealing was that Spencer had made her fall in love with the very sound of the name Tracy.

It was not difficult to see why she wanted to act with Spencer onscreen. From a strictly commercial standpoint he was hot. Four Tracy films had been released in 1940—*I Take This Woman, Northwest Passage, Edison, the Man,* and *Boom Town*—and all were commercial successes.

Kate had yet to meet him, but like millions of fans, she assumed that Spencer must embody many of the same qualities he projected onscreen: quiet strength, wry wit, a stubborn integrity, a gruff, no-nonsense exterior masking the tender soul at the core. In short, the perfect foil for Tracy Lord.

She would have to "settle" for her old friend and frequent costar Cary Grant, who demanded not only a salary twice the size of Kate's but top billing. She agreed. Another top MGM star, Jimmy Stewart, replaced Van Heflin as the reporter who falls for Tracy—a performance that earned Stewart the Academy Award for Best Actor of 1940 over the likes of Henry Fonda in *The Grapes of Wrath*.

Stewart and a few of the other actors were more than a little apprehensive when shooting on *The Philadelphia Story* began. "We had read all those stories about how difficult and demanding Katharine Hepburn could be," he recalled. "But she wasn't. Kate was absolutely first-rate—open, warm helpful, incredibly easy to work with and very patient. Cary and I used to talk about how Kate had made the whole experience wonderful for everyone—cast and crew. I have never worked on a picture that went any smoother."

There was, however, the morning she asked Stewart, an experienced pilot, to take her up for a ride in his single-engine plane. As they started to taxi out onto the runway, Hepburn began tapping all the instruments with her finger. "Look," she said, "the oil pressure is low." Stewart told her that the gauge was broken and the oil pressure was just fine. Then, he recounted, "Kate proceeded to complain about everything. The needle on one of the other instruments wavered a bit. 'That's dangerous,' she said. I reassured her again that I had checked the plane out carefully. 'Well,' she told me in no uncertain terms. 'I don't care for that at *all*.' "

Still grumbling, Hepburn eventually agreed to let Stewart take off. He offered to fly over some of the pretty countryside north of Los Angeles, but his passenger declared she had "had enough" and ordered him to return to the air field.

Then, as the airstrip came into view, Kate informed Stewart, "You're too high! You're going to land halfway down the runway."

"I told her, 'It's going to be all right, Kate, believe me.'" said Stewart. "Well, I landed, but it was really more like a controlled crash." Hepburn then got out of the plane, walked over to her car and drove off. "To this day," Stewart laughed a half-century later, "she has never said a word."

As consumed as she was with engineering her comeback, Kate could still go out of her way to do a favor for someone she liked. Laurence Olivier and Vivien Leigh, who were friends of both Spencer Tracy and Kate Hepburn, had been lovers for years while married to other people. On August 31, 1940, Olivier and Leigh were at last free to marry each other. Kate and another mutual friend, Garson Kanin, dropped everything and rushed to Santa Barbara to be matron of honor and best man at their spur-of-the-moment midnight wedding.

The justice of the peace, by now thoroughly sloshed, kept calling Vivien "Lay," and the groom "Oliver." After a mercifully brief three-minute service he pronounced them man and wife. Then the world-famous couple kissed, at which point the justice of the peace yelled, "Bingo!"

Kate also found time in the fall of 1940 to support Franklin Roosevelt in his quest for a third term in the White House. One weekend Kate was invited to join some of her fellow artists for lunch with the President at Hyde Park. Rather than follow the White House travel plans, the independent-minded Kate chartered a single-engine seaplane and ordered the pilot to land on the Hudson River right behind the Roosevelts' stately house. Hiking up her pants, she waded through mud to the riverbank, then trudged up a steep slope toward the mansion itself. "Kate," FDR said, "you cannot imagine how flattered I am that someone would go through all this just to see *me*." (Spencer Tracy, though politically more conservative than Hepburn, was also a lifelong Democrat and an ardent supporter of FDR.)

In March 1941 Kate was overlooked by Oscar. In a field that included Bette Davis in *The Letter* and Joan Fontaine in *Rebecca*, she lost to Ginger Rogers in *Kitty Foyle*. But her return to the movies in *The Philadelphia Story* was nothing short of triumphant. The film broke box-office records around the country, making it the perfect antidote to "Box Office Poison."

But Kate remembered what it was like to be momentarily on top with *Little Women* and *Stage Door*. If she was going to avoid that inevitable plunge on the roller coaster, she needed a strong follow-up to *The Philadelphia Story*. Enter Garson Kanin, who had just been handed a story outline tentatively titled *The Thing About Women* by the son of Tracy's old Lambs Club crony, Ring Lardner, Jr. The young Lardner was looking for a collaborator, but Kanin, who had just enlisted in the service, suggested Lardner work with his brother, Michael Kanin, instead. Kanin also suggested they write the story expressly as a vehicle for Katharine Hepburn.

From the moment she read the seventy-eight-page outline for the newly retitled *Woman of the Year*, Kate knew she had found the property that would keep her on top. As the acclaimed foreign affairs columnist Tess Harding (Garson named the character after Kate's friend Laura Harding)—a character loosely fashioned after Clare Boothe Luce and the celebrated journalist Dorothy Thompson—Hepburn falls in love with and marries Sam Craig, a tough Irish sportswriter who works for the same paper. The balance of power shifts back and forth as each tries to gain the upper hand in the relationship. This oddest of couples quarrels, makes up, separates, and reconciles—one assumes for good—as the film ends.

Garson Kanin knew Tracy and Hepburn before they knew each other. So he felt eminently qualified to tell them both that Tracy was perfect for the part of Sam Craig. Suddenly Kate expressed doubt. "Oh, I don't know. I wonder whether we'd be good together. We're so . . . different."

Tracy shared her concerns, almost verbatim. "Oh, really?" he asked Kanin. "Do you think we would be good together? We're so, uh, sort of . . . different."

It did not take long for Kanin to convince her—or, rather, for Kate to convince herself—that she wanted Spencer Tracy. She shared the opinion of her peers that he was a breed apart: the finest actor in the medium of motion pictures. Even the great Laurence Olivier conceded that he "learned more about acting from watching Tracy than any other way. . . . The rest of us struggle to achieve the purity, the truth that he appears to convey effortlessly. We act, and you can see the gears whirring. He just *is*."

Kate was also just as aware as everyone else in the Hollywood community that the great Tracy had what could only charitably be called a drinking problem, an addiction to alcohol that was serious enough for MGM to have a clause in his contract forbidding him from imbibing so much as a single beer while making a film. She also knew that he did not always abide by his contract and that rather than show up on the set, he simply disappeared, sometimes for days at a time. He then invariably materialized and delivered the sort of powerful, seemingly effortless performance that was well worth the wait.

Before she could snag Tracy, Kate had to sell the script to Metro. Neither Lardner nor Mike

Kanin had made more than three thousand dollars for a project, so she decided to keep their identities a secret. Even after she had hired Joe Mankiewicz, who had produced *The Philadelphia Story*, to produce *Woman of the Year*, she refused to divulge the screenwriters' names.

Rumors flew that it was the work of none other than *The Front Page* creators Ben Hecht and Charles MacArthur. "I can't tell you who the writers are—it's a secret for now," she said, "but I can promise you the price will be high." It all might be a moot point, she added, if she didn't get the actor she wanted to play opposite her. "If I can't get Spencer Tracy," she told Mankiewicz, "then I'm not selling it."

Mankiewicz agreed that *Woman of the Year* was perfect for the two of them and approached Tracy. Spencer, who purportedly had never seen a Katharine Hepburn film, asked Mankiewicz to arrange a private screening of *The Philadelphia Story*. When it was over, he proclaimed Kate to be "a damn fine actress." And as much as he resented any woman who insisted on wearing pants in public, he agreed to do the picture.

Now it was time for Kate to sell L. B. on the movie. Hepburn called herself one of the "giant ladies" of Hollywood, and at just five feet seven and a half inches she actually was taller than many of the leading men of the day—not to mention nearly all the studio chiefs. "When a woman looks down on a man, it does something to his ego," Kate said. "It's quite extraordinary.

They become so uncomfortable that they give you practically anything you ask for just to get rid of you. Works every time."

To maximize the effect, Kate slipped on what she called her trick shoes—heels that boosted her height a full four inches. Add to this an upswept hairdo and ramrod-straight posture, and Kate could make any man of smaller stature feel inconsequential indeed. "The idea," she said, "is to put the man in his place."

The ploy worked with the five-foot-seven-inch-tall father figure of MGM, who could be so shamelessly manipulative that he would get down on his knees and beg an actor to take a part. "She just stood there looking down—I mean, straight down—on L. B. with one hand on her hip and a finger wagging at his nose, sort of like a teacher scolding a very naughty, bald little boy," said Mankiewicz, who was present at the meeting. "It was all very cordial. They respected each other immensely, but there was never any doubt who was in the driver's seat."

Still unable to pry the names of the writers out of Kate, Mayer eventually gave her what she wanted: $211,000—$100,000 for the writers and $111,000 for her. "After we left I kissed her on the top of the head," Mankiewicz said. "When she asked why I did that, I just told her I wanted to kiss the Blarney stone."

Faced with having to get sixty more pages of a working script to Mayer overnight, Kate closeted herself with Lardner, the Kanin brothers, and two typists in a bungalow at the Garden of Allah Hotel, puffing her way through several packs of cigarettes as they worked aloud on the dialogue. She called in an expensive meal from Chasen's "to keep up their strength," and by dawn they had 106 pages perfectly tailored to the nascent team of Katharine Hepburn and Spencer Tracy. Her colleagues were exhausted, but Kate "practically ran" to L. B. with the pages.

Kate met Spencer for the first time just a few days later. Unfortunately she was wearing her "trick heels" when she emerged from the side entrance to the Thalberg Building at MGM and, on the steps outside, encountered Mankiewicz and Tracy as they left the comissary.

"They got nearer and nearer," she recalled, "and I got more and more excited. I hope he likes me. . . ." As she got closer, Kate realized that she was two inches taller than the five-foot-nine-inch Tracy.

"There was a long silence," she said. "I didn't know what to say." She grasped his hand and shook it, he later said, "like a stevedore."

"Sorry I've got these high heels on," Kate said, trying to break the ice. "But when we do the movie I'll be careful about what I wear."

Tracy looked at Kate with "those old lion eyes of his." Then Joe Mankiewicz spoke up. "Don't worry, Kate," Mankiewicz said. "He'll cut you down to size."

Afterward Kate rushed to Mankiewicz's office, eager to hear what opinion the great Tracy had of her. "What did he think? What did he think?" she demanded. "He must have said something."

"Well . . ."

"What did he say?"

Mankiewicz shifted nervously in his chair. "He said, 'Katharine Hepburn has dirty nails, hasn't she?' "

Mankiewicz did share the fact that Tracy disapproved of the mannish suit she was wearing (custom-made for her by the leading men's tailor Eddie Schmidt) and her too-firm handshake. "Not me, boy!" he told Mankiewicz the moment she left. "I don't want to get messed up in anything like this."

"I'm quite certain," Kate said, "that the first time he met me he thought I was a lesbian. It was not long before he was disabused of that notion, however."

Kate decided that for once George Cukor was not the right director for the film. She needed someone who could get the most out of a "man's man" like Tracy and was also a master of physical comedy. She turned to her old love from *Alice Adams*, George Stevens.

Kate in fact had been dating Stevens periodically over the past few months, and when she chose him over Cukor, there was rampant speculation that the Stevens-Hepburn relationship might be more than merely casual. Sparks did fly on the set. But even Stevens, who bore a physical resemblance to Tracy, recognized from the first day of shooting that whatever sexual tension existed on the set was between Tracy and Hepburn.

Kate quickly realized that she had met her match—"and then some." She was so nervous when they started the picture that she knocked over a glass of water while filming a restaurant scene. She expected Tracy to stop everything and call a propman to clean it up, but instead "he never batted an eyelash. Looking straight into my eyes and continuing with his lines, he picked up a handkerchief out of his breast pocket and handed it to me. I thought, 'You old son of a bitch,' and began damping up the mess. Then it started dripping through the table, so I just said, 'Excuse me,' and bent down to mop it off the floor—all the while saying our lines as if nothing unusual had happened! It worked beautifully, and we kept it in the film."

At first Stevens, Mankiewicz, and the rest of the cast watched as the two screen giants adjusted to each other. "It was rather like a very intricately choreographed ballet at first," Mankiewicz noted. "Very self-conscious as they tried to figure each other out. Early on in the filming I noticed that Spencer was sounding sort of highbrow and Kate's very distinctive, metallic-sounding voice was much lower, her delivery slower. Then it hit me. My God, they were unconsciously imitating each other!"

When they stopped and reverted to their old ways, they realized that their differences made them oddly compatible—the magical, indefinable "he-she chemistry" that came from being locked in an eternal male-female struggle for dominance.

Stevens believed Kate was "the rarer beast of the two." When Stevens visited Spencer in his dressing room, there would invariably be a knock on the door. The door would swing open, and there would stand Kate.

"What are you two conspiring about?" she would ask.

"Kate, I like guidance about things, and this man is our director."

"And what about my guidance?"

Spencer Tracy did his famous slow boil. "How could I be such a damn fool as to get into a picture with a woman producer and *her* director?" he said, shaking his head. "How can I be such a dumb bastard as that?"

Not much meat on 'er, but what there is is cherce.

—SPENCER ON KATE,
IN *PAT AND MIKE*

Not everyone is lucky enough to understand how delicious it is to suffer.

—KATE

Five

It was to be the longest-running star partnership in history—onscreen and off. But the entity known to generations of admirers as Tracy and Hepburn got off to an expectedly rocky start. At first he simply called her "That Woman" or "Shorty" in sly reference to their historic meeting outside the Thalberg Building. Over the years his list of pet names for her grew to include Olive Oyl, Zasu Pitts, Madame Defarge, Madame Curie, Dr. Kronkheit, Molly Malone, Carry Nation, Mrs. Thomas Whiffen, Laura La Plante, Flora Finch, Miss America, and Coo-Coo, the Bird Girl. When he wasn't needling her affectionately, it was simply Kath or, most often, Kathy.

With typical Yankee constancy, Kate started calling him by his full Christian name and stuck with it for twenty-six years. When she called him Spen*suh*, she always gave it the patrician spin that invariably elicited the same exasperated response. "Christ!" Tracy would say. "Why do you always have to sound like you've got a broomstick up your ass!" (The only exception to Spencer was Ratty, a seldom used moniker that was probably borrowed from Spencer's boyhood friend.)

In the beginning it seemed likely that the irascible Tracy and the overbearing Hepburn would collide spectacularly, leaving in their wake a shell-shocked cast and crew. "Everybody was sort of on tenterhooks waiting to see who would blow first," Mankiewicz said. "One day he was talking to George Stevens about 'that woman,' and the next he showed up calling her Kathy. Everyone was immensely relieved."

Life imitated art as Sam Craig–Spencer Tracy sized up Tess Harding–Kate Hepburn and vice versa. From the first day of shooting, recalled Stevens, "Spence's reaction to her was a total, pleasant, but glacial put-down of her extreme effusiveness." She "wanted to do a hundred and one things at once . . . everything except hang the arc lights." He stuck to his job. She wanted to rehearse and rehearse, to study every nuance of her character, and then do retake after retake until she was satisfied. He hated rehearsing and, said Stevens, "loved to do nothing but 'be' the part." When she asked for a retake, he muttered under his breath, "Bore, bore, bore."

Hepburn did not hesitate in bowing to him as the more skilled actor. "Watching him," she told a friend, "is like being grabbed by the front of the shirt and held." She also, reluctantly at first, came to respect his very different approach to the job. "The daily reworking of the script—the whole creative process—always fascinated me. I've always found it to be more fun than the actual acting. But it bored Spencer. He just went out there and made it work." To be sure, Tracy was responsible for the single most-quoted piece of advice on the art of acting: "Learn your lines, and don't bump into the furniture." (Many years later, when a young New York–trained actor was holding things up demanding to know the "motivation" for entering a room, Tracy took him aside. "You come in the fuckin' door," Tracy said, "because it's the only way to get in the fuckin' room. *That's* your motivation!")

"They were not just different," their friend Garson Kanin observed. "They were two very different sorts of people—altogether separate breeds, worlds apart. He was deeply religious, I believe. She is not religious at all. Kate's more of a freethinker, and if she worships anything, it's nature. Kate is actually the most nature-struck creature I've ever known." Even when it came to such mundane considerations as how to get from point A to point B, they had radically different preferences. Hepburn was born to fly; Tracy was terrified of leaving the ground and required a few stiff drinks to even consider boarding a plane.

Garson Kanin believed that the differences were especially glaring on the job. "He was a subjective actor. She is a cerebral actor. She wants to think everything through—every line, every nuance, every gesture. He just wanted to go out there and *do* it. Spontaneously. He liked to tell directors, 'Look, all I have in life is instinct, and if you take that away, I got nothing.' "

Yet no one could ignore the simple fact that these two extreme opposites were falling in love. As with the characters they were portraying, the real-life scenario being played out was between a stubborn man of the people with his own unshakable code of morality and an equally strong, financially independent woman who had, by her own account, behaved like any man in a world dominated by men. "He could read a person," their friend Angela Lansbury said of Spencer, "and he read Kate perfectly."

For both, the choice was neither easy nor logical. Kate was thirty-four when they began work on *Woman of the Year* on August 29, 1941. Tracy was forty-one. Both had come with entire cargo holds full of emotional baggage. Motivated more by concern for his children and personal feelings of remorse than by religious conviction, Spencer was more adamant than ever about not divorcing Louise. He still visited his family most weekends and phoned Louise without fail every day.

Certainly he could have found a less challenging lover than Kate, someone whose habits and personality traits were less at loggerheads with his. Yet at this time of life Spencer needed someone who was more than merely beautiful and smart. "He could find that anywhere," Mankiewicz said. "Spencer wanted someone who would match him point for point, who would put up a fight—not too much of a fight, mind you—someone who was exciting to be around, someone *stimulating*. God knows Kate was all those things.

"Remember, Leland Hayward couldn't tame Kate, and neither could Howard Hughes. Spencer knew all about them; the whole country knew. So, if Spencer was understandably wary of her at first, he had to take some pride in knowing he could accomplish what these other rather formidable gentlemen couldn't."

Kate's reasons for being drawn into an affair with the famously difficult Spencer Tracy were no less complex. She knew that Tracy had once been passionately and very publicly in love with Loretta Young and that if he would not divorce Louise to marry her, it was almost inconceivable that he would make the break for any woman.

Spencer's ineligibility for marriage was actually a plus. As fond as she was of Luddy, Kate had always resented being pushed into marrying him. Similarly, she had toyed seriously with the idea of marrying both Leland and Howard but in the end had come to the unavoidable conclusion that marriage was an institution for which she was ill suited.

By now she had reached the firm conclusion that members of her profession were too egocentric for marriage. "You can't have the whole bargain," she said. "An actor should never marry, not even another actor. You're too involved with yourself, and your work is too demanding, to give the necessary amount of attention to another human being. Inevitably that person feels left out. And becomes unhappy. We must never make people unhappy. Life's too short for that."

To make matters worse, Kate was not just another actor. "I am a total me, *me*, *ME* person," she said. "Always have been. Always will." Nor did it bother her at the time that she might miss out on motherhood. "I did not want to be married," she later stated. "I just wanted to be myself, and if you want to be yourself, you should not try to be the mother of four and the companion of a fascinating man. I never thought of having *one* child. I thought of having four. . . .

"I didn't have it both ways," she continued. "I didn't have a career *and* a family. Being a housewife and a mother is the biggest job in the world, but if it doesn't interest you, don't do it. It didn't interest me, so I didn't do it. Anyway, I would have made a terrible parent. The first time my child didn't do what I wanted, I'd kill him."

Her reasons for not wanting a family probably ran far deeper. "Why do you want to be weighed down with a husband, Kath?" Dr. Hepburn would ask. "You'll only be stuck at home raising the kids." Kate, who blurted out the very revealing "My father doesn't want me to have any babies!" line to John Barrymore, clearly put great store in her father's opinion. Moreover, although she never actively tried to dissuade Kate from marrying, much of the senior Katharine Houghton Hepburn's life had been spent alongside Margaret Sanger on the barricades of the birth control movement. As cofounder of a group that became Planned Parenthood, Kate's mother did little else but exhort women not to have children if they so chose.

"I knew right away," Kate recalled, "that I found him irresistible. Just exactly that, irresistible. . . . I found him totally, totally—total." Tracy was unlike the other men in her life, with one major exception. Physically and to some degree in temperament he resembled her father. Like her father, Spencer seldom bestowed words of praise or approval on even those closest to him. "I don't think he ever complimented Kate to her face," Mankiewicz said. "He would say wonderful things about her, but never *to* her. It just wasn't his style."

Yet there were important differences between Spencer and her father. Kate soon discovered that unlike Dr. Hepburn, Tracy was a deeply troubled and painfully insecure man who required a not inconsiderable amount of mothering. It would make Tracy irresistibly appealing as both a father *and* child surrogate.

It was a role to which Kate was unaccustomed but one that, curiously, she had an undeniable knack for—at least when it came to Spencer. Well aware of Tracy's affinity for booze, she made sure there was an endless supply of hot tea on the set. Other than that, she harbored no illusions about her ability to turn him into a tee-totaler.

Amazingly, Kate did not ask Spencer to go on the wagon, and never would. She subscribed to her father's philosophy when it came to drinking. "If you must drink," Hep told his daughter, "drink when you're happy. It'll make you happier. If you drink when you're miserable, it'll only make you more so. Drinkers are people who're looking for easy solutions to their problems. The shortcuts. There aren't any. Problems have to be faced and solved. You don't do anything with them by getting besotted and pretending they don't exist."

Kate made an exception in Spence's case. She did not approve of Tracy's overriding vice; neither did she condemn him for it. "He had a drinking problem, no doubt about it," Kate later said. "His drinking was no problem between us. Drinking is your own problem, and the only person who can do anything about it is you."

Tracy did do something about it—again and again. "I admired Spencer for his ability to just *stop*. Spencer was amazing. He never went to Alcoholics Anonymous, yet he would quit with a case of bourbon in the cupboard. And he wouldn't touch another drop for two or three years." Sadly, Kate had no inkling that Tracy's drinking had taken a huge toll on his health; by the time they met, his kidneys were already irreparably damaged by twenty years of binge drinking.

1

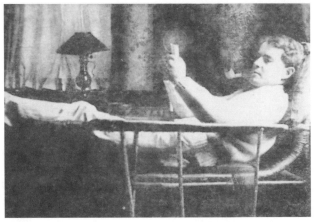

Kate's gruff, no-nonsense father, Dr. Thomas Hepburn, bore more than a passing resemblance to Spencer Tracy.

Tom Jr., four, and his little sister Kate, two, were inseparable.

Nine-year-old "Jimmy"—as Kate liked to be called—at Fenwick in the summer of 1916.

A cozy chat between scenes. It was clear to everyone on the *Woman of the Year* set that the couple was falling in love.

Pipe-smoking *Woman of the Year* director George Stevens, who had been dating Kate when the film started, stepped aside for Tracy.

35

In *Woman of the Year*, Tess Harding refuses to share Sam Craig's bed. Toward the end of his life, Kate actually slept on the floor and talked Spencer to sleep.

When the Kate's away . . .
Hard-drinking Tracy
parties with two
WASPs—members of the
Women's Air Force
Service Pilots—at Ciro's.

Kate was by far the superior
athlete, but she was no match
for Spencer on horseback.

Tracy escorts fifteen-year-old
Susie to the premiere of his film
Cass Timberlane in 1948. After his
death, she would become
friends with Kate.

Smiles on the set of 1948's *State of the Union* belie the fact that Kate had been targeted by the House Un-American Activities Committee.

39

40

George Cukor, probably the couple's closest friend, directs Tracy and Hepburn in a scene from *Adam's Rib*.

41

For their duelling husband and wife lawyers in *Adam's Rib*, they were dubbed "the ideal U.S. Mr. and Mrs. of upper-middle income" by *Time*. It was a different story in real life. "One person invariably does the adjusting," she said, "and in our case that person was me. Had to. Certain characteristics of mine were wildly irritating to Spencer, and for his sake I gave them up."

42

Kate and Spencer "caught" emerging from a barn during a break in the filming of *Adam's Rib* in 1949.

Father of the Bride Spencer Tracy hit it off with his screen daughter Elizabeth Taylor. Liz and Kate, however, remained cool toward each other.

Toting several souvenirs, Kate gets off the plane in London with Bogie and Bacall after two months in the Belgian Congo shooting *The African Queen*.

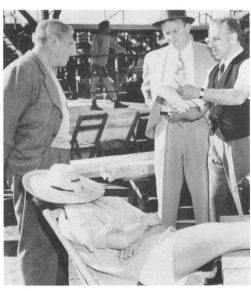

While Kate snoozes on the set of *Pat and Mike*, director Cukor goes over a scene with Tracy and actor Aldo Ray.

As a Runyonesque sports promoter and an upper-class athlete, Spencer and Kate scored their biggest joint hit to date in 1952's *Pat and Mike*. Offscreen, their romance was in serious trouble—and she was on the verge of a breakdown.

50

While Kate insisted on touring in *The Millionairess*, an angry Spencer embarked on an affair with his *Plymouth Adventure* costar (and former JFK paramour) Gene Tierney.

51

In 1955, Grace Kelly added Spencer to a string of older lovers that included Clark Gable, Ray Milland, and Gary Cooper.

Nearly killed while filming *The Mountain* with protégè Robert Wagner, Tracy reacted by tearing off on a drunken rampage.

52

53

Louise, then sixty-one, shows up in court with thirty-three-year-old John Tracy during John's messy 1957 divorce. It was an excuse, Spencer admitted, for the elder Tracy to go on another binge.

54

Kate turned fifty when *Desk Set* was released in 1957—the year they were both devastated by the death of Humphrey Bogart.

Tracy hides beneath a sheet as he is wheeled into St. Vincent's Hospital after collapsing at the beach house he shared with Kate *(right)*. A distraught Louise leaves the hospital; she and Kate took turns at his bedside.

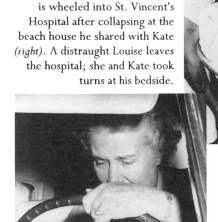

55

56

Their friend Oskar Werner *(left)* looks on as director Stanley Kramer takes a break with his *Guess Who's Coming to Dinner* stars in 1967.

57

58

Himself gravely ill, Tracy shares a tender moment with Hepburn between takes of *Guess Who's Coming to Dinner (above)*. Going over the script, Kate takes her customary place at Spencer's feet.

59

Just as they had for more than twenty-six years in life, Kate and Spencer share the bathroom mirror in *Guess Who's Coming to Dinner*.

Frank Sinatra, Jimmy Stewart, and George Cukor *(behind Sinatra)* were among the pallbearers at Spencer Tracy's funeral on June 12, 1967. Kate drove her car to within a block of the church, but, out of respect for the family, did not attend.

Spencer's strange blend of strength and vulnerability aroused feelings in Kate that were totally unfamiliar. "Those other fellows didn't really need her, and she knew it," said an actor friend. "Just the fact that someone needs you can be a powerful aphrodisiac."

Kate conceded that these stirrings "changed my life." Just as it pertained to this one individual, the ultimate "ME person" now, as she put it, "adjusted. In every relationship that exists, people have to seek a way to survive. If you really care about the person, you do what's necessary or that's the end. For the first time I found that I really could change, and the qualities I most admired in myself I gave up. I stopped being loud and bossy. . . . Oh, all right. I was *still* loud and bossy, but only behind his back."

This was Spencer's main contribution to the relationship. He kept her "down-to-earth," Garson Kanin observed. "She can be flighty, whimsical, impractical, wildly overimaginative, and often unrealistic. Spencer kept his sharp eye on her and used the tender weapon of humor to reveal her to herself, to show her a better way." Mankiewicz agreed: "Spence was the anchor and she was the sail. Unless, of course, he was drinking. Then it was the other way around."

As for Spencer's foibles, it was later reported that midway through the filming of *Woman of the Year* Tracy went on a bender and that after scouring neighborhood bars, Kate found him, sobered him up, cleaned him up, and brought him back to the set. In truth Tracy remained sober throughout the making of *Woman of the Year*.

Kate had already had a profound impact on Tracy. Suddenly looking happier and fitter than he had in years, he had no troubles to drown in alcohol. Thus, during the crucial early months of their relationship, Kate was spared any exposure to Spencer's drinking or to the terrifying transformation that took place when he was drunk.

Would it have made a difference if she had seen him knock a stranger unconscious for no earthly reason or toss a chair through the plate glass window of a crowded restaurant? It is doubtful she could have been scared off by anything. "Looking back, I was blinded from the moment I met him," Kate said. By the time she witnessed his first, truly terrifying alcoholic rage, she was deeply, irrevocably in love.

Almost as much as they delighted in each other's company, Tracy and Hepburn found the *situation* ideal. The lifeblood of Hollywood was hype, yet no two stars with the exception of the hermetic Garbo craved privacy more. Certainly Kate, now famous for refusing to do interviews and for smashing the cameras of hapless news photographers, resented seeing details of her private life trumpeted in headlines and splashed across the covers of fan magazines. As a consequence, she shared a kind of bunker mentality with Tracy when it came to the press.

With Leland Hayward and Howard Hughes, any semblance of a private life was impossible.

In Spencer, however, she had not only a man who was worthy of her but someone who was, curiously enough, virtually scandalproof. "Mrs. Spencer Tracy," as Louise preferred to be called, was now revered for her selfless work on behalf of the deaf. Her dignified demeanor, her quiet, selfless acceptance of his peccadilloes, and their joint decision not to divorce, ostensibly on religious grounds, made the Tracys off limits to the prying press. Columnists and reporters who once filled their papers with stories about Spencer now did not want to be responsible for causing unnecessary pain to the long-suffering Louise.

"Contrary to what most members of the press believed, Spencer Tracy's decision not to divorce his wife was *not* a Catholic thing," said James Bacon, a friend and frequent drinking buddy. "I graduated from Notre Dame, and Spence was a big Notre Dame fan. We'd talk about the church and religion, and he was pretty casual about the whole thing. Guilt over his deaf son—that was the only thing that kept him from divorcing Louise. But religion? No way."

Although he was still master of the cutting, even cruel remark, Tracy remained in uncommonly good spirits during the last few weeks shooting *Woman of the Year*. He was also continuing to work his wonders on Kate. She was less strident, calmer, *softer* in both demeanor and appearance. She wore more makeup, spent more time on her hair, and while she was not about to wear a dress, her once-baggy pants were now tailored to accentuate the feminine curve of her hip.

"It was obvious to everyone on the sound stage," Michael Kanin said of Tracy and Hepburn, "that they had fallen in love." Somehow, after years of careening from one failed relationship to another, each had managed to find a soulmate. "I believe in miracles," she later observed. "God help you if you don't."

Before the press at large suspected even the remote possibility of an offscreen romance, a reporter innocently asked Kate if she was in love with Spencer Tracy. "Of course I am," she replied. "Isn't everybody?"

When Kate explained the part of Tess Harding to reporters, the real-life parallels were overt: "I'm alive, alert, enthusiastic—and also egotistical. I love Spencer, but I won't give up too much of myself to him. . . . I try to dominate him, put things over on him. I almost lose him."

If she was worried about losing Spence, it was not to the titular Mrs. Tracy, whose position was immutable. In the first weeks of filming, another love of Tracy's lingered in the wings, unwilling to concede defeat. According to Mankiewicz, the romance between Tracy and Ingrid Bergman that had begun on the set of *Dr. Jekyll and Mr. Hyde* had not yet cooled. "Ingrid Bergman," said the producer-director, "was still crazy about Spence. Don't forget, she was there before Kate came on the scene. Bergman was the most beguiling, wide-eyed creature. And smart. Kate hated her, of course."

Always a keen competitor, Kate had not hesitated to snatch movie projects out from under the noses of other actresses. In her private life she would never openly confront another woman over the affections of a man—that would be unseemly—but this did not preclude Kate from harboring a deep-seated, lifelong grudge. "Kate never liked Ingrid Bergman," said a friend, "and she never forgave Bergman for trying to come between her and Spence." In her memoirs Kate makes only one brief mention of the three-time Academy Award winner: "Ingrid Bergman played the whore; she won an award, I think."

Between the completion of *Woman of the Year* in October 1941 and its release the following February, Kate and Spencer settled into a comfortable arrangement that baffled those who knew them. Kate would curl up at Tracy's feet and gaze up at him as he stroked her hair lovingly. In this, she differed radically from Louise, who was loving but never adoring. "I could be his toughest critic," Louise said. "He valued my honesty. But I was also someone he could turn to. I was a safe harbor."

Louise may have been Spencer's first safe harbor, but from this point on it was Kate who assumed the role. "I loved Spencer Tracy," she said, admitting that from the very start "he and his interests and his demands came first." Her unbridled devotion ("It must be complete, or it ain't love") confounded their tight circle of friends and colleagues. "None of them," Kate shrugged, "more so than I."

Still, no sooner did shooting stop than Tracy and Hepburn, torn by previous commitments, went in separate directions—he to prepare for his next solo project, a screen version of John Steinbeck's *Tortilla Flat,* she to New York, where she was to meet with the Theatre Guild's Langner and Helburn to discuss a new play.

The first week of December 1941 MGM gave a sneak preview of *Woman of the Year.* Audiences loved everything about the film—except the ending. As originally written, the film ended with Tess Harding becoming such an ardent baseball fan that she outshouts her sportswriter husband at a game. Stevens, Mankiewicz, and Mayer agreed that it was not enough that Tess Harding grow in the relationship.

"The average housewife was going to look up at this beautiful, brilliant, accomplished goddess up there on the screen," Mankiewicz said, "and, well, hate her guts." A new ending was written and shot with L. B.'s blessing. It showed Tess Harding bungling an attempt to make her husband breakfast. "Now," Mankiewicz said, "women could turn to their schmuck husbands and say, 'She may know the president, but she can't even make a cup of coffee, you silly bastard.' "

Kate hated the new, blatantly sexist ending in which the strong woman finally "gets hers." Audiences, however, went wild for it. And critics noted that Kate had clearly mellowed in the presence of the great Tracy. *"Woman of the Year,"* wrote *Time's* James Agee, "was made to order for bold Katharine Hepburn. She saw to it that it was." The *Baltimore Sun* noted that Tracy had somehow banished Kate's "mannerisms, the tricks, the superficiality which marred much of her previous work. Her performance in *Woman of the Year* shows even more subtlety and depth." As for Tracy, the *New York World-Telegram* crowed, "There isn't a false note in his characterization of the sportswriter. And the things he can do with a gesture, with a smile—what an actor!"

Woman of the Year did bigger business than *The Philadelphia Story* and earned Kate another Academy Award nomination (she would lose to Greer Garson in *Mrs. Miniver*). Most important, it set the tone for the next eight Hepburn-Tracy films.

"People talk about their he-she chemistry," Kanin said, "and there is something in it. Spencer Tracy and Katharine Hepburn were two of the most interesting people who ever lived, but together they were even *more* fascinating. These were two people who brought out the best in each other and complemented each other and teased each other and created a tremendous sense of empathy. It was something that we all reveled in. And the amazing thing is, Kate and Spencer did this instinctively *from the beginning*— and when they were together, there was something electrifying about them."

"I think on film we came to represent the perfect American couple," Kate later reflected. "Certainly the ideal man is Spencer: sports-loving, a man's man. Strong-looking, a big sort of head, boar neck, a man. And I think I represent a woman. I needle a man. I irritate him, I try to get around him, yet if he put a big paw out, he could squash me. I think this is the sort of romantic, ideal picture of the male and female in the United States. I'm always skitting about, and he's the big bear, and every once in a while he turns and growls, and I tremble. And every once in a while he turns and says some terrible thing, and everybody laughs at me and I get furious. It's very male-female."

The public at large would remain unaware of their offscreen romance for decades, despite the fact that it was common knowledge in Hollywood even before cameras stopped rolling on *Woman of the Year*. This was partly due to the extreme discretion Kate and Spencer exercised from the beginning. Unlike other movie star lovers, they took great pains never to be seen together off the set. They maintained separate residences and, when they traveled, checked into separate hotels. "We learned to be invisible," Spencer said, "in all the right places."

But it was more than that. All three parties involved—Kate, Spencer, and Louise—commanded an unparalleled degree of respect among members of the Hollywood press corps. There was the occasional hint—"the love scenes in *Woman of the Year* look like the real thing," wrote Hedda Hopper—but for the most part reporters adopted a strictly hands-off approach to Tracy and Hepburn—"the greatest love story," wrote columnist Sheilah Graham, "never told."

Kate was visiting her family in Connecticut and Spencer was midway through shooting *Tortilla Flat* with John Garfield and Hedy Lamarr when the Japanese attacked Pearl Harbor. A month later Clark Gable's wife, top screen comedienne Carole Lombard, was returning from a war bond tour to her home state of Indiana when her plane crashed outside Las Vegas, instantly killing everyone on board. Lombard was thirty-three.

Not long before, a poll showed that Tracy had supplanted Gable as America's No. 1 star, and Spencer had not been able to resist sending his old friend and drinking buddy a note addressed "Dear Former King." Now Tracy consoled his friend. Later Spencer was among the handful of mourners at Lombard's private funeral. Kate, scrupulously adhering to their unspoken agreement never to be seen together outside the confines of their tight circle of friends and coworkers, did not attend.

"Gable and Tracy loved each other," said James Bacon, a drinking companion of both men. "They were both very down-to-earth guys. It never bothered Gable that Tracy was always considered the better actor, or Tracy that—no matter how good he was—he could never be quite as big a star as Gable."

When they got together, the occasion nearly always called for a drink, or several. "Gable was a big martini drinker," Bacon said, "and Tracy preferred Scotch, although he really wasn't too choosy." Once, Bacon remembered, Tracy and Gable were drinking after a polo match at the Riviera Country Club and then vanished. They turned up three days later in a Tucson hotel room. "They were blind drunk, and [Mayer] was madder than hell."

Kate quickly came to consider each of Tracy's bar buddies as the enemy. "She resented Gable," Bacon said. "Perhaps she was even a little jealous of the close bond he had with Spence. Kate called Gable an 'evil companion' for Tracy."

Gable, who never fully recovered from Lombard's untimely death, signed up with the Army Air Corps and flew perilous bombing runs over Germany that later earned him a Distinguished Flying Cross. Tracy, too old at forty-one and not physically fit for service, was shattered by Lombard's death and the effect it had on his friend.

It was not a good time for Spencer to be alone, but he was. While he mixed alcohol with barbiturates on the California set of *Tortilla Flat*, Kate was in New York rehearsing a new Philip Barry play, *Without Love*.

Kate had agreed to do *Without Love* for two reasons: She felt she owed Barry for *The Philadelphia Story*, and despite its weaknesses, the play carried a patriotic message. An American diplomat returns to Washington to convince neutral Ireland to join the Allies in battling Hitler and allow British submarines to use Irish ports. Toward that end he takes on the identity of an Irish butler in the home of Jamie Rowan, a rich Washington widow. Once she discovers who he really is, Jamie offers to enter into a platonic marriage. That arrangement—surprise—eventually blossoms into true romance.

Kate had wanted Spencer to return to the stage as the undercover diplomat, but Langner and Helburn had heard all the stories of Tracy's drinking and did not want to take the risk. Instead they hired the blandly debonair Elliott Nugent for the part. After an early tryout in Wilmington, Delaware, Kate asked Garson Kanin for advice on how to improve the play. "You and Nugent change parts," he replied. She would not speak to Kanin for the next year and a half.

Those first few months of 1942 Kate was torn between her allegiance to Barry and the Theatre Guild on the one hand and Tracy on the other. She had agreed to tour with the play before its limited engagement on Broadway, and that meant she and Spencer would be spending several months apart.

Tracy offered no ultimatums, but his behavior during the making of *Tortilla Flat* sent Kate a clear message. "Jim Backus told me he always liked to work on a Spencer Tracy picture because there was always a nice two-week break when

Tracy just disappeared in the middle of filming," James Bacon said. "Tracy became nasty when he drank. He would yell at the other actors and raise holy hell. I never saw him turn violent, but he was so famous for tearing up saloons that bar owners cringed when he walked in the door."

The stories that reached Kate in New York were particularly disturbing. For the first time she learned that Spencer was mixing alcohol with the pills that had been prescribed to combat his chronic insomnia.

And Spencer was not the only substance abuser she now had to contend with. The mild-mannered Nugent was failing to connect with his leading lady; it was impossible to imagine any sexual spark between them. The play itself, meanwhile, was problematic. Barry could not seem to decide whether he was writing a comedy or a political tract. The pressures on all parties were enormous, but perhaps no one felt them as keenly as Nugent, who felt rightly that he was constantly being compared with Tracy. Not long after the play opened in New Haven on February 26, 1942, Nugent began drinking heavily. Now the producers faced the very problem they had hoped to avoid by not hiring Spencer Tracy.

Whether acting onstage or making a film, Kate had always acted as a sort of cheerleader for her fellow actors, buoying their spirits with words of encouragement and, when necessary, Knute Rockne let's-get-out-there-and-win-one-for-the-Gipper pep talks. This time, however, Kate was far too distracted for that. Only one person commanded her attention, and that was Spencer Tracy.

The tour began at Princeton, New Jersey, and limped along from Wilmington to Baltimore to Washington to Philadelphia and Boston before landing in Hartford on April 28. This marked the first time Kate had appeared in her beloved hometown, and locals turned out in force to greet her, breaking all attendance records at Hartford's cavernous, thirty-five-hundred-seat Bushnell Theater.

On opening night Kate's parents and other family members filed into the sixth row. They had, *Life* magazine pointed out, done "everything to squelch" local interest in Kate, "even calling on the police to preserve their daughter's aloofness." After the curtain fell on the first performance, Kate spoke of her love for the city of Hartford and the people in it. "It was a nice speech," wrote *Life*'s reporter, "and sounded as if she really meant it."

Beyond that, however, Kate was too worried about Spencer to do anything else. She refused to speak to any local reporters or to meet with any Hartford dignitaries. *Life* complained that "she didn't follow the gracious custom of setting aside an hour or two for interviews and greeting all comers." As for her performance, *Life* declared that Hepburn acted "with superb style and all the heatless brilliance of fluorescent light."

On the evening of May 11, 1942, Spencer Tracy slouched in a rear seat at Pittsburgh's Nixon Theater and watched Kate try against insurmountable odds to get *Without Love* off the ground. At intermission he slipped into a box-office anteroom but not before he was spotted by a reporter for the *Pittsburgh Press*:

> Cornered in his secret retreat, Mr. Tracy appeared relieved that I didn't want his autograph and readily admitted that, yes, he was keenly interested in *Without Love*. He said that he had been in Washington and had stopped over here en route to the Coast, just to see the play. . . . Mr. Tracy said he was going to leave for the Coast immediately after the performance, but I noticed at the final curtain that he was not in too great a hurry to get out of town or neglect to run backstage and congratulate Miss Hepburn.

The notion that Tracy and Hepburn were now launched on a torrid affair and that he was actually following her as she toured the country simply had not occurred to the Pittsburgh reporter—or to any journalist outside the Hollywood sphere. So long as they traveled separately and registered at different hotels, their ruse succeeded.

Unfortunately for the harried Kate, Spencer's presence on the tour was anything but soothing. On the heels of their triumph in *Woman of the Year*, MGM had wanted to team Tracy and Hepburn in another romantic comedy as quickly as possible. But Kate had another idea. Donald Ogden Stewart, who had written the script for *Holiday* and *The Philadelphia Story*, had brought Kate a script about a young woman who discovers the dead husband she idolized was actually hatching a fascist plot to take over the country at the time of his death. There was also a meaty part for Spencer in *Keeper of the Flame*: the role of the journalist who finally exposes the dead man as a traitor. The movie's strong antitotalitarian message appealed greatly to Tracy and Hepburn, now both actively searching for ways to contribute to the war effort.

Kate again convinced the powers-that-be to hire George Cukor to direct, and plans were made to begin shooting *Keeper of the Flame* on June 1, 1942. Tracy had resented Kate's long absence from Hollywood as she toured in *Without Love*, and she was equally anxious to be back where she could keep a watchful eye over him. But Kate also had a moral and legal obligation to return to *Without Love* when it opened on Broadway three months later. She assured Lawrence Langner and Philip Barry that as soon as filming stopped, she would keep her end of the bargain.

Tracy admired Kate's sense of honor as much as anybody—as long as it did not interfere with his plans. He did not want her to leave him again in September, and he took every opportunity to let her know how he felt. As the pressure to quit the play mounted, Kate got increasingly testy. When a photographer clicked off a few shots of her as she entered the theater for a matinee, she flew at him, tearing the camera from his hands and clawing him with her fingernails. A passing policeman pulled the two apart.

With Tracy settled into "temporary" quarters at the Beverly Hills Hotel (he did not formally move out of the Encino house until 1943), Kate set out to find a suitable residence for herself during the making of *Keeper of the Flame*. Although she would wind up living and working there for well over a half century, Kate never owned property in California. "She always considers herself a California transient," Garson Kanin once explained. "She loves it there, but she always rents or borrows houses. One day she went out looking for a house to rent and I went with her and the agent and she ran through the house very, very swiftly—the whole thing in about three minutes. Then she started through it again and this time slowly. I said to the agent, 'I think she's interested—that's why she's going through it slowly.' Then Kate disappeared. We waited, and we waited. And I thought she was lost. And the agent looked upstairs and I looked out front and we couldn't find her.

"Finally she turned up standing out in the garden, looking very scrubbed and fresh and rosy, as she always does. We got in the car, and I said, 'Where were you all that time?' "

"What do you mean, where was I?"

"You were gone an awfully long time."

"Well," Kate said, "I was taking a shower."

Kanin was flabbergasted. "Taking a shower? What did you want to do that for?"

"Well, you ass," Kate shot back, astounded at Kanin's ignorance, "if I'm going to live in a house I have to see what it's like to take a shower there, don't I?"

"To her," Kanin said, "it seemed perfectly logical."

After trying out the showers in a half dozen of Beverly Hills' finest houses, she decided to stay put in the John Gilbert house, which after all was only a short drive from Spencer's bachelor pad at the Beverly Hills Hotel. For the rest of the war years Tracy's world revolved around these two addresses and the ranch in Encino. "Spencer's world was very carefully circumscribed," Joe Mankiewicz observed. Kate agreed: "He'd lived there practically his entire adult life, but I knew my way around Los Angeles better than Spencer did. His sense of direction was such that if he wanted to get somewhere, he'd have to drive all the way back to the Beverly Hills Hotel and leave from there. He only knew how to get places from that starting point!"

On the set of *Keeper of the Flame* Tracy and Cukor became fast friends—and instant allies against Kate when she reverted to her old bossy ways. After the filming of one scene she told Cukor, "I don't think that was done correctly. I think Spencer should have been sitting when he spoke those lines." Cukor said nothing. Another time she informed Cukor in no uncertain terms that he had botched a scene by not giving a supporting actress sufficient direction. "She should speak those lines more softly," Kate said. "It wasn't done properly." Again the director remained silent.

In one climactic scene Tracy and the same supporting actress are interrupted in mid-sentence to be told that the house is on fire. "I don't think that they should have to be told about the fire," Kate interjected. "They would smell the smoke."

This time Cukor responded. "It must be wonderful," he shouted, "to know all about acting *and* all about fires too!"

Spencer thought this was so hysterical a break had to be called for him to regain his composure.

Away from the set Kate was anything but bossy and confident. In the early months of their romance, Kate continued to be blissfully unaware of the Jekyll and Hyde metamorphosis that took place when Tracy went on a bender. It was easy for him to be on his best behavior when he was around Kate. He was so intoxicated by her that he would have found liquor redundant.

But things changed when Kate left his side to tour in *Without Love*. That spring of 1942 she was getting her first horrifying glimpses of the creature Tracy could become when he fell off the wagon. There were new reasons for Spencer's mounting melancholia. Gable was not the only major star in uniform. By mid-1942 the front ranks of leading men were depleted as the name-over-the-title stars like Robert Taylor, Robert Montgomery, James Stewart, Tyrone Power, and Henry Fonda enlisted in the military. John Ford, George Cukor, and Garson Kanin also rushed to sign up.

Those left behind for age or health reasons often felt as if they were somehow shirking their patriotic duty. For Tracy, who had always regarded his chosen profession of acting as somehow unmanly, these feelings of guilt were all but unbearable. While friends like Stewart and Gable were risking their lives in enemy skies, Spencer was staying behind, enjoying all the creature comforts as he portrayed war heroes in films like *A Guy Named Joe* and *Thirty Seconds Over Tokyo*.

However valuable these films were as propaganda, Tracy brooded over his contribution to the war effort. By way of compensation, he narrated Kanin's documentary *Ring of Steel* and showed up to wash dishes and meet and greet servicemen on leave at the famous Hollywood Canteen. But he could have done more, and he knew it. At one point Tracy was about to embark on a USO tour to entertain troops overseas when he fell off the wagon and came to days later in a Chicago mental ward. He eventually made up for this lapse by visiting wounded soldiers in Hawaii.

Kate, meanwhile, narrated another documentary, *Women in Defense* for the Office of War Information, and showed up regularly at the Stage

Door Canteen in New York. In 1942 she also appeared (along with nearly every recognizable face from the worlds of Broadway and Hollywood) in the film *Stage Door Canteen*, with the proceeds going to finance the canteen's operations.

Even if Tracy had wanted to enlist—at forty-two he was younger than many of the other stars being given commissions—his health would not permit it. In 1942 he learned that he had already sustained irreparable heart damage and that years of drinking had taken its toll on his kidneys and his liver. He was also a hypochondriac for whom the slightest headache or stomach upset signaled the onset of stroke or cancer. "He was so afraid," said a family friend. "The fear led to more severe and frequent anxiety attacks. It was a vicious circle."

By August 1942 Kate was catering to Spencer's every whim. She picked him up at the Beverly Hills Hotel and drove him to the studio, brewed pots of coffee on the set, attended to his needs throughout the day, fed him lunch, drove him to her house after work, cooked dinner for him (over the years she had mastered a small but serviceable repertoire of dishes), massaged his ego, then drove him back to his hotel.

Kate was chauffeur, wife, cook, maid, nurse, psychiatrist, lover, professional advisor, and confidante. She straightened his tie, combed his hair, and screened his phone calls. She kept him distracted with constant talk about their work and their friends and the war and the mutual acquaintance they both most admired above all others, FDR. His off-the-cuff remarks—he routinely called her his "Bag of Bones" and often dismissed her most heartfelt observations with a curt "Who in the hell asked *you*?"—came across as verbal abuse to coworkers and friends.

The thoughtless comments did not just roll off Kate's back; in a curious way they endeared him even more to her. "If Tracy didn't like someone he simply ignored them," Mankiewicz said. "But if he liked you, he gave you holy hell. It meant he really *cared*. They both thought it was slightly hilarious that other people got so overwrought about the way he teased her. It was just Spence's way." George Cukor concurred: "He could be extremely gruff with her—that was the little roughneck boy from Milwaukee filtering through—but he had enormous respect for her, and he *listened* to her."

Even among those who understood Tracy's unconventional way of expressing affection, there was considerable speculation that the Tracy-Hepburn relationship was essentially platonic. Not likely. Tracy boasted a long string of sexual conquests, and Hepburn had always had a free and open attitude toward sex. They both were intensely physical creatures, and this extended to their personal relationship. "It's a force of life, sex; you can't deny the thrill of riding high, wide, and handsome with someone you love," Kate later said of their affair. "The only thing is that age doesn't bring any sexual wisdom. You're just as confused forty years later as you were when you first heard about it."

As a woman of childbearing age, however, Kate had the usual practical matters to consider. Tracy's strict Catholic beliefs made it impossible for him to take an active part in preventing an unwanted pregnancy. Kate, who told anyone who would listen that Mother was a founder of Planned Parenthood and Dad an expert on sexually transmitted disease, was particularly well prepared to take responsibility for birth control. Dealing with such nettlesome problems, as one acquaintance remarked, "came with the territory."

Kate's biggest challenge in the relationship had nothing to do with sex, however. Hepburn, who had once been dispatched by L. B. himself to have a heart-to-heart chat with the troubled Judy Garland, knew what the task of protecting Spencer from himself entailed. "If you are going to help anybody who is in trouble, this is not a two-hour-a-day job. It is a twenty-four-hour-a-day job. You won't do anything else if you decide that you are going to resurrect and rearrange a human being."

She seldom let him out of her sight. On those occasions when he did come crashing off the wagon, she would track him down at one of his favorite watering holes, drive him back to the Beverly Hills hotel, clean him up, change his clothes, and put him to bed. Sometimes he did not want Kate's help and, after ordering her out, locked the door behind her.

Undaunted, Kate merely camped in the hallway outside his door for hours, listening for sounds of mayhem. When all finally fell silent, she used her key to enter the room, washed Spencer's face and body where he had soiled himself, and made sure he could sleep comfortably. It was often dawn before she tiptoed out the door, got into her car, and drove up the narrow, serpentine road to her house high atop Tower Drive.

"He was there—I was his. I wanted him to be happy, safe, comfortable," she explained. "I liked to wait on him—listen to him—feed him—talk to him—work for him. I tried not to disturb him—irritate him—bother him—worry him, nag him." Kate Hepburn had never felt more useful—or more loved—in her life.

This total devotion would be at the expense of Hepburn's own career. From 1942 on, every professional decision Kate made—every stage and movie role she accepted or refused—was arrived at on the basis of how it affected Spencer. Over the next eight years she starred in only ten films, six of them with Tracy. Eight of the fourteen pictures he made during that same period were without Kate, including some of the most successful of his career: *A Guy Named Joe, Thirty Seconds Over Tokyo, Cass Timberlane,* and *Father of the Bride.*

Keeper of the Flame meanwhile stumbled badly.

Woman of the Year fans who expected another effervescent romantic comedy featuring America's favorite onscreen couple were confronted with a murky Gothic melodrama that did not even feature any romance between Tracy and Hepburn. Tracy, as usual, was lauded for his acting. Kate, along with the film, was criticized for being stiff and unconvincing. In an attempt to find a film that would showcase Spencer's skills, she neglected to consider how audiences might react to her in a serious role. Instead of building on the success of *The Philadelphia Story* and *Woman of the Year* with another bubbly romantic comedy, she now left audiences more confused than ever about which Katharine Hepburn they could expect to see when they shelled out twenty-five hard-earned cents for a movie ticket.

Kate was intent on finding another script that would duplicate their triumph in *Woman of the Year* and keep Spencer's mind off his troubles, both real and imagined. The "vicious circle" of anxiety over his health was robbing him of sleep; he was now getting less than three hours a night. So long as she remained by his side, both Kate and Spencer reasoned, he would have the strength to resist temptation. "Between the drinking and the lack of sleep, I think she worried that he might lose his mind," Ginger Rogers said, "if the booze didn't kill him first."

As Tracy became increasingly unhinged, Kate had to decide what to do about *Without Love*. After weeks of trying unsuccessfully to reach its elusive star, the Theatre Guild's Theresa Helburn sent her an urgent telegram on August 9, 1942: DEAR KATE: WHAT ARE YOU UP TO THAT YOU KEEP CHANGING YOUR PHONE NUMBER?

The letter Helburn received in response was devastating. Kate had no intention of returning to open on Broadway in *Without Love*. She pleaded with her friends at the Theatre Guild and particularly with playwright Philip Barry to understand the predicament she was in. To return to New York for the sixteen-week run of the play meant she would be abandoning her one true love at the time he most needed her—and that, Kate said, would "destroy" her.

"While we sympathize with you very deeply in the emotional disturbance you seem to be in," Helburn wrote back, "there are duties and obligations both to Phil Barry and to us which we do not feel you can overlook." Helburn went on to say that Kate's departure from *Without Love* would be "disastrous" because the play "revolves around you." Adding that Barry was "thunderstruck" by Kate's refusal to leave Los Angeles, Helburn suggested that the main reason Kate had soured on the production was that Elliott Nugent, not Spencer, played opposite her. "The fact that you are in pain while you are playing with Elliott is merely because you see Spencer in it, but the audience doesn't and everybody thinks that you and Elliott make a good team in it, and you are surely too good a trouper to let a

purely personal point of view stand in the way
of an objective success."

Still unable to reach Kate by phone, Helburn
traveled to California for a face-to-face confron-
tation the first week in September. Hepburn, furious that she was being asked to leave Spencer
at this critical time in their lives, stood her
ground. When Helburn threatened a breach of
contract lawsuit against MGM on the grounds
that the studio had kept Kate from fulfilling her
commitment to *Without Love*, Kate exploded in a
tearful rage. Before she would give in to the Theatre Guild's demands, she said, "I will retire
from stage and screen."

It was a bravura performance, but Helburn
was unmoved. Back in New York the following
week Helburn wrote another letter to Kate reminding her of her contractual obligations. She
started out as if scolding a naughty child:
"Come, come, my dear Kate . . ."

But there were other things weighing on Kate's
mind. Everyone, including Kate, was convinced
that her quickie 1934 Mexican divorce would not
be recognized by the U.S. courts. Because she
had never bothered to follow through with an
American divorce, Luddy still clung to the belief
that someday she would eventually come to her
senses and return to him.

Spencer told Kate it was patently unfair to
string Luddy along and urged her to set him free.
Almost reluctantly she agreed, knowing full well
that to ask the same of Spencer would end their

relationship instantly. That September Louise Tracy announced the establishment of the John Tracy Clinic for the deaf at the University of Southern California. Spencer, cited as the non-profit clinic's chief benefactor, let it be known that he was never prouder of his wife. "You honor me because I am a movie actor," Tracy said at the dedication ceremonies, "a star in Hollywood terms. Well, there's nothing I've ever done that can match what Louise has done for deaf children and their parents." Spencer and Walt Disney were among those on the John Tracy Clinic's original board of directors; Louise served as president.

Louise was certainly not someone Kate could ignore. Newspaper and magazine articles lauded her efforts on behalf of the deaf, and in her own way "Mrs. Spencer Tracy" was as much a fixture of the Hollywood film community as were her husband and his lover. She was regarded by everyone—most significantly by Spencer—as a selfless, tireless humanitarian. At the time, and for many years after, Kate claimed she felt that way too. She really had no choice.

Eventually Kate wondered if she had made the right decision in not forcing Spencer to choose between her and Louise. "I was complacent," she said. "I didn't push for action. I just left it up to him. And he was paralyzed. I must say it taught me a lesson—one must figure out how much you care for this or that. Then put up a fight. Or don't . . ." Had Louise asked for a divorce, Kate mused, "it would have been ennobling to her. And supremely honest . . . his guilt would have been removed . . . but if she had done that, she would have had to have been a saint. . . . Too much to ask, I agree."

On September 18, 1942, Hartford Superior Court Judge Patrick B. O'Sullivan heard the case of *Ogden Ludlow* v. *Katharine H. Ludlow*. Luddy told the court that he doubted the validity of the 1934 Mexican divorce, which he had obtained on grounds of desertion "because she had decided that she couldn't continue her career and be married, too." This time, again with his wife's blessing, the official grounds were desertion.

Kate was not present, but her father stood up to acknowledge that she was indeed a legal resident of the state of Connecticut. Why, the judge wanted to know, had Ludlow waited so long? "I was—I am—very fond of her, Your Honor," Luddy replied. "I always had in the back of mind the possibility of getting her back." It was not until the hearing was over that Judge O'Sullivan realized Katharine H. Ludlow was the famous Katharine Hepburn.

Eight days later Kate's first and only husband married Elizabeth Alders, a Boston divorcée. Luddy and Kate would remain friends, and after he became a widower, she would help care for him until his death in 1979 from prostate cancer.

Just as she knew she owed it to Luddy to cut him loose, Kate realized she must live up to her contract with the Theatre Guild. She finally agreed to return to New York—provided Spencer could accompany her. With his brother Carroll, Tracy took a suite at the Waldorf Towers, less than two blocks from Kate's Turtle Bay townhouse. He was in the audience, at the St. James Theater on November 10, when Kate opened in *Without Love*. As predicted, the reviews were terrible. "It is hard for her to sustain a scene," wrote *The New York Times'* Brooks Atkinson of Kate's performance, "in a trifling play that is generally uneventful." But Kate, it turned out, was critic-proof. On the basis of Hepburn's megawatt star power, the show was sold out for the entire sixteen weeks.

Now it was Tracy's turn to bolster Kate's spirits as she slogged through one mediocre performance after another. He often lingered backstage, smiling encouragement as he watched from the wings. Evenings she cooked dinner for him at her Turtle Bay town house, then, coat collar turned up against the cold night air and hat brim pulled down to disguise his face, America's No. 1 box-office star crossed Third Avenue toward Lexington and the back entrance to the Waldorf.

For the first few weeks Tracy occupied himself going over the script for his next MGM production sans Kate, *A Guy Named Joe*. But the death of his mother Carrie that year hit Spencer hard, and soon he was seeking solace in familiar surroundings. With its swing bands and leggy cigarette girls—not to mention the breathtaking sixty-fifth-floor view of the Manhattan skyline—the Rainbow Room atop Rockefeller Center epitomized the glamour and excitement of New York nightlife during the war. Tracy had already had a few drinks at the bar when a male fan approached him. Without warning Tracy whirled around and knocked the stranger unconscious.

MGM's publicity director Howard Strickling managed to keep the story out of the papers, and Tracy quietly paid the fan's hospital bill. But for Kate it was a sobering reminder that the man she loved was, under the influence of alcohol, violent and unpredictable.

Incredibly, in 1943 Tracy was prescribed powerful doses of the amphetamine Dexedrine to combat his depression. A potent form of what was later commonly known as speed, the Dexedrine merely aggravated Spencer's insomnia, pushing him even closer to the edge. Understandably, neither Hepburn nor Tracy ever thought to question the medication he was receiving. It was in fact more than two decades before the medical profession began to comprehend fully the drug's potentially devastating side effects.

As soon as her sixteen weeks in *Without Love* were over, they returned to Los Angeles. Tracy was once again drinking heavily whenever the cameras were not rolling on *A Guy Named Joe*. In the movie Tracy plays the ghost of a dead combat pilot given the assignment of bringing together his grieving girlfriend (played by Irene Dunne) and his best pal (Van Johnson).

Tracy showed up for work on time and fully prepared, but the strain of having to confine his drinking to after hours made him even more irascible than usual. The properly prim Dunne, already a major star, became the hapless victim of his teasing and practical jokes. Dunne felt the endless taunts about her "needle" nose and her well-endowed figure were anything but good-natured and went to Louis B. Mayer himself to complain. She simply could not, Dunne told him bluntly, work under such tense and unnerving conditions.

But the director, Spencer's old buddy Victor Fleming, was not about to force a change on Spencer's part. In fact, Dunne accused Fleming of being almost as tactless as Tracy. She was on the verge of walking off the picture for good when Van Johnson was nearly killed in a motor-cycle accident. Once he learned that plans were afoot to replace Johnson, Tracy marched into the offices of top MGM executive Bennie Thau and threatened to quit if Johnson wasn't kept on.

Mayer agreed to postpone *A Guy Named Joe* for several months while Johnson recovered from his skull fracture and other injuries. In return Tracy had to promise to treat Dunne with re-spect. "Without Tracy," Johnson later said, "my career could have ended then and there." In-stead, propelled to stardom by the success of *A Guy Named Joe*, the blond all-American Johnson was cast as the boy next door in dozens of films throughout the 1940s and 1950s.

Kate, now spending more nights sleeping in the hall outside Spencer's room at the Beverly Hills Hotel, had career troubles of her own. She had desperately wanted MGM to buy the rights to Eugene O'Neill's *Mourning Becomes Electra*. But after L. B.'s resident Scheherazade, Lillie Messenger, read Mayer the classic tale of incest, he exploded. "No! Disgusting! Filthy!" Mayer shouted. "We'll sully the nest!"

For the first time Kate went public, continuing her campaign in the press. "Really deep consideration of the issue of sex," Kate lashed out, "has no chance to be translated onto the screen under the present system of censorship." She complained that MGM musicals and other light fare dealt with the same subject matter in "a vaguely peeking sort of way" that was "false, and unintelligent and even harmful."

Mayer was unmoved, but he did give the green light to another, equally weighty drama that Kate found intriguing. MGM had scored a huge popular and critical hit with Pearl Buck's *The Good Earth*, and now Kate was eager to play the Chinese peasant heroine in Buck's *Dragon Seed*. For Mayer, there was a bonus to making the film: The film's unflinching depiction of Japanese aggression was certain to appeal to post–Pearl Harbor audiences.

An epic production (its three-million-dollar budget made it one of the most expensive films ever made up to that time), *Dragon Seed* was stressful for all involved. Jack Conway, who had directed *A Tale of Two Cities* and Tracy's *Boom Town*, collapsed from nervous exhaustion midway through filming and was replaced by Harold S. Bucquet.

No one was under more strain than Kate. The success of *Dragon Seed* hinged on whether or not she could make herself remotely believable in the role of Jade. Commuting for an hour to the 120-acre San Fernando Valley set, she spent another hour having her eyelids taped back and disguised under heavy makeup.

Tracy, meanwhile, was not exactly enjoying himself on the set of his new film, either. While Kate made *Dragon Seed*, he portrayed an escapee from a Nazi concentration camp in *The Seventh Cross*. The demands of the part were physically as well as emotionally taxing, and the subject matter served as a constant reminder to Tracy that he was among the few major stars not in uniform.

Tracy was acutely sensitive to the fact that he might be perceived as a shirker in some quarters. Attending the Hollywood Legion Stadium boxing matches in 1943, he was publicly humiliated when a band of sailors heckled him with cries of "chicken" and "draft dodger" before they were hauled off by stadium police. As soon as she heard of the mortifying incident, Kate rushed to Spencer's side with words of encouragement and plenty of hot coffee. Being branded a coward in front of thousands of people could have easily pushed Tracy off the wagon, but instead he vented his frustration at the one person he needed most.

In his memoir *A Terrible Liar*, actor Hume Cronyn recalled Spencer's callous attitude toward Hepburn when she visited him during the making of *The Seventh Cross*. The encounter took place in Tracy's dressing room.

"I hope I'm not interrupting anything," Hepburn said after shaking the awestruck Cronyn's hand for the first time. "Please sit down."

It was clear to Cronyn that she was there out of concern for Spencer. "How are you doing, old man?" she asked.

"On my ass," he answered with a sneer.

"Problems?"

Tracy sat in surly silence until Cronyn offered to get her a drink. "She told you to sit down!" Tracy snapped. (Recalled Cronyn: "It was said as though I was hard of hearing.")

Cronyn and Hepburn chatted amiably, and when the younger actor offered to light her cigarette, Tracy thundered, "Why don't you two find a bed somewhere and get it over with?" Cronyn was so stunned that he scarcely noticed the match burning his fingertips.

"Sit down, for Christ's sake!" Tracy continued. "You keep bouncing around like corn in a popper!"

Kate, thoroughly accustomed to Tracy's outbursts, puffed on her cigarette as if nothing out of the ordinary had happened. She knew that Spencer was scraping by on less than three hours of sleep each night and that he was not accountable for his words. Besides, she had come to view Tracy's moodiness and irascibility as just another symptom of his singular genius. As for Cronyn, "It wasn't the last time I was invited to Tracy's dressing room. I liked and admired him, and he could be just as funny as he was sometimes savage." (Later, Cronyn and his wife, the actress Jessica Tandy, became close friends of Kate's.)

Tracy had good reason to lose sleep over *The Seventh Cross*. When it was released, audiences found it hard to buy the all-American Tracy as a German antifascist. By contrast, *Dragon Seed*, which seemed to stretch credulity even farther, was a major success. Somehow audiences managed to get past Kate's patented Yankee clip and painfully reconfigured eyes, turning what stood to be a major embarrassment into one of the most compelling films ever made about wartime China. Kate could breathe a sigh of relief; *Dragon Seed* had not derailed her comeback.

Still, what Tracy and Hepburn needed—and what the public craved—was for the couple that lit up the screen in *Woman of the Year* to return in a romantic comedy. Kate thought they had that when MGM agreed to bring *Without Love* to the screen as a Tracy-Hepburn vehicle. This time screenwriter Donald Ogden Stewart threw out the whole Irish political angle. Now the Irish-American butler played onstage by Elliott Nu-

gent was an American scientist-inventor coping
with the housing shortage in Washington, D.C.
Kate, still the rich widow, offers to let him use
the basement of her mansion as a laboratory. For
appearance's sake, they enter into their marriage
"without love."

As soon as Tracy finished playing Jimmy Doo-
little in *Thirty Seconds Over Tokyo*, filming started
on *Without Love* in the fall of 1944. True to form,
Kate offered her unsolicited comments on every
facet of production from costumes to lighting.
Without Love's producer, Lawrence Weingarten,
finally told her, "Even looking at photos of you
makes me tired!" But she persisted. "People always said to me, 'She's trying to do everything.'
And my reply was, 'The thing I'm afraid of, and
you should be afraid of, is that she *can* do everything.' Producer, director, cameraman! That's
what she was! Her idea of everything was always better than you could ever have envisioned." Lucille Ball, who shone in a supporting
role in the film and would one day own RKO
Studios, agreed. "Like E. F. Hutton," she said.
"When Katie spoke, you listened—if you were
smart."

Hepburn's self-imposed aura of authority extended far beyond moviemaking. Kate always
believed she knew best and brooked no disagreements. As far as she was concerned, there
was one and only one proper way to brew tea,
scrub a floor, water a philodendron, grasp a tennis racket, hoe a garden, take a shower, chop

wood, scramble an egg, sail a boat, bank a fire, brush one's teeth, shell peas, fly a kite, make a chip shot, drive a car, fold a napkin, or decorate a Christmas tree. "She had ironclad rules for *everything*," Kanin observed, "and the total, utter conviction to back them up."

Tracy, no less set in his ways, viewed Kate's authoritarian streak with an air of bemused detachment. Yet to those who had known him it seemed that now Tracy listened only to Kate. His old friends at MGM's Culver City studios lamented the fact that he no longer shared meals with them at the commissary; he nearly always ate in his dressing room with Kate. As for after-hours socializing: "It was all different," said MGM talent executive Billy Grady. "We had all been Tracy's pals—the executives, the directors, everyone—and he had been our favorite guy. I suppose he still was, but we weren't close anymore. We didn't do things together anymore. You saw Spence only at the studio, and now you were just casual friends."

Now that they were a couple—albeit a clandestine one—it was only natural that Spencer and Kate would gravitate toward a similarly talented two-some, the husband-wife team of Garson Kanin and Ruth Gordon. A blunt-spoken, opinionated New England Yankee like Kate, Gordon, who went on to win an Academy Award as Best Supporting Actress in 1968's *Rosemary's Baby*, had made her stage debut in *Peter Pan* in 1915 and been an established star on

Broadway since the 1920s. She and Kanin went on to write *A Double Life* and *Born Yesterday*, as well as two of Tracy and Hepburn's biggest hits. Gordon and Kate, it turned out, had something else in common: Kate's old lover Jed Harris was the father of Gordon's only son.

Next to George Cukor, Gordon and Kanin could lay claim to being Kate and Spencer's closest friends even before they moved into the town house next door to Kate's Turtle Bay brownstone. No wonder. Stimulating raconteurs, the Kanins thrived on gossip and the *mot juste*. And while they always stayed within the boundaries of civilized conversation, they chose for the most part to overlook Tracy's penchant for inflicting psychic pain.

Still, with four such strong personalities there were the inevitable blowups. "I must confess we had a thirty-year friendship but it was not without its bad patches," Kanin said of his relationship with Tracy. "He was a difficult man; he was terribly set in his ways; he had to be left alone. We had terrible disagreements and fights. There were times we didn't talk for months or even years. But that's the magical thing. . . . A broken friendship is like a broken bone: When it heals, it is that much stronger."

They hit one of those bad patches in 1945, when Tracy returned to the Broadway stage in the Kanin-directed *The Rugged Path*. Tracy had been back to the stage only once in fifteen years—to narrate Aaron Copland's *Lincoln Por-*

trait when it was performed by the Los Angeles Philharmonic Orchestra in 1944. Now Kate, who unlike Spencer was a proven risk taker, prodded Spencer to take a chance on a new play by Robert Sherwood.

At six feet eight inches, Sherwood cast a looming shadow as both a man of letters and a trusted confidant to Franklin Roosevelt. The four-time Pulitzer Prizewinner had written *Waterloo Bridge, The Petrified Forest, Idiot's Delight, Abe Lincoln in Illinois*, and *There Shall Be No Night*. During the war Sherwood ran the overseas operations for the Office of War Information and was one of FDR's chief speech writers.

Sherwood was at the White House the first week in April when Tracy arrived for a meeting with the President. FDR had asked Spencer to undertake a morale-boosting tour of troops stationed overseas and a special covert mission on Roosevelt's behalf. The President wanted Tracy to deliver a top secret message to someone in Europe and would withhold the name of the recipient and the content of the message until shortly before Spencer's departure. A humble Tracy agreed.

A week later, on April 12, 1945, the nation was plunged into mourning when Roosevelt died of a brain hemorrhage at Warm Springs, Georgia. Tracy's tour was canceled, and he never found out the nature of the message he was to deliver or the identity of the recipient. It haunted him for the rest of his life.

Tracy wept as he and Kate listened to Sherwood's moving tribute to the late President over the radio. When Sherwood approached him the following month with his first play in five years, *The Rugged Path*, Tracy sent back a telegram—his preferred form of communication—saying he would do the play. He had been so moved by Sherwood's radio tribute to FDR, he felt there was no way he could refuse.

Tracy regretted his decision almost immediately. The studios knew how to handle Tracy's periodic lapses in his ongoing war against alcoholism. If he disappeared for a few days or even a couple of weeks, they merely shot around him, confident that he would eventually turn up. But theatergoers were obviously paying to see their favorite movie star in the flesh, and if he disappeared, the results for the cast, the producers—and, most of all, Sherwood—would be catastrophic.

Eager to see the usually cautious Spencer take on a new challenge, Kate turned a blind eye to *The Rugged Path*'s somewhat farfetched plot: A distinguished reporter gets fired for his antifascist articles, serves his country as a cook on a Navy destroyer, and winds up getting killed in action. Having seen him in 1930's *The Last Mile*, Hepburn knew Tracy was a great stage actor as well as a movie star. Now, she reasoned, the world would know. "She was as excited about Spencer returning to the theater," Olivier said, "as I've ever heard her. I think she wanted success and happiness for him more than he wanted it for himself."

Before rehearsals began that summer of 1945, Kate took Spencer to share Sunday dinner with her family at Fenwick. "First time I got invited to the Hepburn home in New England—home, hell! a palace! On half an island and facing a private fenced-off beach a mile long," he told director Frank Capra. "Well, you know Madame Do-Gooder here. She'll donate to the committee for the Protection of Fireplugs. She'll parade for the civil rights of the three-toed sloth. And you know what? Her family are all bigger fruitcakes than she is. You know—ultraliberal New England aristocrats that work their ass off for the poor, poor folk, but never see one. Take Father. A big doctor. They won't let charity letters go through New England's mails unless his name's on the letterheads. And their mother helps Margaret Sanger with young girls that got knocked up—"

"Mother helps with birth control—" Kate interjected.

"OK, Mother helps young girls from *getting* knocked up. And all the grown Hepburn kids've got pet social rackets of their *own*. What a clan! Well, at dinner, my head's this big. Can you imagine listening to Hepburns all talking at *once* about the Negroes, the slums, the Puerto Ricans, abortions, the homeless, the hungry?"

Recalling the events of that day to Garson Kanin—as always, in Kate's presence—Tracy marveled at the Hepburns' ability to talk nonstop. "Even when they look like they're listening," Spencer said, "they're really only sitting there thinking what they're going to say next."

Then, Tracy continued, talk turned to the dawn of the new era known as the Century of the Common Man.

"Don't tell this, Spence," Kate said.

"Why not?"

"Because the way it happened isn't the way it sounds when you tell it."

"I'm a liar, is that it?" Tracy asked.

"I didn't say that," Kate replied, "but it was the whole *ambiance* and the suddenness—well, what I'm trying to say—"

Tracy resumed the story. After listening to the Hepburns volley back and forth on the subject of the "Common Man," Tracy excused himself. "So I get up and say, 'If you don't mind, I'll step outside and lift the lamp beside the golden door.' So I go out on the porch for some peace and to watch the sunset.

"The beach is empty. Had to be empty with those barbed-wire fences on each side. And I see a guy, with a fishing rod, a little guy, crawling through the barbed wire about a half mile away, so far away he was a speck. 'Hey,' I yelled to them inside, 'better put on another plate. Here comes a wretched one yearning to breathe free!'

"Old Man Hepburn came out running with fire in his eye. 'Where is he?' I pointed to the fence. Dr. Hepburn took down a megaphone off the porch wall and ran out on the beach, yelling, 'This is private property! You are trespassing! Get off this beach immediately or I will fill your tail with buckshot! Now git!'

"The poor old fisherman dove through that barbed wire and gits for his life up the beach trailing barbed wire from his legs. . . . And by this time Dick and Bob, and Emma Goldman here, and the whole slew of kids were all tear-assing after this poor brute on the beach."

Then, Tracy continued, "they all came back to the table, out of breath, and I'm a son of a bitch if Dr. Hepburn didn't pick up right where he'd left off and went on for another five minutes about the rights of the common man!"

Thought by many in the Hollywood community to be politically conservative, Tracy was actually a moderate Democrat. Not only was he a fervent supporter of FDR, but he numbered among his friends liberal Supreme Court Justice William O. Douglas and the Kennedy clan. "All the Kennedys," said Tracy, who played tennis with Joe in California and at the Kennedy family compound at Hyannis Port, "remind me of my father." But he saw the Hepburns as "fruitcakes" and their nineteenth-century brand of patrician liberalism as nothing short of hypocritical.

Kate's parents were not overly fond of Tracy either. "They were never close," Kate said. "I *think* that they liked him, but Spence felt a bit uncomfortable with them. After all, he was a married man."

According to Kanin, Spencer was "a revelation" during rehearsals for *The Rugged Path.* "Imaginative, resourceful, malleable. Kate was around, helping us all in the most self-effacing way." After the play opened in Providence on September 28, 1945, Kate rushed backstage to embrace Spencer and congratulate him on a brilliant performance. But it was clear to all involved that the play had serious deficiencies.

There were frantic rewrites and more rehearsals before the play moved on to Washington. Spencer fell ill with the flu and was soon running a 103-degree temperature. But he insisted they press on. Fearing that any missed performances would be chalked up to heavy drinking, Tracy "struggled to the theater night after night, trembling with chills, sweating with fever, throwing up in the wings, but playing the play," Kanin said.

After being savaged by the critics in Washington, the play went on to Boston, where Tracy's doctors finally ordered him to take four days off. Spencer was so demoralized that he announced his intention to quit. Sherwood and Kanin pleaded with Tracy to stick it out, but it was Kate who convinced him that if he left, people would assume it was because he had fallen off the wagon.

Everyone involved in the production was on edge during the two weeks before the all-important New York opening. Tracy and Kanin were now barely speaking to each other. And even though Kanin conceded that "Katie was the only one who kept her head" while the rest of the company panicked, he upbraided her for daring to coach one of the actresses behind his back.

This was a mistake. "Spencer," Kanin recalled, "rising to Kate's defense, blasted me powerfully."

Early on November 10, the day of the Broadway opening, Kanin checked Tracy's dressing room at the Plymouth Theater and discovered Kate in the bathroom on her hands and knees, scrubbing the floor. She looked up. "Damn place," Hepburn said, "is filthy . . . *was*."

That evening Tracy paced the floor of his dressing room as Kate read aloud from the pile of congratulatory telegrams on his desk. She rubbed his shoulders, poured him another cup of coffee, and bolstered him with words of encouragement. Then Kate watched proudly from the wings as Tracy stepped onstage to a thunderous ovation. When the play ended, the audience leaped to its feet and cheered. Spencer Tracy's performance was a tour de force; he had confounded skeptics and returned to the stage in triumph.

The same could not be said for the play itself. After opening night Spencer, Kate, and the Kanins attended a small dinner party at the Sherwoods' and waited for the reviews. Kate read them over Spencer's shoulder, periodically glancing at his face to study his reaction. Sherwood came in for some of the most scathing criticism of his career.

On the basis of Tracy's star power, *The Rugged Path* limped along for ten more weeks before quietly closing on January 19, 1946. Kate never let on to Spencer, but during the run she shared her doubts about the play in a letter to Cukor:

> *Dear George,*
>
> *Thanks for good thoughts—it went well—but it is almost a super human task—the show is* too *complicated—too too—and the hall's huge— look front and scream—*
> *Love and Thanks,*
>
> > *Kate*

Without fail, each day of *The Rugged Path*'s run Kate was on hand in Spencer's dressing room, endlessly tidying up and always making sure there was a bottomless supply of coffee and tea. Still keyed up after the show, Tracy often invited several cast members and others involved in the production for a late-night snack at his Waldorf Towers suite. Kate was always there, listening attentively and saying very little. "Kate adored Spencer, worshiped him," Mankiewicz said. "When she was around him, she sometimes did behave like some awestruck kid. But she *enjoyed* it. It was something very different for her. How many people were there in the movie business for Katharine Hepburn to look up to?"

Kate's overriding mission was to get Tracy through this particular ordeal in one sober piece. One temporary casualty of *The Rugged Path* debacle was their treasured friendship with the Kanins. "His resentful gray eyes rejected me," Kanin recalled. The two headstrong couples did not speak for the next eighteen months.

When they did reunite, it was over a tense dinner at Romanoff's in Los Angeles (true to her credo, Kate did not attend). The Kanins complained about how difficult the husband-and-wife acting duo of Fredric March and Florence Eldridge had been during the Broadway run of Ruth's autobiographical play *Years Ago* and confessed they wanted Spence and Kate back. With that Tracy fell to his knees in front of Ruth. "Promise me," he pleaded, "that this little son of a bitch isn't lying." Then Spencer took the Kanins to Kate's house on Tower Drive, where their reunion—sans liquor, of course—continued until 2:00 A.M.

During the run of *The Rugged Path*, Spencer had remained assiduously sober. His proudest moment came when he sat young John Tracy in the front row so he could read his father's lips. That night, Spencer said, "I put on my best performance of the run."

Once the play closed, Kate was reasonably confident that he would "stay off the booze," as Tracy put it, while she made a picture on her own. Directed by Vincente Minnelli, the new husband of their old friend Judy Garland, *Un-*

dercurrent was another unusual choice for Kate: the story of a gullible young woman who marries a powerful industrialist (played by Robert Taylor) and learns that his brother (Robert Mitchum) is a homicidal maniac. After several Hitchcockian twists and turns, Kate's character cannot decide which is the real psychopath—her husband or her brother-in-law. Unable to perfect "the right horrified expression," Kate, not surprisingly, proved utterly unconvincing as the terrorized, helpless wife.

Off camera Kate was in fact trying to save an increasingly helpless wife—Minnelli's—from herself. Having done what she could for Spencer, Hepburn made yet another attempt to get Judy off alcohol and drugs. She took long early-morning walks with Garland and asked about her infant daughter by Minnelli, Liza. Knowing what it was like to live with someone battling substance abuse, Kate sympathized with Minnelli and did what she could to make the director's workdays as trouble-free as possible. No matter. There was no way Minnelli could help feeling intimidated by the strong-willed Kate. "She," he confessed, "made me nervous."

But while she tried—without success—to help Judy Garland, word filtered back to Kate that Spencer had fallen off the wagon in New York. Spectacularly. After bingeing with his old cronies from the Lambs, Tracy became violent and was taken, in a straitjacket, to Doctors Hospital on Manhattan's East End Avenue. By way of damage control, the studio had Tracy registered under a female alias and moved to one of the floors reserved for women. Suffering from delirium tremens, Tracy remained in the hospital for more than a week.

. Once he was back in Los Angeles, Kate was more protective than ever. There were long walks and long drives through the countryside. They picnicked, flew kites, and painted in oils and watercolors—mostly landscapes, seascapes, and, when they took to the road, the views from their hotel windows. They sat by the fire at her house on Tower Drive and read for hours. She preferred biographies and the classics; he devoured mysteries by the carload. He smoked cigars, cigarettes, pipes—whatever it took to keep his mind off that other addiction. "She lived in constant fear," said Tracy's friend James Bacon, "that he was going to go off any minute. She begrudged anyone and anything that might push him in that direction. But people have got to give Tracy credit for *trying*." Mankiewicz agreed: "Spence loved Kate and respected her, and for all his bluster it killed him when he disappointed her. But who was the stronger of the two? My God, was there ever any question? Hepburn. Hepburn . . ."

Kate's career took a backseat to Spencer's welfare once more. She turned down several screen offers, including *The Ghost and Mrs. Muir*, just to devote herself to finding a suitable project for herself and Tracy. In selecting *The Sea of Grass*, based on Conrad Richter's sprawling novel about a nineteenth-century cattle baron and the sensitive city girl who marries him, Kate and Spencer again resisted being typed strictly as a comedy team.

With only one film (albeit a major hit) to his credit, *A Tree Grows in Brooklyn*, Elia Kazan was hired to direct Tracy and Hepburn's first and only western. The producer, Pandro Berman, warned Kazan to "photograph Katharine right—it's not easy. Mr. Mayer is worried about that—and keep Spence together, if you know what I mean. You've heard the stories. Thank goodness Kate is with him now."

Tracy, now fattened up by Kate, was too soft to be believable as a leather-tough cowboy. Nor did he show any inclination to invest too much of himself in the role. At the moment "portly, dignified, much-honored" Tracy "squeezed out of the studio car, to be precise," Kazan made the conscious decision "to be friends—with everybody. . . . I'd given up on the picture."

Tracy made it easy for Kazan to like him. The young New York director broke up when Tracy poked fun at some of MGM's biggest names. "At lunch," he told Kazan, "Mervyn LeRoy was raving about a book he'd bought. 'It's got everything,' he said. 'Surprise, great characters, an important theme, fine writing! But,' he said, 'I think I can lick it.' Honest. That's what he said!"

Hepburn was another matter. "I was scared of Kate. I was overpowered by her. After all, she was 'royalty.' " He soon discovered that "the cause Hepburn believed in was Tracy. She'd watch him do a scene, and before I could comment on his work even favorably, she'd say, for my ears to hear, 'Wasn't that wonderful? How does he do it? He's so true! He can't do anything false!' and so on. Which didn't leave much room for any criticism I might wish to offer. Was she protecting him from me? I don't think it was that. She truly adored him."

Kate did not have to protect Tracy from the director. "I couldn't help coddling Spencer," he confessed. "He was a man devoured by guilt—so he seemed and so I've been told—about the son who'd been born deaf. He blamed himself and his 'sins' for that tragedy."

Kazan did, however, overcome his reticence and asked Kate to break down crying in one scene. She was happy to accommodate him, but when L. B. saw the footage, he complained that "the channel of tears is wrong. They go too near the nostrils." Kazan was nonplussed. "Some people cry with their voice," Mayer explained, "some with their throat, some with their eyes, but she cries with everything, and that is excessive."

Like the comparably somber *Keeper of the Flame*, *The Sea of Grass* disappointed audiences. "You should have almost smelled the land," Kazan said. "You should have got the stink of horse shit. Instead it was a miserable picture. . . . The whole point of the story was lost."

Perhaps, but critics were especially kind to Kate, who walked off with the film. When Tracy, who still valued his wife's candid appraisals of his work, asked her what she thought of *The Sea of Grass*, Louise pulled no punches. "You let her steal it," she told him bluntly.

For her next project Kate wanted to bring Anita Loos's Broadway comedy *Happy Birthday* to the screen. The story of a straitlaced librarian who gets tipsy on her birthday and is surprised to wake up the next day with a husband, it seemed the perfect vehicle for Kate. But the Motion Picture Association's censorship board, which had to approve all scripts before they went into production, vetoed *Happy Birthday*. Given Kate's heroic efforts to help Spencer battle the bottle, the reason given by the censors was especially hurtful: that the movie was "pro-alcoholism."

Unwilling to put up a fight, Kate undertook yet another costume drama: *Song of Love*, a film biography of Clara Schumann, the brilliant nineteenth-century pianist who gave up her own career to marry the composer Robert Schumann and bear his seven children. Ever the perfectionist, Kate studied with pianist Laura Dubman, a student of Arthur Rubinstein's, so that for the close-ups her hand movements would match Rubinstein's sound track. "If I hadn't seen it with my own eyes," Rubinstein marveled, "I wouldn't have believed it. That woman is incredible! She actually does play almost as well as I do! And when she ends and I begin, only I in the whole world could tell the difference!''

Tracy dropped in on the *Song of Love* set when he could, ostensibly to offer advice. "You know your lines?" he would bark at her. "Well, say them, loud and clear." Then he would turn to her costar, Paul Henreid, and say so that she could hear, "Watch her. She'll always start to smile at the wrong time."

"She was very much under his influence and control," said Henreid, perhaps best known for his roles in *Casablanca* and *Now, Voyager*. Henreid and Tracy whiled away the time between takes playing chess—until Spencer shouted, "Katie, where *are* you?" in the middle of a game.

"And she'd always come running, just as soon as he called," Henreid recalled. " 'Get us some Scotch,' he'd say, and she'd come along with two glasses, although I could see that she disapproved. She would pour it out very meagerly—two very small glasses."

While Kate swished and swooned through her period piece, Spencer worked on a film project of his own, playing a widower judge opposite Lana Turner's "nice young girl from the wrong side of the tracks" in *Cass Timberlane*.

Cass Timberlane's Hollywood premiere jolted Spencer back to the reality of his marital status. Now a popular twenty-three-year-old college student with a string of girlfriends, John Tracy was a son any father could be proud of. But Tracy still had not accepted John's deafness and refused to talk about it publicly. When Louise arranged with the studio for *Cass Timberlane* to benefit the John Tracy Clinic, Spencer grudgingly delivered a brief speech thanking the clinic's supporters. Then he posed with John for photographers. There was a flurry of stories about the benefit, but this time Tracy felt exploited; the issue of his son's deafness was behind him, and he resented anyone who reminded him of it. He did not speak to the MGM publicist responsible for the press coverage for months.

Based on the novel by onetime Hepburn neighbor Sinclair Lewis, *Cass Timberlane* was enough of a success to put Spencer back on top among MGM stars. But everyone agreed that the Lana Turner–Spencer Tracy pairing had failed to strike a spark. "Lana and Robert Mitchum—great. Lana and John Garfield, wonderful," Kanin said. "Lana and Spence? Nothing. Nothing at all. In the public mind it was becoming more and more difficult to imagine Tracy *without* Hepburn."

The moviegoing public would not have to wait long. But before Hollywood's greatest male-female team would go before the cameras again, Kate would become embroiled in an all-too-real political potboiler. Working title: *The Lady in Red*.

Sometimes I wonder if men and women really suit each other. Perhaps they should live next door and just visit now and then.

—KATE

Six

Long before she landed in a seaplane on the Hudson
and waded ashore at Hyde Park, Katharine Hepburn was a vocal supporter of Franklin Roosevelt. However, she grew disenchanted with what
she perceived as the less progressive policies of
his successor, Harry Truman. In 1947, with Truman facing election as President on his own,
Kate decided to back the second of FDR's three
vice presidents, Henry Wallace.

Regarded as too left-wing by the Democratic
rank and file, New Dealer Wallace had been
dumped from FDR's 1944 ticket and replaced by
Truman. Roosevelt had appointed Wallace secretary of commerce shortly before his death in
1945, but Wallace lost his cabinet post after
openly criticizing Truman's hard-line policy
against the Soviet Union.

Now Wallace, running for President on the
third-party Progressive ticket, was being labeled
a Communist dupe before the House Un-

American Activities Committee. In the spring of 1947 HUAC Chairman J. Parnell Thomas launched an investigation into the supposed Communist subversion of the American movie industry. Thomas's hyperbolic claim that his committee had uncovered "hundreds" of Communist sympathizers in Hollywood—among them some of the industry's biggest names—ignited a firestorm of controversy.

The HUAC hearings that began that May led to the infamous blacklist, the jailing of the Hollywood Ten, more than a dozen suicides, and hundreds of wrecked careers. Behind it all, supplying the raw material that made the whole nightmare possible, was J. Edgar Hoover. Responding to Thomas's urgent plea for help, the lionized FBI director supplied the names of actors, producers, writers, and directors who at one time or another may have actually belonged to the Communist party or one of its front organizations. He also supplied HUAC with profiles of thirty-two people Hoover thought would be "cooperative or friendly witnesses," Hollywood figures who would be willing to go before the committee and publicly "name names." Among these witnesses was Screen Actors Guild president Ronald Reagan, who since 1943 had been an FBI informant, and Kate's old friend and *Morning Glory* costar Adolphe Menjou.

Kate had been too preoccupied with Spencer to become actively involved in Wallace's campaign. But when the former vice president was prohibited from using the Hollywood Bowl for a rally, she was indignant enough to join an anti-censorship rally at L.A.'s Gilmore Stadium. She was, after all, still very much one of those "rabble-rousing Hepburns."

On May 12, 1947, Kate turned forty without anyone taking special notice. No one, *including Spencer Tracy*, knew that this—not November 8—was her real birthday. Like the rest of the world, Spencer was also under the impression that Kate was two years younger.

One week later she stepped up to the microphone at the Gilmore Stadium rally and, to the cheers of twenty thousand Wallace supporters, denounced HUAC. "Today J. Parnell Thomas is engaged," Kate told the crowd, "in a personally conducted smear campaign of the motion picture industry. He is aided and abetted in this effort by a group of super-patriots who call themselves the Motion Picture Alliance for the Preservation of American Ideals. For myself, I want no part of their ideals or those of Mr. Thomas. The artist, since the beginning of time, has always expressed the aspirations and dreams of his people. Silence the artist and you have silenced the most articulate voice the people have."

What she said had less of an impact than what she wore. Instead of her customary uniform of a man's jacket and tailored slacks, Kate chose to show up at the rally in a dress. A red dress. "At first I was going to wear white. And then I thought they'd think I was the dove of peace. . . . How could I have been so dumb!"

Mayer wasted no time summoning Kate to his office, where he scolded her for wearing a dress the color of the Soviet flag. He said she had not only imperiled her career but placed the studio in jeopardy as well. Once the hearings got underway in October 1947, directors Sam Wood and Leo McCarey testified that Kate had helped raise eighty-seven thousand dollars for a "very special" political cause that, said the smirking McCarey, "certainly wasn't the Boy Scouts." Although the reference was to fund-raising efforts for Wallace's Progressive party, in those heated times many may have drawn the inference that Kate had been a fund-raiser for the Communist party.

What neither Kate nor Mayer realized was just how close they had come to disaster. For years J. Edgar Hoover's agents had been spying on Hollywood. By 1947 the FBI had amassed thousands of dossiers on virtually every figure of any significance in the entertainment industry. These went far beyond information on political affiliations. Every transgression, every peccadillo, every addiction, every affair—real or imagined—were painstakingly chronicled. If an individual had received so much as a traffic ticket, it was noted in the file. Every fragment of potentially damaging gossip, particularly rumors concerning an individual's sexual habits or incidents of alcohol and drug abuse, was also included.

In part these top secret files satisfied Hoover's voyeuristic appetites. Although he periodically upbraided agents for quoting profanity in their reports, the more lurid the detail, the better. At the time Hoover's own vaunted reputation for moral rectitude—however false—was unparalleled. But instead of befriending only those with unblemished records, the FBI director, according to an aide, "didn't associate with people unless he had something on them." It was not until he reviewed Mervyn LeRoy's file that Hoover approved him as director of *The FBI Story* because he was confident "we have enough dirt to control him."

Back in Washington, Hoover now debated whether or not to give HUAC the FBI's extensive files on both Hepburn *and* Spencer Tracy. By her own admission, Kate felt her mother leaned toward communism. Certainly the Hepburns' long-standing friendships with left-leaning Emma Goldman and Margaret Sanger, as well as Kate's friendships with Donald Ogden Stewart, Ring Lardner, Jr., and others whose careers were being destroyed by the witch-hunts, were duly noted in Kate's bulging file.

The dirt Hoover had on Spencer was another matter. Aside from his unswerving support of FDR, Tracy stayed above the ideological fray. His oft-repeated line—"Remember who shot Lincoln"—was his way of saying actors should for the most part stay out of politics. What the FBI had managed to glean in the way of personal transgressions—Tracy's visits to brothels in the 1930s, the violent drunken sprees, the unprovoked assaults, the arrests, the disappearances and blackouts that ended with Spencer's being straitjacketed and hospitalized, not to mention numerous extramarital affairs with top stars ranging from Joan Crawford and Loretta Young to the guileless Ingrid Bergman—would have destroyed the most venerated film star in America.

There was more. Ever since the Tracy-Hepburn Affair began on the set of *Woman of the Year*, Hoover had been tracking it. If the American public had been told that the movies' Father Flanagan was cheating on his sainted wife with Hepburn, the personal and professional damage would have been incalculable. "In that climate," Joe Mankiewicz said, "neither would have worked for a long time—maybe never again. Besides, it would have killed Spence, and that would have left both Kate *and* Louise brokenhearted."

Without revealing the precise contents of the FBI files, Hoover informed HUAC's Thomas and a couple of other key committee members that he had some euphemistically "interesting" information on Tracy and Hepburn. One of the committee members, a freshman congressman from California who was to use the committee as a stepping-stone to higher office, believed Hepburn and Tracy were so admired by the

American public that any attempt to drag them through the mud would trigger a backlash. The congressman's name was Richard Nixon.

Hoover shelved the files, and neither Kate nor Spencer was called before the committee. Aside from a few passing references during the hearings, they escaped the firestorm that consumed so many of their friends and colleagues. Still, Mayer was irked by the fact that Kate's "Lady in Red" speech had spawned a boycott of the newly released *Song of Love*. To avoid further controversy, and by way of teaching his rebellious star a lesson, he waited several months before casting Hepburn in another picture.

When he did put Kate before American audiences again, oddly enough, it was with Spencer in a movie that amounted to an indictment of American politics. In such film classics as *It Happened One Night, Mr. Deeds Goes to Town, You Can't Take It With You, Mr. Smith Goes to Washington, Meet John Doe*, and *It's a Wonderful Life*, director Frank Capra sang the virtues of the common man. In 1948 he bought the Howard Lindsay–Russel Crouse play *State of the Union* with the same purpose in mind. Only this time Capra was taking aim at those who were willing to betray their principles to achieve the highest office in the land.

As averse as he was to becoming enmeshed in political causes, Tracy was eager to portray a politician for the first time in his career. "What Irish-American wouldn't?" he asked. "It's in our blood." In *State of the Union* he played Grant Matthews, a wealthy Wendell Willkie–like presidential candidate torn between his high ideals and a burning desire to occupy the White House. In a role that was to prepare her for her later part as the scheming mother in *The Manchurian Candidate*, newcomer Angela Lansbury played Kay Thorndyke, the wicked newspaper publisher who plots to get Matthews the Republican nomination and breaks up his marriage in the process.

It is left to Matthews's estranged wife Mary, a part originally given to Claudette Colbert, to bring him to his senses in true Capra-esque fashion. Two days before shooting was to begin, Colbert had informed the director that her doctor (who happened to be her husband) would not allow her to work late. Her agent—Colbert's brother—also insisted that she would not work past 5:00 P.M. When Capra would not agree to her last-minute demand, Colbert walked off the picture.

Capra was frantic. He called Tracy and asked if he had "any girlfriends—I mean, actresses"— who could step into the role.

"Waaal, come to think of it, Katie isn't hamming it up at the moment," Spencer answered.

"My God . . . Hepburn! Oh, no, Spence. You think she'd do it?"

"I dunno. But the Bag of Bones has been helping me rehearse. Kinda stops you, Frank, the way she reads the woman's part. . . . She might do it for the hell of it." Then he handed the phone to Kate.

"Sure!" she said. "What the hell? When do we start?"

Single-handedly, and without making any special demands, Kate had saved the picture. But there were other problems. Adolphe Menjou also played a pivotal part in the movie. Because of his role as a star witness before the House Un-American Activities Committee, Kate and Spencer now detested the mustache-twirling, perennially dapper Menjou.

A clash between Hepburn and Menjou seemed inevitable, and Capra felt the best he could do was close the set to snooping reporters. But to the director's relief, all parties rose to the occasion and behaved civilly to one another on the set. There were fireworks, all within the confines of the script. Mary Matthews is at odds with Menjou's slippery character throughout the film, but as it reaches a climax, she finally gets the chance to blast him for corrupting her husband and deceiving the electorate. No one, including Menjou, could fail to recognize that Kate was not simply delivering her lines.

For Angela Lansbury, who had earned an Academy Award nomination for her supporting role as the tarty maid in *Gaslight*, *State of the Union* was a watershed experience. "When I walked into Frank Capra's office the first time wearing a pink dress and a ribbon in my hair to match, his mouth fell open. How in the hell was this sweet-faced kid—I was twenty—going to pull off the part of a scheming, hard-as-nails forty-five-year-old? We all crossed our fingers and plunged ahead.

"Spencer Tracy called me Miss Lansbury, and everyone treated me like a seasoned professional—an equal. In one scene I slithered up to Spencer in a slinky robe and tried to seduce him while Katharine watched from the sidelines. Somehow I got through it, but under that robe my knees were literally knocking together. I just couldn't let them know that beneath the cool exterior was a seething mass of nerves. But Katharine went out of her way to make me feel at ease.

"What was exciting about Spencer Tracy and Katharine Hepburn was their presence," Lansbury continued, "I mean *collectively*. Their personalities as well as their talents were orchestrated so marvelously. It was almost as if they had a secret language all their own. I began to think of them as one person, really. I suppose most people did."

From that point on Kate took a special interest in Lansbury's career and often recommended her to producers. "I'm grateful to Katharine," Lansbury later said, "for taking me under her wing early in my career. She became my champion, and we are great friends to this day. I feel I owe her a great deal."

Judged by the reaction of the cast and crew, *State of the Union* was destined to be a hit. "Word got around when Spence and Katharine were about to act for the camera," said another actor, Howard Smith. "A crowd would gather, first watching, then applauding." As a slinky incarnation of evil, Lansbury walked away with more than her share of raves. But the movie clearly belonged to Kate. After Tracy's idol Lionel Barrymore previewed the movie, he told Spencer as much. "Really?" Tracy beamed proudly. "That's wonderful!" More than anything, *State of the Union* did what their last four films together had not: it cemented Tracy and Hepburn together in the public mind as a *permanent* team.

Tracy loved and respected Kate too much ever to begrudge the rave notices she received for *State of the Union*. But when critics used words like "restrained" and "lackluster" to describe his performance, he began to worry that he was slipping. Eager to latch on to any challenge, he accepted the part of a ruthless millionaire who commits arson, goads two people into committing suicide, and turns his wife into a hopeless alcoholic in Cukor's screen version of Robert Morley's hit play *Edward, My Son*.

Kate, originally slated for the role of the tragic wife, bowed out. After *Keeper of the Flame* and *The Sea of Grass*, she was determined not to star in another heavy drama with Spencer. Instead, Deborah Kerr stepped into the part that earned her the first of six Academy Award nominations.

Edward, My Son was to be filmed on location in England in the autumn of 1948. Before he departed for London, Tracy, full of enthusiasm for the project Cukor self-deprecatingly called his "mess," cabled ahead to Cukor at London's Savoy Hotel. In his cable he used a new nickname for Kate, the Loop: DEAR GEORGE YOUR WONDERFUL MESS HAS MADE ME VERY HAPPY BUT REMEMBER WITHOUT YOU IT NEVER WOULD HAVE BEEN DONE—LEAVING FROM COAST, NOW BE SURE KEEP ME POSTED—AND I EVEN INCLUDE THE LOOP'S DEEPEST AFFECTION. SPENCE

Kate accompanied Spencer, taking a suite at Claridge's in London while Tracy and Cukor stayed with Laurence Olivier and Vivien Leigh at their cavernous home, Notley Abbey. Kate busied herself browsing through antiques stores and reacquainting herself with Cukor and the Oliviers. But Tracy did nothing to disguise his unhappiness.

"Spencer was a Californian," said Olivier, who only the year before had been knighted and had just released his 1948 Academy Award–winning *Hamlet*. "He hated the damp and was accustomed to such American luxuries as central heating." Then there was the matter of *Edward, My Son*. "He decided not to try a British accent, which I think he rightly believed would have been rather jarring for audiences. But as it turned out, here was this quintessentially American figure in the midst of a story that was really very British. There was really no way to win on that one, I'm afraid. Spencer was truly a great actor— I think he had the potential to be the greatest onstage as well as on film and told him so. Many times."

Kate made her customary visits to the set to watch Spencer work but made a point of not being on hand when an old friend of Tracy's asked to drop in. Ingrid Bergman kissed Spencer chastely on the cheek, wished him well and then, sensing her former rival waiting in the wings, departed. Spencer would say that Bergman "was the greatest actress I ever worked with—except one."

Before they left for England, Kate and Spencer were spending even more time than usual with Ruth Gordon and Garson Kanin. The previous winter, while driving from New York City to their country home in Sandy Hook, Connecticut, the Kanins had begun to cook up the story of a prosecutor and his lawyer wife pitted against each other in a sensational attempted murder trial. Over the phone to London, Garson told Kate the script for *Man and Wife* was almost finished. Given Tracy and Hepburn's offscreen relationship, Mayer thought it would be tempting fate to release the film under that title. It was changed to something subtler: *Adam's Rib*.

From start to finish *Adam's Rib* was decidedly a family affair. In addition to the scriptwriting team of Gordon and Kanin, Lawrence Weingarten and George Cukor were brought in, respectively, to produce and direct. Kate turned to another old friend, Cole Porter, for a favor. She drove to his Rockingham Drive house in Beverly

Hills, walked into his famous Glass Room (the ceilings, walls, fireplace, furniture were all made of glass), handed him a script and asked him to write a song about Madeline, her character in the film. Porter agreed, but only if Kanin and Gordon would change the name of Hepburn's character to "Amanda." A week later Porter arrived at the studio and played "Farewell, Amanda" while cast and crew looked on.

A welcome newcomer in their midst was Judy Holliday, cast as the woman who shoots her philandering husband (Tom Ewell) and is defended by Kate. Tracy and Hepburn were actually instrumental in getting Holliday, who was convulsing Broadway audiences in Kanin's *Born Yesterday*, to join the cast.

After buying the rights to *Born Yesterday*, Columbia's dictatorial president, Harry Cohn, had refused to hire Holliday to play the role she made famous. He preferred a proven commodity like Rita Hayworth or Lucille Ball. So Kate and Spencer hatched a scheme: If Harry Cohn would not even deign to see a screen test of Holliday, her performance in *Adam's Rib* could be her test. Kanin and Gordon agreed to beef up the part of the wife, and Cukor, at Kate's insistence, would showcase Holliday's comedic strengths in the supporting role.

After their considerable effort Spencer and Kate were astounded when Holliday turned down the role in *Adam's Rib*. Kate and then Cukor called her up and explained their clever ruse to get her the *Born Yesterday* movie lead, but she still said no. Finally she pointed to a line in the script. "I don't want to play a part," said the zaftig Holliday, "where somebody calls me Fatso."

"Good God!" Kate howled. "Is that all? One word! It happens *once*." After Kate promised that the offending word would be excised from the script ("They're writers—they know lots of words"), Holliday signed up. Later Judy, feeling more confident, insisted that the word "Fatso" be put back in the script.

During filming, Kate insisted that Judy get as many long speeches and lingering close-ups as possible. Cohn, as hoped, was bowled over by the result. Directly as a result of Kate and Spencer's efforts, Holliday would go on to win an Academy Award as Best Actress for her role in *Born Yesterday*.

In preparing for *Adam's Rib*, Kate and Spencer were their usual study in contrasts. She attended a murder trial with Cukor in Los Angeles, carefully noting every movement and gesture of the opposing attorneys—and how the statuesque defendant, obviously on the advice of counsel, dressed more dowdily with each subsequent appearance. Tracy, as always content to rely on his instincts, refrained from doing any special research.

Much of *Adam's Rib* was shot on location in Manhattan during the summer of 1949, so Kate and Spencer shuttled between his Waldorf Towers suite and the house in Turtle Bay. On weekends Kate made her customary pilgrimages to Fenwick or the house in West Hartford, usually with Spencer. As for the work itself, gone were the apprehensions and anxieties that had, to one extent or another, marred their earlier collaborations. They were more confident and comfortable—personally and professionally—than they had ever been in their lives.

And it showed. Calling each other Pinky—actually Pinky for him and Pinkie for her—Adam and Amanda Bonner ducked under their counsel tables to flirt in the middle of a trial, conducted nonstop conversations as they dressed (off camera) for dinner, and came to blows in the middle of a massage ("I know your touch. I know a slap from a *slug*!").

"Home movies" of the Bonners clowning in Connecticut might just as well have been taken of Kate and Spencer in an unguarded moment. As cameras rolled on scene after scene, the stars were so convincing that had moviegoers not known he was "happily" married, they might have thought Tracy and Hepburn were an actual couple in real life. "A line thrown away, a lifted eyebrow, a smile or a sharp, resounding slap on a tender part of the anatomy is as natural as breathing to them," wrote Bosley Crowther in *The New York Times*. "Plainly, they took pleasure in playing this rambunctious spoof."

"THE FUNNIEST PICTURE IN TEN YEARS!" screamed the posters for *Adam's Rib*. "IT'S THE HILARIOUS ANSWER TO WHO WEARS THE PANTS!"

All hype aside, *Adam's Rib* was a huge hit—arguably the best of the nine Hepburn-Tracy films. It also marked another turning point for the team. In the two years since *State of the Union*, both had undergone a discernible physical change. Kate, now a mellower forty-two, still cut the trim, athletic figure of a woman in her late twenties or early thirties. Conversely, gray, stocky Spencer, clearly suffering the ravages of alcoholism, looked at least a full decade older than his fifty years. Yet to an unsuspecting public, he merely seemed only that much more fatherly, more charming and distinguished. "Chocolates," Spencer now liked to say, "broadened me into a character actor."

Indeed Tracy was never more popular. In 1950, not long after the Christmas 1949 release of *Adam's Rib*, women were asked which man "most strongly influences American women emotionally." Spencer, who was named by twice as many women as any of his peers, graciously accepted the framed award certificate. Later he had it reframed and sent to Clark Gable, who doubled over when he read the added inscription: "Lest You Forget."

To mark the century's midpoint, the Associated Press conducted a poll asking thousands of Americans to name the greatest movie actor and actress of silent and talking films. Greta Garbo (who was now an infrequent member of Tracy and Hepburn's tight social circle) took the honors in both categories, and Charlie Chaplin was chosen king of the silent screen. As for talkies, there was no contest. In a field that included—to name only a few—James Stewart, Cary Grant, James Cagney, Clark Gable, Humphrey Bogart, and Henry Fonda, the American public voted Spencer Tracy the greatest actor the medium had produced. No one else was even close.

As comfortable as he was with his elder statesman status, Tracy did not want to confine himself to cerebral dramas and domestic comedies. He had, after all, fought and sweated his way through more than his share of action-packed adventures and war movies. So, while he and Kate played their customary waiting game for another script that even approached the caliber of *Adam's Rib*, Tracy starred with Jimmy Stewart in the wartime adventure *Malaya*.

Championed by the brilliant and ambitious Dore Schary, whose arrival at MGM as production chief presaged Louis B. Mayer's eventual demise, *Malaya* told the story of American efforts to steal much-needed rubber out from under the noses of Japanese occupation troops. For Tracy, there was plenty of opportunity for onscreen derring-do: The film's climactic scene has a wounded Tracy avenging the death of Jimmy Stewart's character by killing their Japanese nemesis. Backed by an all-star supporting cast that included Lionel Barrymore, Sidney Greenstreet, Gilbert Roland, and John Hodiak, *Malaya*'s success reassured Tracy that he had not completely lost what he called his "sex appeal."

Privately, however, Spencer was never more sedentary. After the deaths of several of its members, the Irish Mafia's meetings were now fewer and farther between. He spent nearly all his evenings at home with Kate and their few friends—principally Cukor, the Kanins, producer-director Chester Erskine and his wife Sally, and of course, the Carroll Tracys.

Even after Kate turned in, Tracy, still suffering from insomnia, stayed up for hours chugalugging coffee and smoking as he pored over scripts. The anxiety he experienced evidenced itself in an array of nervous tics. His jaw muscles rippled as he clenched his teeth. He chewed on his lower lip or rolled his tongue against the inside of his right cheek. Even when he managed to calm down, he was seldom relaxed enough to sleep. Often Kate emerged from the bedroom in the predawn hours to find him alone listening to Brahms, his cigarette an orange glow in the dark.

Perhaps for the same reasons that Tracy felt compelled to assert his masculinity in *Malaya*, Kate decided it was time for a change. At an age when other women heard their biological clocks ticking loudly, Kate felt it was time to give birth to a new career—as a Shakespearean actress.

Even before the cameras had stopped rolling on *Adam's Rib*, Kate made the courageous decision to play Rosalind—far and away the largest of any female role in the Shakespearean repertoire—in the Theatre Guild's Broadway production of *As You Like It*. "I realize I'm putting my head on the line," she told one writer, "but for me, the personal satisfaction justifies the risk."

There were practical considerations. In June 1949 HUAC finally released its long-expected list naming hundreds of Hollywood figures with supposed Communist sympathies. Unlike most of the other stars named, including Frank Sinatra and Lena Horne, Kate chose to ignore the committee. But, with the televised hearings of the McCarthy era still ahead, she realized that Hollywood was more and more becoming a dangerous place to do business.

That is, if Hollywood was going to survive at all. After years of legal wrangling, the courts had finally ruled that the studios and the theaters they owned constituted a vertical monopoly. Loew's, Inc., which owned both the huge Loew's theater chain and MGM, was ordered to divest itself of its movie houses. With television beginning to siphon off some of their audience, movie executives feared the worst.

There were other, more personal reasons for Kate to steer her career in a direction away from Hollywood. Increasingly Kate was bothered by the feeling that her mother was disappointed that her movie star daughter had not chosen to tackle more socially relevant material. The films that clearly delighted the public—including the ones in which she starred with Spencer Tracy— may have seemed a bit silly for Mrs. Hepburn; she favored the avant-garde and the classics. "I just don't think," Kate said, "that Mother really thought I was doing all I could with my life. She made me wonder if I wasn't just wasting my time." When she told her mother about her decision to do Shakespeare, she got the reaction she hoped for. "Wonderful, wonderful," Katharine Sr. said. "It's about time!"

Spencer did not share either of the Kates' enthusiasm. On the contrary, he objected to any project that would take her away from him for an extended period—in this case, at least several months. To prove he could not do without her, he began drinking again. He was too proud to come right out and say he needed her, that he might self-destruct without her, but she got the message.

This time, however, Kate was determined not to repeat the mistakes of the past. She had long marveled at Spencer's ability to stop drinking cold turkey, but now she realized that he had to seek professional help if he was going to beat the problem once and for all. She urged him to join Alcoholics Anonymous or at the very least to see one of the battery of Beverly Hills physicians who had built entire careers on treating alcoholic movie stars.

Tracy responded by only drinking more. At one point he lost control and did the one thing he had never done before: Spencer struck Kate. He was too drunk to realize what he had done at the time, and too mentally fogbound the next day to remember. Kate certainly would not tell him, though years later she described the inci-

dent to an acquaintance, writer Martin Gottfried.
She knew that if she had told Spencer he had hit
her, he would have been so overcome with remorse that it would have changed the nature of
their love for each other. She did not want him
to be bound to her by guilt, as he was to Louise.

Nevertheless this period marked the nadir of
the Tracy-Hepburn Love Affair. "He was clearly
very upset, almost panicky," said society writer
Doris Lilly, who spoke with Tracy at the time.
"She seriously considered breaking it off. For the
first time he was deathly afraid of losing her."

Now more than ever Kate was committed to
leaving Hollywood for a time—to reassess her
complicated relationship with Tracy, but also to
forge a new and entirely independent career for
herself onstage. Even before rehearsals began at
New York's Cort Theater on November 14, 1949,
Kate went into training like a prizefighter ready-
ing himself for a championship match. Each
morning she jogged around Central Park, usually with her trusted chauffeur, Charlie Newhill,
shadowing her. If he spotted a photographer,
Newhill honked the horn to warn Kate; then she
ducked into the car and sped off. Each day she
hiked to the "secret spot" where she had studied
the scripts for all her stage roles—a small rock
outcropping overlooking the park's Belvedere
Castle.

The real training took place at the Turtle Bay
town house, where for three hours a day she
studied with her friend Constance Collier. Ever

since the classically trained Collier had appeared as the over-the-hill actress in *Stage Door*, she and Kate had been fast friends. Kate's mother, who attended several of her *As You Like It* performances, provided moral support. But Kate relied on Collier to coach her through the difficult and exhausting role.

Spencer meanwhile was on the phone to Kate constantly, sometimes calling three and four times a day. The calls became more and more desperate. Finally she agreed to let him join her on the road. At their rendezvous in Cleveland, a repentant Spence convinced Kate that he was "off the sauce" for good. Over the next few weeks they resumed their usual masquerade. At various stops on the tour, he would slip quietly into town, take a room under a pseudonym, then join her for a quiet dinner at her hotel.

By the time *As You Like It* opened at the Cort on January 26, 1950, Kate's return to Broadway after a seven-year absence had taken on the proportions of a national homecoming. Noting that she had done more than anyone to popularize pants for women, *Life* magazine ran a cheesecake shot of Kate wearing her Elizabethan doublet and hose. The magazine's writers were "surprised and delighted to discover that her gams are as good as her iambics."

Since they were so seldom seen uncovered, more was made of Kate's stunning chorus girl legs than of her performance. Many critics, in fact, felt that she was ill suited to the role. *The*

New York Times' influential Brooks Atkinson allowed that Kate was "lovely to look at" and "an honest and straightforward actress whom it is easy to admire. But she is not a helpless, bewitched, moonstruck maiden.... And is this a New England accent we hear twanging the strings of Shakespeare's lyre?"

Other critics agreed that Kate's forceful Yankee personality had overpowered Shakespeare's swooning Rosalind, but their opinion still carried little weight with audiences. Hepburn's public flocked to the theater.

Spencer spent the first few weeks of *As You Like It*'s Broadway run in New York. Left to his own devices while she performed onstage, Tracy soon broke the promise he had made in Cleveland. Still, when she returned home from the theater each night, she would find him waiting for her, drunk or sober. Just as religiously he walked—sometimes staggered—the one and a half blocks back to the Waldorf Towers, just for the sake of appearances.

Again, work proved to be Tracy's salvation. When Dore Schary purchased Edward Streeter's best-selling novel *Father of the Bride* for MGM, there was no question in his mind that the title role was tailor-made for Tracy. MGM also had under contract the perfect actress to play the part of Tracy's daughter.

Since enchanting filmgoers in *Lassie Come Home* and 1944's *National Velvet*, Elizabeth Taylor had played the child teetering on the brink of womanhood in movies like *Life with Father* and the 1949 remake of *Little Women*. Other attempts had failed, but as Tracy's daughter in *Father of the Bride*, audiences would allow her to grow up. To Spencer's delight, his friend Vincente Minnelli, no longer just Mr. Judy Garland, was hired to direct. All that remained was to bring Kate on board as the mother, but that was impossible. Kate could not get out of the Theatre Guild contract even if she wanted to, and she didn't. Instead the part of Spencer's beautiful, unflappable wife went to Joan Bennett, one of his favorite leading ladies from the 1930s.

Before long life was imitating art on the *Father of the Bride* set, as Spencer began doling out advice to Taylor on her impending marriage to hotel mogul Conrad Hilton's son Nicky. The engagement was announced on February 20, 1950, and the next day Taylor showed up on the set wearing a doorknob-size square-cut diamond engagement ring.

"Strangely," Joan Bennett said, "she didn't seem overly pleased, almost as though she understood the impending marriage might not be easy for her." According to Bennett, Taylor and Tracy "huddled for hours in his dressing room. He confided to me later that she had certain misgivings about Nicky Hilton. Spence delivered a rousing pep talk in an effort to convince her that young Hilton effused boyish charm and would make an excellent husband. I'm not sure he himself believed any of this. I think Spence thought they were both too immature and unformed to walk down the aisle." Still, Spencer and Bennett both turned up in the hundred-degree heat at Beverly Hills' Church of the Good Shepherd when Taylor married Hilton on May 6, 1950. This first of Taylor's eight marriages soon disintegrated, but the timing of the wedding—one month before *Father of the Bride*'s release date—could scarcely have been better.

Without Kate as competition, Tracy had no trouble stealing *Father of the Bride. Newsweek* praised everyone involved in the making of the film but allowed that "in the final analysis this is the story of a defenseless, ordinary man caught up in events far greater than himself, and as that man, Spencer Tracy hilariously sparks *Father of the Bride* with one of his surest comedy performances."

By the time *Father of the Bride* was released, *As You Like It* had closed and Kate had rushed back to Los Angeles to spend the summer with Spencer before taking the play on the road. With *Adam's Rib* still in general release, it struck both Kate and Spencer as strange that the press was now pointing to Tracy's "triumphant comeback" in *Father of the Bride*.

What's more, Tracy was too agitated to savor his success. Against his own best instincts he had agreed to film a sequel, *Father's Little Dividend* even before the original was completed. Kate had been among those who suggested he go ahead and make the film, if only to stay busy (and presumably off the booze) while she finished up her Broadway run.

But Tracy found the filming of *Father's Little Dividend*, the predictable story about the travails of grandfatherhood, a chore. Recalled Bennett: "Spencer's favorite expression pertaining to the production of the sequel was 'boring . . . boring . . . boring.' We both felt one family film had been enough; I imagine Elizabeth shared our sentiment."

That summer Kate had moved into the sprawling Beverly Hills estate of her friend Irene Mayer Selznick. The move had actually been arranged by Cukor, who by now had assumed the roll of principal California caretaker to both Hepburn and Tracy. Hundreds of notes and cables passed between Cukor and his two friends over five decades, and in one dispatched from Kate not long before *As You Like It* closed, she thanked him for masterminding her new California rental—complete with the hire of butler and cook. The tone was quintessential Hepburn:

Dear George,

It all sounds so thrilling. The cook sounds wonderful. . . . What an angel you are to do this. I just cannot tell you with what longing I look forward to the luxury of not working nights. Oh God, to get up early and go to bed early. Christopher Columbus, what richness! I leave Monday on the Century with my silver, my towels and my sheets. I have not called before because of my voice, but, if you ever want to get me, after the performance is always safest.

Affectionately,
Kate

As she "lolled in the luxury" of the Selznick mansion ("Can you imagine? A projection room with a screen that comes up from the floor at the press of a button?"), Kate pondered her future with Spencer. Her absence from California had been disastrous for him, and had it not been for the back-to-back filming of *Father of the Bride* and *Father's Little Dividend*, there was no imagining how much more trouble he would have gotten into alone.

Kate was committed to the play's national tour, and once that was over in March 1951, she needed a film project. But in age-conscious Hollywood, starring roles for women in their midforties were practically impossible to come by. Her Dietrich-caliber "gams" aside, even when she covered up her neck with high collars and scarves, there was no disguising the fact that Kate was entering middle age.

Ironically, the film she chose to bring her back to Hollywood was to wind up taking her farther away from Spencer than she had ever been. Sam Spiegel, the rotund producer who would go on to make such film classics as *On the Waterfront*, *The Bridge on the River Kwai*, and *Lawrence of Arabia*, called Kate with an offer. He told her that he and John Huston, who had directed *The Maltese Falcon*, *Key Largo*, and *Treasure of the Sierra Madre*, planned to bring a C. S. Forester novel to the screen.

She had never heard of the book before, but if Spiegel would send her a copy, she would read it right away. Kate loved the offbeat adventure-romance—about Charlie Allnut, a gin-swilling riverboat pilot in German East Africa during World War I, and a British spinster named Rose Sayer—but wanted to know who Spiegel had in mind as her leading man. They kicked around the names of several actors before he came up with one of Hollywood's most bankable stars, Humphrey Bogart.

What Kate did not know was that she was the first of the three principals to be approached by Spiegel. At the same time he was telling her he had Huston, he was telling Huston he had already signed up Kate and Bogart, and Bogie he had already signed up Huston and Kate. All the parties would have been even more appalled if they had known Spiegel did not yet even own the rights to the book, which had been acquired by Warner Brothers for Bette Davis.

Keeping these various plates spinning, Spiegel somehow managed to pull the entire project together. It was settled. The following spring, Kate, Bogie (along with wife Lauren Bacall), and Huston would undertake a Herculean task: They would journey to the jungles of the Belgian Congo to film *The African Queen*.

I don't give a damn about marriage. But I do care about honor.

—KATE

We learned to be invisible in all the right places.

—SPENCER

Seven

❦

During the closing months of 1950 Spencer Tracy was not a happy man. He was not happy that his next film, *The People Against O'Hara*, was already promising to be among the most forgettable of his long career. Most of all, he was not happy that Kate had left him in September to return to the road in *As You Like It.* They were able to spend the holidays together in California—she continued to stay at Irene Selznick's house, though they found themselves spending more and more of their precious time together at George Cukor's estate—but with the exception of these three weeks and trysts in one or two tour cities, they kept in touch exclusively by telephone. Once again rudderless without his Kate, Spencer started drinking alone. There were sightings of Tracy behind the wheel of his black Thunderbird as it weaved through the streets below Sunset Boulevard.

He did not force the issue, but Spencer plainly

did not want Kate to make *The African Queen*. Coming directly on the heels of the *As You Like It* tour, it meant they would be apart at least until July 1951. Once she told him she had signed the contract with Spiegel, Spencer called her bluff: He renewed his contract with MGM for another three years—a clear statement that his working life, apparently unlike Kate's, would continue to be centered in Los Angeles.

Fearing that, in her absence, Spencer would wind up in a mental ward or dead behind the wheel of his car, Kate racked her brain for a solution. Finally it hit her. She asked George Cukor if he would invite Spence to move into the small guesthouse he was building at the back of his St. Ives Drive property, on a gentle, tree-shaded slope just above Sunset. That way, while both could retain some semblance of privacy, Spencer would be less likely to succumb to his bouts of loneliness and depression.

Tracy loved the idea. On February 8, 1951, while vacationing in Tucson, he wrote Cukor in England. Spencer described the progress being made on St. Ives Drive. As part of the ongoing cloak-and-dagger effort to keep the Tracy-Hepburn Affair secret, Tracy and Cukor alternately referred to each other as Corse Payten: apparently a loose anagram for "Spencer Tracy":

Dear Corse . . .

I have taken it upon myself to send you the

*plans of the Tracy Residence in the new Cukor Development (otherwise known as "*THE-LAST-STOP - BEFORE - THE - MOTION - PICTURE - RELIEF - HOME*").*

To satisfy a certain Touring Actress—we are draining the malarial swamp on which this residence is to be erected. She will be pleased to know that the sun hits the property regularly once a week and that the smog condition that has made this land uninhabitable for years is gradually being corrected.

The Hollywood Freeway does pass directly over the site, but the concrete mixers and riveters will be finished in about three short years.

Confident that Cukor could be counted on to keep a close watch on his mercurial tenant, Kate closed out the tour in Buffalo, her mother's hometown, with Katharine Sr. in the audience. The next day they returned home to West Hartford.

March in the northwestern corner of Connecticut was notoriously bleak, and Kate adored it. She loved the stately houses on Bloomfield Avenue, hidden behind a thick green wall of vegetation in the spring and summer, now laid bare—their turrets and chimneys and widow's walks exposed for all the world to see. The most impressive of these was the Hepburn residence at 201 Bloomfield Avenue—a three-story, twenty-four-room, brick-and-stone manse set on five wooded acres.

Normally the house at 201 Bloomfield overflowed with family and friends. But on St. Patrick's Day 1951, a chilly gray Saturday, Kate was the only visitor. Still, even as she approached her forty-fourth birthday, she could not help thinking of this place as home and herself as dutiful eldest daughter. The airy downstairs rooms, with their gleaming antiques, overstuffed chairs, and cherry wood wainscoting, had not changed in thirty years. Kate's own beige-walled room was much the same as it had always been. The maple bureau with the brass handles still stood against the south wall, and the four-poster—like the other beds Kate slept in—was still heaped with stuffed animals from her childhood. "You see," she later confessed to Spencer, "I never really left home. Not really."

Kate spent most of the morning and early afternoon with Mother in the parlor, happily chatting about *As You Like It* by the crackling fire. Then she took a brisk walk with her father. Bracing herself against the bitter cold, clouds of white vapor billowing from her mouth, Kate excitedly told her father about her future plans. Shooting on *The African Queen* was to begin next month; in two weeks she was to fly to London for wardrobe fittings.

The most punctual star in Hollywood, Kate did not have to look far for the source of this particular trait. "If Dad was going to pick you up and you were two minutes late," she said, "he'd leave without you." They hurried back to the house for four o'clock tea.

When they got back to the house, Kate warmed her hands over the fire in the parlor. Noticing that the tea service had already been set out by the maid, Kate realized that the house had fallen quiet. Too quiet.

She called upstairs. No answer. "We just looked at each other," Kate said, "and without a word ran upstairs. We knew what we would find." Kate's mother was lying on her bed, eyes closed, one hand still clutching the sheet. There was a peaceful look on her still-handsome seventy-three-year-old face.

Later they were able to piece together what had happened: After her bath she was apparently pinning up her hair when she suddenly felt dizzy and decided to lie down. Presumably within a few short minutes she had died of a massive stroke.

"The death of Kate's mother," Garson Kanin said, "hit her hard. Her mother had been a friend and a confidante, a person to whom Kate had often turned for advice of the most intimate sort." The loss of her mother was doubly devastating to Kate. Not only was it unexpected—to Kate it had always seemed her vital, dynamic parents would live forever—but like Tom's death, it changed the dynamics of the family that had always been her refuge.

Three days after her death Mrs. Hepburn was cremated. Her ashes were then buried beside her son Tom's in the Hepburn family plot at Hartford's Cedar Hill Cemetery. Scores of family members, friends, admirers, and allies from countless social campaigns waged over a half century paid their respects.

Spencer Tracy was not among the mourners at the funeral. Within a couple of hours after Mrs. Hepburn's death Kate called to tell him the news. Spencer, who was still so saddened by the death of his own parents many years earlier that he could not discuss them without becoming emotional, told her how deeply sorry he was and that he would catch the next flight east and join her. But Kate insisted that he stay put in California. There was no reason to interrupt work on *The People Against O'Hara*, and his presence would serve only to raise eyebrows. Spencer obeyed her wishes but called even more frequently than usual to see how she was bearing up under the strain.

It was not Kate's way to wail and keen; in stalwart Yankee fashion she kept her grief to herself. However, she was disturbed at first to learn that not long after the funeral her father had burned practically everything pertaining to her mother— from personal letters to anniversary cards to hundreds of news clips chronicling the elder Katharine's pioneering efforts in the suffrage and birth control movements. He had already shown the same disregard for his own papers, going so far as to burn his lengthy correspondence with George Bernard Shaw on the subject of venereal disease.

"Dad was such a nut, he destroyed all the correspondence," she said. "Destroyed it all. Just tore it up and threw it away. Can you believe it? The important thing to Dad was that he be unencumbered by old letters, so he never saved anything. 'Don't clutter up your life,' he'd always say. But it's sad, isn't it?"

True to his vow not to "live in the past," Dr. Hepburn remarried only a few months later. The bride: his longtime nurse and Hepburn family friend Madelaine Santa Croce—"Santa" to the Hepburn children. "Well, when you've had a wife for forty-five years," Kate told a friend, "I suppose it's pretty hard to get along without one. I like Santa—she'll be fine for Dad. We all should be damned grateful to her—she's taking on quite a handful."

Rather than confront her feelings, Kate escaped them. Only three weeks after her mother's funeral, she sailed aboard the *Media* with Constance Collier and Collier's secretary, Phyllis Wilbourn, to prepare for *The African Queen*. From Liverpool they drove eight hours to London, where Sam Spiegel and John Huston called on Kate in her flower-filled suite at Claridge's.

From the beginning she was intrigued, enchanted, and most of all frustrated by the elusive, evasive, and chronically late Huston. "I didn't know what to make of him," said Kate, who had long admired his father, the Academy Award–winning actor Walter Huston. "That scrawny neck, the Kentucky colonel charm—was he for real? Definitely one of the boys. Terribly full of himself. Had to be irresistible to all women and I suppose he felt I was no exception."

Huston, who preferred to talk about big-game hunting or riding to the hounds—anything but Kate's problems with the script—impressed her as being "full of himself, definitely. Maddening in the extreme. Infuriating! But brilliant." The director was, like Leland Hayward and Jed Harris and Howard Hughes and John Ford and George Stevens, precisely her forceful, mesmeric, center-of-attention type. She almost certainly would have fallen for him were it not for her total devotion to the most powerful personality of them all.

While she was sizing up Huston, he and Bogart were no less tentative about the Madame, as Spencer called her. "We had heard the stories about her," said Bogie, who joined Huston when he paid a call on Kate at her hotel. "How she drove hard Yankee bargains with producers, that Hollywood was only a necessary evil to her, her real interests being the stage and her home in Connecticut, that she wouldn't sign autographs for film fans and detested publicity. We knew too that she had been fired from plays because she tried to direct them, and today insists on editing and cutting her films. If she chose, she could be difficult."

But Bogart also wondered about "the zany

side, which we figured threw the lie at her shy, publicity-hating nature. Like the five baths a day she took because, she said, they helped her to think; like the story that she couldn't sit without propping her slack-clad legs almost as high as her head. She'd say, 'ya' for 'yes,' 'rally' for 'really,' sweetened tea with strawberry jam, shined her freckled face with rubbing alcohol; wouldn't use makeup except on her lips, or wear stockings, and had never used jewelry or perfume."

There was a press conference at Claridge's, where Kate bantered with Bogie. "Katie starts out as a missionary," he said, explaining the story to reporters, "but after going down river in Africa with me, she ends up as a woman."

Kate, sitting by a crackling fire in beige sweater and slacks, disagreed. "I'd say I start out as a woman," she said, "and end up a missionary trying to save Bogart." What Bogart's young wife most remembered of the press conference was that "I got all done up in my Balenciaga suit and Katharine Hepburn stole the show in her pants!"

While Huston and Spiegel scouted locations in the Congo, Kate flew quietly on to Rome. Bogart and Betty Bacall (real name: Betty Perske) were already there. In Rome Kate stayed in the apartment of her friend the American sculptress Fran Rich.

Meanwhile back in California Cukor smoothed the way for Spencer to rendezvous with Kate in Italy. He cabled a friend in Paris: SPENCER TRACY

ARRIVING IN ROME FOR THE FIRST TIME, FROM MAY
THIRTEENTH TO THE TWENTIETH. IT WOULD BE VERY
NICE IF SOME CHARMING, KNOWLEDGEABLE PEOPLE
TAKE HIM IN HAND AND SHOW HIM ALL. HE IS VERY
SHY BUT AN AWFUL NICE PERSON. COULD YOU DO
ANYTHING ABOUT THIS GREAT PROBLEM? REGARDS
GEORGE CUKOR.

Nowhere did he mention Hepburn, whose
presence in Italy was still top secret. After sightseeing with Fran Rich, Kate and Rich drove the
sculptress's tiny Fiat down to Naples to pick up
Spencer. "What's that?" he said, pointing to the
Fiat. "Needless to say," Kate remembered, "we
switched cars with the MGM limousine sent to
pick him up."

Ever mindful of appearances, Tracy checked
into the Grand Hotel. Each day Rich picked him
up at the hotel and brought him to her apartment. "We had a glorious time," Kate recalled of
their Roman sojourn. "Picnics, sightseeing,
churches, dinners in Fran's flat with the local
friends, walks in the country. Spencer loved
Rome. The press never caught on that I was in
Rome too. We drove all over the place, but they
never got a picture of us together of any kind."

After a few days Kate called the Grand Hotel
and was surprised to find that Spencer had already checked out and left for London. "Did he
leave because he was bored," she later mused,
"or did he leave because he couldn't bear to say
good-bye? The eternal question."

For Kate, the making of *The African Queen*

turned out to be one of the most terrifying, exhilarating experiences of her life. From Rome, Kate and the Bogarts flew to Léopoldville, the capital of the Belgian Congo. They traveled to Stanleyville, crossed the Congo River and boarded a "Toonerville Trolley" for Ponthierville, and then on to the village of Biondo and the black-as-ink Ruiki River.

"At first," Bacall later wrote, "Katie seemed nervous and talked compulsively.... I concluded her talking stemmed from being a woman alone, in an inaccessible part of the world, at the mercy of Huston and Bogart, about whom she'd heard all sorts of stories, the least of which was that they drank. I thought she was apprehensive—was trying to make it appear that she could handle any situation, that she knew all about men like them. As it turned out, she could—and she did."

It marked the beginning of an enduring friendship between Hepburn and Bacall. "She's a complete original," Bacall later said. "She has not fallen into any category—never has and never will. Katie never had an ordinary life, never lived by anyone else's rules. She has dealt with her life on her own, and I think that makes for a somewhat awesome woman."

Bacall readily admitted that she was intimidated by Hepburn at first. "Katie is a formidable woman, no doubt about it," she said years later. "We kid each other about being difficult. I mean, we both are. She is very demanding and has no patience with anything but the best. Neither do I. She can be very abrupt and say things quite bluntly at times. I do the same thing."

Even after they had been friends for decades, Bacall would admit that being Kate's pal was never easy. "I would never call her just to chat," she said. "And sometimes she makes me feel like she doesn't want me around. With Kate you just go along, and if she is in a good mood, that's terrific. If she's not, don't take it too personally, that's all."

For ten weeks, seven days a week from 6:30 A.M. until dark, cast and crew worked nonstop. Everyone had to endure the torrential rains, the sweltering heat, swarms of flies, mosquitoes, and hornets ("every creature that crawled or flew")— not to mention the ever-lurking threat from crocodiles, venomous black and green mamba snakes, poisonous spiders, scorpions, and worse. At one point the camp was attacked by ants and Kate was "literally covered up to my neck in ants, bitten everywhere except on my face and hands." At dinnertime giant moths flew into the overhead lights, were electrocuted, and plopped into the food. One night the *African Queen* sank and had to be pulled by rope up from the mucky river bottom. Kate, along with the cast, crew, and several villagers, stood on the riverbank and pulled.

The women faced added indignities. "There were no dressing rooms, no toilets—hell, there weren't even any *chairs*." Through it all Hepburn and Bacall uttered not a word of complaint, watched out for each other when they were forced to relieve themselves in the snake- and insect-infested bushes—the menfolk merely peed off the side of the boat—and forged a bond that would last a lifetime.

Conversely, Bogart, a confirmed city dweller who would have much preferred to shoot *The African Queen* on a comfortable sound stage, grumbled constantly about conditions in "this stinking hole. . . . While I was griping," he said, "Kate was in her glory. She couldn't pass a fern or a berry without wanting to know its pedigree and insisted on getting the Latin name for everything she saw walking, swimming, flying, or crawling.

"Here is either a twenty-four-carat nut or a great actress working mighty hard at being one," Bogart added. Along with Huston, he belted down sizable quantities of Scotch each night while Hepburn looked on disapprovingly. "She won't let anybody get a word in edgewise and keeps repeating what a superior person she is. . . . She pounces on the flora and fauna with a home movie camera like a kid going to his first Christmas tree, and she blunders within ten feet of a wild boar's tusks for a close-up of the beast. About every other minute, 'What divine natives! What divine morning glories!' Brother, your brow goes up. Is this something from *The Philadelphia Story?*"

Exasperated, Bogart told Kate, "You ought to come down to earth."

"You mean," she replied coolly between drags on her ever-present cigarette, "down to where you're crawling?"

He called her "an old crow"; she called him "the bag of bones." They were getting along famously.

Hepburn called Bogie a "no-bunk person" and admired his professionalism: "Always knew his lines. Always was on time. Hated anything false." After work he was "grumpy" until he'd "had a drink or two," at which point he would begin to needle Kate. "I was adorable and malleable," Kate recalled, "and well trained to handle the male grumps."

Still, Kate left no doubt that she disapproved of the marathon drinking. She was determined to "shame" them by drinking only life-giving water at mealtimes. Then she was struck with dysentery. So, while the boys kept draining the liquor bottles, she drank more water. Gallons of it.

And the sicker she got. Unable to keep food down, Kate, already rail-thin, lost twenty pounds. Cast and crew were so hard hit by dysentery and malaria that filming stopped for two full weeks. Yet no one was more deathly ill than Kate.

"Now, all this time neither Bogie nor John had been sick at all," she recalled. "They were fine." It turned out, of course, that the water was contaminated. "And I—the queen of water drinking, the urologist's prize—was the sickest. And those two undisciplined weaklings had so lined their insides with alcohol that no bug could live in the atmosphere. . . . I took to champagne."

At her sickest, while she was still trying to cure herself with polluted water, Kate passed out in her cabin. Huston dropped in to check on her and, she recalled, began massaging her back ("and my head and my neck and my hands and my feet") with his "smooth, strong hands." All the while Huston whispered, "Just stay asleep, Katie dear. Stay asleep. Asleep . . . asleep . . ."

"Took the trouble from me," she said. "It is true—the laying on of hands. So quiet—so sweet—soothing. He was gentle. I slept. I don't remember when he stopped. Dear friend."

She was also grateful to Huston for providing the key to Kate's character. On the second day of shooting he told Hepburn that she was being too glum. Aware that her mouth had a natural tendency to turn downward at the edges, she listened.

Huston asked Kate if she had seen newsreels of Eleanor Roosevelt visiting wounded soldiers during the war. Did Kate remember Mrs. Roosevelt's smile? Yes, she did.

"Well, I was . . . thinking of your skinny little face. . . . And those famous hollow cheeks. And that turned-down mouth. You know—you do look rather serious." So he suggested Kate smile "like Mrs. Roosevelt—she felt she was ugly—she thought she looked better smiling. . . . So, chin up. The best is yet to come—onward, ever onward. . . . The society smile."

Rose Sayer's smile would be the key to her courageously optimistic nature. "I was his," Kate said of the director, "from there on in."

Even when it seemed she might die from what she indelicately called "the Mexican Trots," Kate's thoughts never strayed far from Spencer. In the equatorial jungles of East Africa, she still could not stop worrying about him. Runners took Kate's daily letters to Tracy from *The African Queen*'s base camp back to the village each week. They were then picked up by launch and delivered to the closest post office, in Léopoldville. But with no way of receiving either phone calls or telegrams, Kate seldom, if ever, heard from Spencer.

Nevertheless, a day did not go by when she failed to bring up Tracy. "It was 'Spencer said this' and 'Spencer thinks that,'" said a crew member. "I remember the many nights I sat with Kate on the top of the deck of the paddleboat," Huston said, "and watched the eyes of the hippos in the water all around us." According to the director, they "talked about nothing and everything. But there was never any idea of romance— Spencer Tracy was the only man in Kate's life."

Back home in Los Angeles Spencer, whose ulcers were now acting up, was a nervous wreck. He worried about Kate's safety, but he was also an intensely jealous man who must have wondered what Kate and the fatally charming John Huston were up to during ten weeks in the sultry jungle. These fantasies, and his own work pressures, pushed Spencer back in the direction of his drinking buddies. Even Cukor, acting as his guardian in Kate's absence, could not keep him from joining reporter James Bacon or Clark Gable for a belt at Romanoff's or Chasen's.

On July 17 location shooting on *The African Queen* was completed, and cast and crew flew to London for six more weeks of filming at Shepperton Studios. After all they had been through in Africa, it seemed ironic that several key exterior scenes that wound up in the picture—including one in which Bogie fixes the propeller underwater and then tows the boat while wading—were shot on a sound stage.

Bored and eager for a change of scene, Tracy had sailed to London before Kate was scheduled to arrive. He was anxious to see her for the first time in nearly three months and had climbed back up on the wagon. He did not want to lose her.

To pass the time, he accepted a dinner invitation from producer William Goetz and Goetz's wife, Edie, who in keeping with Hollywood's tradition of nepotism was also Louis B. Mayer's daughter (and Irene Selznick's sister). Tracy was delighted that they would be joined by Joan Fontaine, in London filming *Ivanhoe* with Elizabeth Taylor, Robert Taylor, and George Sanders.

Goetz had produced *Jane Eyre*, in which Fontaine had starred with Orson Welles.

Fontaine, then just thirty-three, welcomed the distraction. She had discovered that her *Ivanhoe* director, Richard Thorpe, "cared more about the performance of the horses than the actors. Elizabeth Taylor was being wooed by Michael Wilding. Bob Taylor was nursing his vanity over his divorce from Barbara Stanwyck. George Sanders was his laconic, moody self."

She was not prepared for Tracy, whose distant gaze through most of the dinner indicated to her that his mind was on Kate. After she returned to her rented flat at 15 Grosvenor Square, Fontaine received a call from Tracy. "He had been so quiet at dinner, and now his tone was completely charming," she recalled. "It took a minute for it to sink in. He was flirting."

"Why don't you join me for dinner tomorrow night?" he asked. "Just the two of us."

Fontaine was still grateful to Hepburn for having put in a good word for her to producers years before she won her Academy Award opposite Cary Grant in *Suspicion*. "What about Kate?" she asked.

"What about her?"

"Well, Spence, out of respect for Kate's feelings I really don't think it's a good idea for us to go out alone," Fontaine said. "I'm afraid I just can't. . . ."

"What? Oh, you don't understand, Joan. You

see, Katie and I are just good friends. Friends—
nothing more."

"Oh, boy," Fontaine responded. "That's what
they all say!" She later recalled: "I made a joke
of it at the time, but I don't mind saying I was
absolutely *stunned*." A few days later she left to
do some location shooting outside Stockholm.
Tracy called her again, this time at her hotel in
Sweden, and continued pressuring her for a date.
Wouldn't she reconsider?

"I'm afraid not. Not only is there Kate to consider," Fontaine argued, "but you *are* a married
man!"

Spencer was unfazed. He told Fontaine that
she had the situation all wrong, that all parties
were free to do as they pleased. "I can get a divorce whenever I want to," he explained, "but
my wife and Kate like things just as they are."

Tracy's comment left Fontaine "floored," but
it had the ring of truth. It had been a full decade,
and since neither woman had forced the issue or
even expressed any dissatisfaction, Spencer was
left to believe that they liked the arrangement.

As for Tracy's overtures to Fontaine, it may
only have been a case of tit for tat; Kate had just
spent months in the jungle, with the exception of
Bacall the only woman among dozens of men.
She could hardly begrudge him dinner with a
friend, albeit a gorgeous one.

When Kate did meet up with Spencer in London, she was sick and weak. Laid up in her suite
at Claridge's, she called up the internist recom-

mended by her father, Sir Horace Evans, who also happened to be the royal physician. She was still wobbly, but within two or three days at least she was able to return to work.

While Kate finished up work on *The African Queen* in London, Spencer had an adventure of a different sort while dropping in on the Kanins in Paris. The couple had managed to convince their hermetic friend to venture forth from his suite at the Raphael Hotel during daylight hours. They then managed to persuade Tracy, who was pleasantly surprised when fans left him alone, to spend an evening at the Lido, the world-famous nightclub on the Champs-Élysées.

A group of acrobats had performed several amazing stunts when they stopped to introduce Spencer Tracy from the audience. A spotlight hit the ringside table, and Spencer, momentarily stunned, stood to acknowledge the thunderous ovation. One of the acrobats reached down to shake hands and—without warning—yanked the fifty-one-year-old screen legend onstage.

Mouths agape, Ruth Gordon and Garson Kanin watched as the acrobats made Spencer part of the act. "I saw the third member of the troupe begin a series of whirling backflips," Kanin later wrote, "moving toward the body tangle of which Spencer was a part. . . . The drumroll increased in volume until, with a crash of cymbals, the whirler leaped high into the air and landed on Spencer's outstretched legs. I saw him wince. The audience cheered."

Later a fuming Tracy returned to the table. A waiter produced the check, which Tracy tore up with a hearty "Shove it! The William Morris Agency will bill you for my appearance here tonight," he told the manager as he flung the pieces of the bill in his face, "and I hope you can *afford* it!" Then he told Kanin to make sure all the photos of his "performance" were rounded up. "Boy!" he said. "That's all I need. Nightclub high jinks pictures plastered all over."

When she arrived the following weekend, Kate refused to believe their outlandish story—until Tracy produced the pictures to prove it. After she saw them, Tracy burned the photographs himself—an impulsive act he later regretted. "What'd you let me burn them for?" he demanded of Kanin. "You don't always use your noggin, do you?"

Released just before Christmas 1951 so that it would qualify for Academy Award consideration, *The African Queen* was a monumental success, unanimously recognized for what it was—an instant classic. In the prim Rose Sayer audiences saw a woman very much like Kate at forty-four: well bred, intelligent, high-principled— yet with the mettle to love a hopelessly grouchy, hard-drinking tough guy. Gone forever was the high-strung, spoiled society girl of *Holiday* and *The Philadelphia Story*, replaced by a mature woman who was the match for any mature man. What's more, Kate proved that she was just as at home in the wilds of Africa as she was on Park

Avenue. At an age when most actresses were settling into supporting parts, Kate stood on the brink of a whole new career.

Bogart was to win his first and only Academy Award as Best Actor for *The African Queen*. Kate was nominated (her fifth time) but lost the Oscar to another woman playing a mature character: her friend Vivien Leigh as the tragic Blanche DuBois in *A Streetcar Named Desire*.

When she returned to California in September 1951, Kate asked a favor of her old love Howard Hughes, now head of RKO. Charles Boyer, who had starred with Kate in 1935's *Break of Hearts*, had built a spectacular château high up on Beverly Grove Drive. Boyer had lost the house to RKO when his career began to slip, and now Kate wanted to lease the house. In less than a week she had it fully furnished—with the help of the MGM and RKO prop departments. She added a few artifacts of her own: a spear and several ebony carvings, mementos of her African adventure.

She spent the next few months there, seldom leaving the grounds, utterly exhausted by her ordeal in the Congo. "Kate is not a Christian Scientist but often behaves as if she were," Garson Kanin observed. "She would not admit she looked drawn, was not functioning properly, and should rest. Eventually it hit her. . . ." Hepburn was so drained that for the first time Tracy stopped in each day to see how *she* was faring.

Like any good tourist, Kate managed to sum-

mon the energy to invite friends over—Cary
Grant and his third wife, Betsy Drake, the Kanins—and then inflict an after-dinner slide show
on them. When the slide projector broke down
and Kate summoned her guests back, Mrs. Cary
Grant begged off with a migraine.

"I've got a migraine too," Spencer told the
Kanins as he slumped into his seat.

"You have not," Kate protested.

"I'm going to have," Spencer muttered.

It was the kind of verbal Ping-Pong that inspired the Kanins' next creation for Hepburn and
Tracy. *Pat and Mike* told of the unlikely romance
between a classy, all-around female athlete and
the Runyon-esque sports promoter who takes
her under his wing. Yet again Kate and Spence
made certain that Cukor was hired to direct.
They read the script aloud one evening in the
library of Cukor's house. "Spencer sat in the corner of the room," Kanin recalled, "his eyeglasses
perched on his nose. He began to read, to act, to
be. The man with whom we had dined a few
minutes earlier was no longer there. Instead we
were confronted by Mike—a personality far
more real and complex than the person we had
imagined—with a way of breathing, thinking,
smoking, coughing, speaking, and munching
peanuts." Kate, the crack golfer and tennis champion (in Beverly Hills she played regularly with
tennis great Bill Tilden), was equally convincing
as Pat.

Pat and Mike was another bull's-eye for that

entity known as Tracy and Hepburn. But it was to be the last under Kate's MGM contract. Dore Schary was now officially head of MGM, and partially out of loyalty to Louis B. Mayer, she had no desire to continue under the new regime. Tracy too lacked confidence in the new management's instincts. His new contract called for him to make only one film a year at MGM, freeing Spencer up to accept offers from other studios.

Even before she left for the Belgian Congo to make *The African Queen*, Kate had decided to take on a fresh theatrical challenge—appearing on the London stage in the role of Epifania, Shaw's shrewish, overindulged heiress in *The Millionairess*. After hearing a speech by Lenin, the Irish playwright had written *The Millionairess* as an indictment of the superrich. "My mother worshiped Shaw," Kate said. "She knew everything he'd ever written. Backwards. So did my father." Her close friend Alice Palache (later Alice Palache Jones) confirmed this: "Mrs. Hepburn was a very forthright person. She'd tell you just what she thought about everything. She had very firm ideas about right and wrong, and Bernard Shaw was the greatest man alive." In fact *The Millionairess* was the next step in Kate's campaign to win her mother's posthumous blessing.

During the making of *Pat and Mike* Kate had done what she could to shore up Spencer's flagging self-esteem. He needed her approval, her care, her adulation in the presence of others, and he got it. But while she was willing to sit at his feet and cheerfully handle his black moods, Kate had no intention of canceling her trip to London. When she was not pouring his tea or combing his snow white hair, Kate was on the phone to London, going over plans with the director of *As You Like It*, Michael Benthall, who was to direct Hepburn in *The Millionairess*.

Tracy nagged, cajoled, threatened, and pleaded for Kate not to go. The implication was clear. He had barely survived their last prolonged separation. Between the mood swings and the alcohol, there was no telling what might happen if she left again.

But Kate believed, as she had when she left to tour in *As You Like It*, that she had become part of the problem. She was his crutch, and he would stay off the booze permanently only if he made the decision to do so on his own. This, coupled with the fact that she felt she owed it to her mother to perform the Shaw play, gave her the courage to stick with her master plan. Besides, she would not be leaving Tracy entirely at loose ends. He was to begin *The Plymouth Adventure*, an epic Technicolor telling of the *Mayflower* saga.

In February 1952 Kate flew to New York to be coached by Constance Collier before continuing on to London. She left behind a furious Spencer Tracy. "As far as he was concerned," Mankiewicz said, "Kate's leaving him behind like that constituted an abandonment, a betrayal."

Tracy decided to act on the inclination he had shown toward Joan Fontaine in London. This time he followed through by starting an affair with his stunning *Plymouth Adventure* leading lady, thirty-one-year-old Gene Tierney.

By the time she starred in the classic 1944 whodunit *Laura*, Tierney had already divorced fashion designer Oleg Cassini and carried on a torrid affair with a young naval officer named John Fitzgerald Kennedy. She had given birth to a retarded daughter after a fan with German measles kissed her during her pregnancy, and the tragedy touched off a series of mental breakdowns.

Just before Tracy, Tierney had been carrying on an affair with rising star Kirk Douglas. But rather than let him ring the doorbell, she left her bedroom window open and insisted he climb through it. "She wasn't married, she wasn't living with anyone, but if that was the way she liked it it was fine with me. . . . Maybe it was an aphrodisiac."

Tierney broke off the affair with Douglas the minute he told her he was not interested in marriage. She had just started work on *The Plymouth Adventure* and within weeks told Douglas that she would be marrying Spencer Tracy. "This all happened so quickly," Douglas recalled. "I didn't believe it. She showed me a saccharine letter that he had written, telling her that he wanted to arrange things so that they could go off together."

"Gene, I don't believe it," Douglas told her. "First, Spencer's married. Second, he has a very intense relationship with Katharine Hepburn, and he'll never give it up."

Tierney ignored Douglas, just as she had ignored Oleg Cassini when he warned her that Jack Kennedy would never marry her either. But it troubled Douglas that Tracy would lead on a gullible, obviously troubled woman twenty-one years his junior. "I don't know what was in Spencer Tracy's head."

Throughout his affair with Tierney, Tracy continued his daily calls to Kate, now staying at the Connaught Hotel in London's Mayfair district. Not once, apparently, did he write her a letter or note. Kanin would claim that after more than thirty years of friendship he had in his possession precisely one letter written in Tracy's elegant hand. Next to the phone, Spencer's preferred method of communication continued to be the telegram—although even those were maddeningly few and far between.

Spencer burned up the phone lines when his son, John, working as an artist for Walt Disney Studios, made Tracy a grandfather for the first time in 1952. Spencer shared his joy over the course of several excited phone conversations with Kate. The perfectly healthy boy, who Spencer feared might be born hearing-impaired, was named Joseph Spencer Tracy.

For the most part Kate kept tabs on Spencer through Cukor. Although the two men lived only steps apart down a garden path, Tracy preferred to communicate with Cukor by calling him up at the main house. Days would go by without them actually seeing each other.

In their letters and cables Kate and Cukor never referred to Spencer by name. Instead they referred to him by a variety of code names: the Tenant, the Old Man in the Gully, the Squatter, to name a few.

Fairly typical was Cukor's April 2, 1952, letter to Kate, which contained words of encouragement for her impending opening in London and an intriguing postscript:

Dearest Kate,

This is "Just Before the Battle, Mother!" I'm leaving tomorrow for New York. A couple of days there, and then to England . . .

On Wednesday, April ninth, don't be surprised if there's a ring at your telephone. It will be me, full of all the latest news.

I hope all is going well with your rehearsal. I know that you are your usual agreeable, charming, cooperative self.

Love

P.S. My tenant, the old man who lives in the gully, gave a brilliant dinner party in my honor—at least he said—at Romanoff's the other night. I have just spoken to him. He has a cold, but seems very cheerful, is just as abusive as of old . . . my loving regards.

Kate needed all the words of comfort she could get. After a brief tour of the provinces prior to the London opening, she had been plagued by laryngitis. Then there were the more arduous physical demands of the part. Back in the summer of 1950, when the Theatre Guild's Lawrence Langner first approached Shaw directly with Kate's plan to do *The Millionairess*, the ninety-three-year-old literary giant asked Langner if Hepburn was an athlete, "as she would have to do jujitsu."

"Yes," Langner replied, "Kate is wonderfully strong and athletic."

"Then perhaps she better not play the part," Shaw replied. "It would be disastrous."

Langner, confused, asked why.

"Disastrous," Shaw explained, "for the actor she'll play with. She'll probably kill him."

Indeed, when *The Millionairess* opened on June 26, 1952, at London's New Theatre, Kate, clad in a jewel-encrusted organdy ball gown by Pierre Balmain, was called upon to throw her six-foot-two-inch tall leading man, Cyril Ritchard, to the floor, destroy an antique chair, sprint up and down a staircase, and bound about the stage in a panicked state while variously denouncing men, threatening to kill herself, and loudly proclaiming the virtues of excess. Ritchard (who would become best known to American audiences in the 1950s as Captain Hook in *Peter Pan*) complained that he was bruised even before the play opened; Kate's passion for authenticity extended to battering him during rehearsals. (In the play's other major role, that of an Egyptian doc-

tor who falls in love with Epifania, Robert Helpmann emerged unscathed.)

It was all pure, manic Hepburn of *The Warrior's Husband* variety, and British audiences and
critics alike adored it. The *Daily Telegraph* compared Kate to "a tornado. The vitality comes
bursting out of her, driving her hither and thither
across the stage." Kenneth Tynan of the *Observer*
crowned her "Katharine the Great" and compared her to a branding iron, a fire—and Adolf
Hitler. The *Manchester Guardian* declared that
"her eruptions were always a great pleasure to
watch," and the *Sunday Times* pronounced her
"staggering. . . . to inhabitants of the tropics, to
people, that is, who are used to having their
homes swallowed by earthquakes and ripped up
by hurricanes, Miss Hepburn must seem a very
naturalistic actress."

For the Americans in the audience, including
Langner, Kate's antics were disturbingly over the
top. The day after the opening Langner wrote to
Theresa Helburn: "Dear Terry, *The Millionairess*:
Saw this last night, and found Kate was too high
in the first act. However, everybody has told her
so, and we hope she will be down tonight. It was
a very swanky audience, and she had an ovation
at the end. She would, I know, like to bring the
entire company over."

Kate's colleagues, notably Cukor and Constance Collier, did think her performance was
perhaps a bit too shrill. Certainly they were concerned that if she kept up the frenzied pace, she

would simply exhaust herself. If nothing else, there was the matter of her voice. In order to conserve her vocal cords, she now spoke sparingly and refused to take phone calls altogether.

There were other, unseen stresses. For the first time Kate learned of Spencer's infidelity firsthand. Arriving in London to shoot scenes for *The Plymouth Adventure*, Spencer checked into Claridge's. Gene Tierney meanwhile rented a flat with her mother on Grosvenor Square, just below the Connaught. Tracy juggled clandestine meetings with both Kate and Tierney, frantic that Kate would find out. Whenever he met Tierney for dinner in the dining room of Claridge's, the young actress later said, "he kept watching the door in case Katharine Hepburn walked in."

Spencer breathed an audible sigh of relief whenever Tierney's mother tagged along. Belle Lavinia Tierney had just returned to her Christian Science beliefs and "could talk about them in an almost mystical way," recalled Gene. Belle and Tracy had long talks about religion. "My mother," Gene said, "thought he was the most tormented man she had ever met."

He may have been unnerved at the prospect of being caught by Kate, but he did little to conceal his affair. Before long, Kate heard about Spencer's cozy dinners with Tierney. She chose, wisely, to ignore the evidence. Eventually, he grew tired of Tierney, and the assignations stopped.

Still, he kept pressuring Kate to give up *The*

Millionairess and return with him to California. After Tierney and the rest of *The Plymouth Adventure* cast and crew broke camp and returned to the United States, Tracy remained behind with Kate.

Midway through the London run Kate fell ill with the flu and was running a fever of 103 degrees. The laryngitis returned. But she soldiered on. The only concession to her failing health was that she would no longer have to play matinees.

Offstage much of Kate's time was spent fending off the very fans who flocked to see her. Kate still adamantly refused to sign autographs. When pressed to the wall, she would sign an autograph book several times and then rip out the pages; if someone thrust a photograph in her face to sign, she would scrawl her name across the front, intentionally ruining it. Signing a book and then slamming it shut, smudging the autograph, was another favorite trick. On her way to play tennis at Wimbledon one Saturday morning she barked at an autograph seeker before clobbering him with her tennis racket.

"One of the fans turned nasty and was going to hit her," recalled someone who had waited outside the theater just to catch a glimpse of Kate. "Tracy intervened, and for a moment it looked as though he were going to smash the fan. The fan fled. Hepburn was totally uncooperative."

When he wasn't standing shoulder to shoulder with Kate against the adoring multitudes, Tracy was pressuring her to return with him to California once her twelve-week run in London was over. But Kate had a hit on her hands—in fact the biggest hit of the London season—and she was determined to follow through with plans to bring it to Broadway.

She seemed to understand why her performance in *The Millionairess*, so worthy of the Marx Brothers, was so well received in London. "American vitality," she told *Time* magazine, "has a great appeal for the British. You can see that in the popularity in England of Judy Garland, Danny Kaye and others. But back home, vitality is not so bloody unique."

After her final London performance Kate emerged from the stage door and waded through the crowd toward her waiting limousine. "Drive on," she shouted to the chauffeur as the crowds pressed in on the car. "We'll sweep up the blood later!"

The next day, September 21, 1952, Kate left for New York. Fed up with Kate's obstinacy, Tracy had cut short his stay in London—his original plan had been to return with Kate—and headed straight for Los Angeles.

Physically and emotionally drained, Kate took a few weeks to rest up at Fenwick before plunging into rehearsals for the New York opening. Just as she had observed to *Time*'s interviewer, critics back home did not find her vitality "so bloody unique" when the play opened on October 17, 1952, at the Schubert Theater. The *New*

York Herald Tribune's Walter Kerr wrote: "Katharine Hepburn is beautiful, radiant, vital and not very good. At times, she sounds like an alarm clock that no one can shut off." *The New York Times*' Brooke Atkinson praised her for having "doubtless more endurance than any actress alive" but concluded that "*The Millionairess* is not worth all the energy she is squandering on it."

Audiences could not have cared less. Kate, getting by on sheer adrenaline, played to standing-room-only crowds for two and a half months. When it was over, she vowed to press ahead with plans to film *The Millionairess* with Preston Sturges as director and Alec Guinness as her co-star.

Meantime Hepburn, her voice almost gone and her famous reservoirs of energy drained by the back-to-back strains of *The African Queen, Pat and Mike*, and *The Millionairess*, was in serious trouble. Pushed to the brink of nervous collapse, Kate finally felt—allowed herself to feel—the delayed impact of her mother's death. Moreover, she worried about Tracy's affair with Tierney and what it meant for the future of her relationship with Spencer.

In January 1953 Kate was briefly admitted to Columbia-Presbyterian Hospital suffering from exhaustion. Her real salvation, however, was Fenwick. Now she had the time to do nothing but stroll the shore, split wood for the fire ("It's terribly therapeutic, gives you lots of time to think—and I'm damn good at it"), and swim in the icy water of Long Island Sound while her brother Dick, who lived at the compound year-round, looked on and shuddered. "They all think I've taken it a little far," she said of her wintry plunges, which she continued well into her eighties. "My father taught me: The bitterer the medicine, the better it is for you."

It was now time, Kate decided, to return to California. On January 9 Kate wrote Cukor telling him she was about to head west. She had wanted to stay at Irene Selznick's, but Betty Hutton was Selznick's tenant and had been slow in leaving. So she asked Cukor if she could move in with him for a time, knowing full well that Spencer, with his rigid sense of discretion, would not approve of her moving into the guest cottage.

Dear George,

As your squatter may have told you there is a good chance that I will be in California. . . . I still think there is a possibility that Irene may get rid of Betty Hutton. . . . If not I hope that you are still in the mood to receive your poor poverty stricken unemployed friend for about ten days. If you have changed your mind I know you will not hesitate to let me know for otherwise you may be stuck with me. . . . It does seem dreadful to land on you but I could really just use the bedroom and go down the hill [to Tracy's cottage] to meals so it may not be too bad—It is thrilling to be idle.

Cukor replied with a telegram four days later:

> DEAREST KATE THE PENSION CUKOR IS ON THE
> AMERICAN PLAN THREE WHOLESOME MEALS
> AVAILABLE DAILY COMFORTABLE CLEAN ROOM
> WITH SEPARATE ENTRANCE BEING HELD FOR
> YOU PLEASE LET US KNOW DATE OF ARRIVAL.
> THINK YOU WOULD LIKE OUR HOMEY ATMO-
> SPHERE.
>
> GEORGE CUKOR
> PROPRIETOR

In a final tribute to her mother and her parents' values, Kate poured her energy, her ingenuity, and her money into making *The Millionairess* into a film. Unable to convince a studio even to buy the property, she used her own funds to acquire it from Gabriel Pascal, executor of Shaw's estate for film rights. They she invited Preston Sturges to move into the Turtle Bay town house so they could collaborate on the shooting script. After months of arduous work they emerged with what everyone agreed was a brilliant script.

But even with a proven stage hit, Kate as the star, a polished script, and Preston Sturges as director—not to mention the genius of Shaw—not a single studio was the least bit interested. Even when she agreed to do it on a minuscule budget, work for free, and pay Sturges out of her own pocket, the answer was still no.

After more than a year of trying, Kate finally surrendered. "I'm licked," she told the Kanins as they sat around the fire in her Turtle Bay living room. "It's gone on too long. . . . I don't think I could bear one more—" (A later film version of *The Millionairess* starring Sophia Loren and Peter Sellers turned out to be a colossally expensive failure.)

Over roughly the same period, Spencer suffered a similar series of mortifying rejections. Garson Kanin had proposed a film biography of Benjamin Franklin to Tracy, and Spencer, a Franklin buff who quoted often from *Poor Richard's Almanack*, was eager to do the part. But after more than eighteen months of trying to get the project off the ground, it died.

In the wake of *The Plymouth Adventure*'s disappointing receipts, Tracy had tried and failed to get MGM to buy film rights to *The Mountain*, Henri Troyat's novel about an old mountain guide who heroically leads a rescue party to stranded plane crash victims. The film, Dore Schary decided, would be just too costly to make.

Tracy spent the early months of 1953 working on the movie adaptation of Ruth Gordon's autobiographical stage hit *Years Ago*, retitled *The Actress* for the screen. The movie was again directed by Cukor, with newcomer Jean Simmons in the Ruth Gordon role. Spencer portrayed Simmons's father, a former seafarer now stuck in a dead-end job.

"He's a sort of sorcerer," Simmons said. "When we met, he was pleasant and professional; later a bit flirtatious, but that was to be expected—it was his habit, I gather. Then we began to shoot. All at once he looked at me, and he wasn't the star—he was the father. *My* father. And I wasn't me—I was his daughter. And it would happen again and again—startling, really. One never quite got used to it. To him."

Kate knew the feeling. She spent a good deal of 1953 in New York working on her ultimately ill-fated *Millionairess* film project, visiting Los Angeles only sporadically. But in August Kate and Spencer accepted an invitation by Garson Kanin and Ruth Gordon to spend some time with them at Les Rochers, the Kanins' villa at St.-Jean-Cap-Ferrat in the south of France. Kate sent Spencer ahead on the USS *Constitution*, with the excuse that she had some work do on *The Millionairess* project. In truth, she was having several skin cancers—the result of her exposure to the subequatorial African sun—surgically removed at Hartford Hospital, and did not want to upset Tracy.

But after a week at Les Rochers, Spencer does find out—and, in Kanin's words, "goes to pieces" when a general strike prevents him from contacting Kate by phone. Eventually he managed to get a call through and relaxed when Kate told him she was fine. The strain, meanwhile, had been enough to cause an angry-looking rash to break out around Tracy's midsection—a painful case of shingles.

Tracy flew to London the next day and was joined by Kate not long after. At forty-seven Kate felt stronger and healthier than she had in years.

Tracy was another matter. Flirting may have been his "habit," as Jean Simmons suggested, but it belied a more serious problem. In the early 1950s he was stricken with a new and, if not life-threatening, at least psychologically devastating malady. In addition to his heart condition, his kidney, liver, and digestive problems, his breathing difficulties, and his chronic insomnia, Tracy now had a wholly unfamiliar complaint—the kind of disorder that magnified his already overwhelming self-doubt.

Spencer Tracy, the love of Katharine Hepburn's life, was impotent.

*There was something exceptionally sweet about it.
Though they were extremely sophisticated people, he
was like a little boy with her and she was like a little
girl with him.*

—GEORGE CUKOR

*People are shocked that I gave up so much for a man.
But you have to understand it gave me pleasure to
make him happy, to ease his agony.*

—KATE

Eight

Kate believed in confronting life's challenges, and the issue of Spencer's impotence was no exception. And as the daughter of both a noted urologist and a birth control expert Kate had never been squeamish when it came to medical matters— particularly when the subject was plumbing, male or female.

As always on such matters, Kate first consulted her father, getting the names of the foremost experts in New York, Boston, and Los Angeles. She then took an active role in Spencer's treatment—accompanying him on visits to the doctor, quizzing the experts on the physical and/ or psychological causes of his impotence, which medications to take, when and under what circumstance they might resume their sexual relationship, and so on. In Boston he underwent surgery for a related "plumbing" problem.

There was no question that the long separations had been taking their toll on Spencer. He was simply miserable when she was not around. "We'd invite him to our place," Gene Kelly said, "and he'd come and sit quietly and sip his Coke. He'd chat amiably enough, and after about two hours he'd leave. He sure was a sad, lonely guy when Katie wasn't there."

To be sure, with the exception of his infrequent benders, Tracy led a Spartan existence in Kate's absence. "The bedroom of his little house was almost like a monk's cell when Spencer lived there," Cukor recalled. "It had an oak chest, a bed, and that's all. It had the air of a place where a man might do penance."

By contrast, Kate gloried in the creature comforts. "I like nothing better than to buy a house and then fill it with all the things I cherish," Kate told Spencer one day. "Buy all those silly wonderful things that make a house a heartwarming experience to return to."

"Not me," Tracy replied. "I don't want to own anything that I can't pack into the baggage car of a train to Chicago."

Yet, with Cukor's quiet complicity, Kate made the rest of the cottage as cozy and inviting as Tracy's bedroom was austere. The wood floor in the living room was covered by a striking white-bordered red wool rug that Cukor—at considerable trouble and expense—had made especially for Tracy in Spain. A life-size carved Canada goose with its wings spread—a gift from Kate—swung from the rafters. Most of the paintings were gifts from Kate. A large, moody Vlaminck in hues of black, blue, and gray ("It reminds me of you," Kanin told Tracy) dominated one wall. Another painting, a large study of the lighthouse near Fenwick that Hepburn had painted herself, hung above Spencer's wooden desk on a wall of exposed red brick. Sunshine poured through a skylight onto the desk, where Kate often perched, her sandal-clad feet propped comfortably on a low-backed wooden captain's chair.

Tracy, like Hepburn, had artistic ambitions. "Spencer tried to paint, but it's a very curious thing," Kate observed. "He'd paint a mountain without a single thing on it or a lake without any boats or anything. Never any people. Very simple, stark, lonely pictures. Single-minded. In the end he decided he was just lousy at it, but those pictures said a lot about him."

Although they never ventured out together as a couple in their own country—in Europe they felt somewhat more free to be seen in each other's company—Kate and Spence still reveled in their time together. "It was fun watching them wandering around my property hand in hand," Cukor said, "looking at the flowers and then sitting down in the sun to read or to listen to a Brahms concerto or a symphony on their portable record player."

Tracy had not stopped needling her, but now Kate, at least in the company of Cukor and the Kanins, sometimes gave as good as she got. At this time only a fortunate few—the Kanins, the

Erskines, Carroll Tracy, Laura Harding, Cukor, of course, and their longtime agent, Abe Lastfogel of the William Morris Agency—were allowed into the inner sanctum on anything approaching a regular basis. They brought with them the bits of news and gossip that Hepburn and Tracy both devoured gleefully.

Their fabled repartee followed a discernible pattern. Spencer more or less held court, sitting in silence while Kate chattered on in the nonstop style of many of her screen characters. He simply watched with a bemused expression on his face as Kate alternately interrogated, contradicted, criticized, prodded, and praised their guests.

Tracy would raise an eyebrow, shift his weight in his seat, but say nothing. Then, in the time-honored manner of all Tracy-Hepburn films, he would calmly utter the few well-chosen words that put Kate in her place. "For God's sake, Kath," went a typical refrain, "will you let the man *finish*?"

"Well, I wasn't a *sap*. I didn't just sit there in silence," Kate recalled. "That really wouldn't be *me*, would it? We had plenty of arguments. That goes with the territory when two reasonably intelligent, stubborn people care about each other. I mean, if you can't express yourself freely around the people you love, well, then, you might as well forget it. My parents taught me that."

"They could bicker and argue and say dreadful things to one another," Cukor said. "But they always came out of it laughing and hugging, like teenagers."

Still, there were the times when Tracy succumbed to his darker impulses. Now completely attuned to his moods, Kate was taking more decisive action when he had one drink too many and looked as if he might tear off on a full-fledged bender. When he was starting to get "loaded" and she saw the storm clouds brewing, Kate, according to Cukor, coaxed him into bed. Once Tracy dozed off, Hepburn tied him to the bedposts and waited for his black mood to pass.

Holding to her belief that "work doesn't hurt anyone—only the lack of it does," Kate urged Spencer to take the role of the cattle baron Matt Devereux in *Broken Lance*. That left her free to spend even more time working with Preston Sturges on *The Millionairess* in New York. As always, she relied on daily calls from Spence and regular reports from her resident spy, George Cukor.

On the second day of shooting *A Star Is Born* with Judy Garland, Cukor took the time to dictate a note to gossip-loving Kate. In it he wrote: "I have not yet glimpsed my distinguished tenant but I have hour-long telephone conversations with him daily. He sure is full of news and seems to me pretty chipper. He *may*—mind you, he's a slippery customer—dine with me this Saturday, at least I'm in hopes—"

In February 1954 Kate was in London, now trying to coax *British* producers into make *The*

Millionairess. At the Connaught she received a letter from Cukor, still hard at work on *A Star Is Born*, updating her on all the gossip:

> [F]or the past few weeks we've been doing the big sad scenes. James Mason plays them most sensitively and movingly, and Judy is a revelation in her emotional scenes. She manages to get the same thrilling quality in them that she does when she's singing a song—at her best. She makes them heart-rending, real and electrifying.
>
> I managed to snag my elusive tenant for dinner one night a few weeks ago. We had a very pleasant time. He left at 9 o'clock, out of consideration, he said, for me because I was so tired and had to get up so early the next day. He didn't fool me for a minute, he was just trying to get the hell out. It's such a pity that he's spent so little time in his house, and yet he keeps on saying how much he loves it and misses it. I've taken up the cook question with him and when he gets back I'll see to it that he gets one. From my brief glimpse of him, I thought he looked very well indeed, and seemed to be in good spirits.

Three weeks later Cukor wrote to say that he had finished *A Star Is Born*:

> Up until the last few weeks everything went quite well. . . . After that, I'm afraid that Judy slipped right back into her Metro pattern—ill-

ness, lateness—all very mysterious and disquieting. . . .

My elusive tenant turns up at his little home from time to time, unexpected and unannounced. Before I know it, he's gone again, so I have not been able to talk to him to get news of you. I hope all is progressing satisfactorily and smoothly for you.

On March 2, 1954, Kate replied from London: "Oh dear! Isn't it sad that Judy couldn't keep up the pace. . . . What an agony for her, to say nothing of you but, at least, she is unique. . . ." Kate went on to praise the work of two "brilliant" young talents—Jack Lemmon and Richard Burton—but was less impressed with another:

Claire Bloom has, somehow, not quite jelled this season. I'm afraid that she is not very interesting. . . .

Guess our neighbor [Tracy] is thoroughly occupied in Arizona and I hope he will be here in May.

PS—Are you coming here—Spence said so—It snowed last night.

His *Broken Lance* shoot in Arizona notwithstanding, Kate was clearly concerned about Spencer's disappearing act. Then, on March 22, Cukor wrote:

I had quite a talk on the telephone with the St. Ives Roy Rogers [Tracy] the day he returned from location. He seemed fine, and they'd had ecstatic notes from [Fox chief Darryl] Zanuck about their rushes—but he also observed, very wisely—that Zanuck was always enthusiastic about all his projects. I haven't set eyes on him [Tracy] but hope to soon. He tells me that he's booked air passage early in May. . . . I suggested we go to Seville for the Feria. After a few days of playing the castanets and shaking our tambourines, we could proceed to England. He fell in with my plans very readily but, as you know, there's many a slip with that gentleman.

By now Tracy had to some degree—although by no means completely—overcome his fear of flying, and he and Kate took full advantage of the freedom that came from traveling abroad. Although they traveled throughout Europe, they felt most at home in London and in Paris, where they freely strolled the boulevards and side streets, dined at the homes of friends, and haunted the galleries and museums. Tracy blushed when Kanin recalled the sight of Spencer staring at the Louvre's Venus de Milo while everyone stared at *him*.

Tracy was so enamored of London and Paris, in fact, that he turned down many invitations from even close friends to visit other European capitals. When Cukor begged Tracy to join him in Rome, Spencer could not resist the opportunity to tweak him. JUST SENT RENT, he cabled Cukor, SO CANNOT AFFORD ITALY HOPE YOU ARE ENJOYING YOUR WEALTH LOVE SPENCE.

Yet even abroad Tracy was concerned that someone might blow the whistle on his affair with the famous Katharine Hepburn. And while there was a gentleman's agreement of sorts with the American press, there was no way of knowing what the foreign press—Fleet Street in particular—might do.

There was one heart-stopping moment in June 1954 when the management of Claridge's asked to speak to Tracy about a "sensitive" matter—Miss Hepburn, to be precise. Kate, as usual, was staying at the Connaught and visited Spence daily at his suite at Claridge's. Convinced that the management was going to object to his carrying on an illicit affair in its fine establishment, Tracy was ready to explode when he was informed that Kate was merely breaking the dress code. Would it be possible, the trembling assistant manager inquired, for Mr. Tracy to ask her to wear a dress when walking through the lobby?

"Good *God!*" Kate replied when Kanin told her the story. "I've never *heard* of anything so *idiotic!*" Hepburn did not own a dress and was not about to buy one. Her solution: From that day on she rode up to Spencer's suite in the freight elevator, making fast friends of the maids, hall porters, and various service personnel. "They may not love me in the front of this hotel," she said, "but they *adore* me backstairs."

The management was satisfied, and Spencer was relieved; he had long considered the hotel a second home. "When I die," he told Kanin, "I don't want to go to heaven. I want to go to Claridge's!"

For all their physical problems and professional disappointments, that summer of 1954 turned out to be one of the most fruitful in years. First Spencer headed back to California to work on a movie for Dore Schary and director John Sturges. Filmed on the Metro lot and in Lone Pine, a godforsaken desert town on the edge of California's Death Valley, *Bad Day at Black Rock* told the story of a one-armed veteran (Tracy) who journeys to remote Black Rock in 1945 to present a posthumous medal to a Japanese-American farmer whose son has been killed in the war. Eventually Tracy's character discovers that the townspeople have murdered the Japanese-American and burned out his farm. Tracy, one good arm or no, brings the killers to justice.

In the weeks before shooting began, Tracy was his usual enthusiastic self, repeatedly praising the script, his director and the supporting cast (which included Robert Ryan, Ernest Borgnine, Walter Brennan, and Lee Marvin). And true to form, as the start date drew closer, he suddenly changed his mind and tried to back out of the picture. Dore Schary, less and less willing to pamper temperamental stars, vowed to sue him if he did.

It was all part of the elaborate dance the chronically indecisive, self-doubting Tracy did before nearly every film project. He often counted on producers like Schary to stand their ground, in essence making his decision whether or not to proceed for him.

Tracy was lucky that Schary stood his ground. A taut melodrama that would stand the test of time, *Bad Day at Black Rock* offered Tracy one of his most challenging roles. *Bad Day at Black Rock*, wrote John O'Hara in *Collier's* when it was released in January 1955, "is simply one of the finest motion pictures ever made." Comparing the movie to a recent film with a similar moral, *High Noon*, critic Robert Hatch wrote in the *Nation* that Tracy "offers a more complex, contradictory, witty, and therefore more interesting impersonation than did Gary Cooper." *Bad Day at Black Rock* would earn Tracy his fifth Academy Award nomination. (Ironically, he would lose to a long shot: *Black Rock's* own Borgnine, in *Marty*. After the Oscars Borgnine visited Tracy's trailer on the MGM lot. Tracy berated him, demanding to know why he had not acknowledged the congratulatory telegram Spencer had sent. Kate popped her head out from the back of the trailer and interrupted. "*He* won the Oscar—not you, dummy.")

While he was working on *Bad Day at Black Rock*, Kate was filming a classic of her own in

Venice: David Lean's *Summertime*, based on the Broadway hit *The Time of the Cuckoo* by Arthur Laurents. In *Summertime* Kate played Jane Hudson, a lonely spinster who goes to Venice, falls in love with a handsome antiques dealer (played by Rossano Brazzi), but in the end decides their differences cannot be surmounted and returns home alone.

In some ways making *Summertime* was more arduous for Kate than filming *The African Queen* had been. Although the cinematic Venice had a shimmering, dreamlike quality, Hepburn suffered from the oppressive heat and humidity. Where Spencer sipped iced tea in his trailer on the *Bad Day at Black Rock* set and emerged for only a few moments to do his single take, Kate stood in the blazing sun for hours, blinded by the rays that bounced off the canals. Overcome by the stench from the stagnant water, she suffered a recurrence of the dysentery she had acquired in the Congo.

At times the technical problems seemed insurmountable. In addition to Lean's relentless, time-consuming perfectionism—maddening even by Kate's standards—there were the happily inefficient Italian crew members, a customs strike that prevented the rushes from being sent to London for processing, and even a threatened strike by gondoliers who feared the filmmaker's presence would disrupt tourism and cost them jobs.

Then there were the fans. Hepburn was far and away the biggest star ever to make a feature film in Venice. Locals and tourists alike crowded around, pestering her for autographs (which she brushed off, as always) and ruining key shots.

Nevertheless, Kate tried to make the most of her stay in Venice. With Constance Collier and Phyllis Wilbourn to keep her company, she moved into a house opposite the Gritti Palace that boasted a butler, a cook, a maid, and a private gondola. But halfway through filming, Collier became ill and departed with Wilbourn.

Without her companions Kate grew as isolated and quietly desperate as the character she was portraying. Assuming that she had plenty of "madly exciting things to do," none of Hepburn's colleagues socialized with her. "I felt very angry about that," she reflected. "I wandered off by myself through Venice, feeling very lonely and neglected and sat down by a canal and looked in the water—and while I was sitting like that a man came over to me and said, 'May I come and talk to you?' Only it wasn't Rossano Brazzi; it was a French plumber. But I was glad to talk to anyone who looked reasonably all right, so we went out together for a walk through Venice."

There were other reasons for the melancholic feelings that now enveloped Kate. Word had reached Venice via the Hollywood grapevine that Spencer Tracy was cheating on Kate with the woman who was set to star with him in his next film, tentatively called *Jeremy Rodock*. Her name was Grace Kelly.

Kelly had just won an Academy Award for *The Country Girl* at twenty-five, and her impressive list of screen credits already included *High Noon* and Alfred Hitchcock's *Dial M for Murder* and *Rear Window*. She was also an inveterate pursuer of leading men, most of them married. Among them: Clark Gable, Gary Cooper, Ray Milland, William Holden, and Bing Crosby.

When asked by MGM's publicity department to talk to reporters about the making of *Bad Day at Black Rock*, Tracy promised to only if they would set him up with Grace Kelly. As he had with Fontaine and Gene Tierney, Spencer pursued Kelly in Kate's absence—perhaps now driven by the need to prove his manhood following his bout with impotence. Kelly, who was drawn to older men, could hardly resist the one figure in Hollywood acknowledged by all to be the greatest actor ever to step before a camera.

According to Joseph Mankiewicz, "Grace Kelly was bowled over at the thought of just *meeting* Spence. No matter how big a star was, he or she always approached Spence with a sense of awe. You know, they called him 'The Pope.' So the idea that he was interested in someone romantically, well, it was tremendously flattering to that person. Grace Kelly was no exception." The affair with Kelly, he said, was "brief. Spencer *loved* one woman and only one woman: Kate Hepburn."

When a photograph of Tracy dining with Kelly ran in the newspapers, he became frantic. As soon as he could, he joined Kate in Venice to reassure her that news of an affair with the comely Miss Kelly was "nonsense." For Kate the whole situation seemed more than vaguely reminiscent of Spencer's infatuation with the young and "innocent" Ingrid Bergman. Still, she was grateful to have his company for at least a few days and accepted his explanation. "What am I supposed to say when this comes up?" she asked a friend. "I mean, he was married to *someone else*. Besides, we never owned each other. If a person wants to stray, there isn't a hell of a lot you can do about it. Is there?"

While still in Venice, Kate picked up an unwanted souvenir. In one scene she was to step backward while taking a photograph of Rossano Brazzi's antiques shop, lose her footing, and fall backward into a canal. "Oh, I knew it was a cesspool, a *sewer*, so I took every precaution I could think of," she recalled. "I had a special sort of antiseptic dressing to protect my hair, covered every exposed area with Vaseline, even gargled with a disinfectant in case I swallowed some water. But I forgot one thing: my *eyes*. You see it in the film: I fall back with my hands up in the air, mouth and eyes *wide open*. Well, immediately my eyes started watering. I got an eye infection from that filthy water—conjunctivitis—and I'll never get rid of it. Dumb, dumb, dumb."

There was at least one beneficial side effect. "After *Summertime* it was never a problem for me to cry on cue," Kate said. "In fact you'll notice that after *Summertime* I seemed to be crying all the time. So intense, so moving. It may look like brilliant acting, but it's just my damn ghastly eye infection!"

In *Summertime* Kate delivered a heartrending, poignant performance reminiscent of her work in *Alice Adams*. The same year Spencer was nominated for *Bad Day at Black Rock*, *Summertime* earned Kate a sixth Best Actress nomination.

On her way home to the United States Kate stopped in London to pay a visit to her *Millionairess* colleagues Michael Benthall and Robert Helpmann. They were firming up plans to tour Australia for the Old Vic, performing three Shakespearean plays: *The Merchant of Venice*, *Measure for Measure*, and *The Taming of the Shrew*. Would she like to join them? they dared ask.

After her experience in *As You Like It*, Kate was convinced that the classics offered the one true test of an actor's worth. "I still wondered, could I only play myself?" she asked. Kate viewed the prospect of tackling the Bard again as "terrifying. These are works that have been performed by the greatest actors and have stood the test of time," she added. "The material itself is not in question, but is the actor up to it?"

It was an all-too-familiar situation. As he had so many times before, Spencer pressured Kate not to leave him. Over the past five years they had spent perhaps six months together. It was time, he insisted, that she return to Beverly Hills.

She was his bulwark against the stresses of life that he found so unbearable.

Constance Collier, Kate's surrogate mother, pushed Kate to accept the Old Vic offer. There was no nobility, she argued, in sacrificing herself for a man. As long as Kate was there to take his verbal abuse, soothe his brow, and even tie him to his bed, he would never take full responsibility for his own behavior.

After Collier died in April 1955 at the age of seventy-seven, Kate felt the same twinge of obligation to her craft that she had when her mother passed away. Over Tracy's objections, she boarded a flight for Sydney on May 5, 1955. She told Spencer she would not be returning until the middle of September.

Tracy felt as if he had been abandoned by the only person who could protect him from himself. He returned to the bottle with a vengeance. A month after Kate's departure he was to start filming *Jeremy Rodock*; only now the film had a new title, *Tribute to a Bad Man*, and a new leading lady. Out of embarrassment over the stir caused by her fling with Tracy, Grace Kelly had bowed out and was replaced by rising Greek star Irene Papas. Tracy, once again brooding, seemed alarmed to learn before she arrived that Papas was taller than he was. She stood a full five feet ten inches in her stockinged feet.

Prior to Kate's departure and at her insistence, he had gone to the doctor to have a small growth removed from his face. It had turned out to be a benign cyst, but given Kate's own experience with skin cancer (the tiny surgical scars were still visible on her face), the hypochondriacal Spencer became obsessed with the tiny scar on his cheek.

Director Robert Wise, who would go on to win Academy Awards for *West Side Story* and *The Sound of Music*, was not concerned at first about Tracy's tendency to brood and to vacillate at the last minute; Wise had been warned. Even when Spencer showed up on the Montrose, Colorado, set five days late, the trunk of his black Thunderbird crammed with his beloved murder mysteries, Wise was not concerned.

But it did not end there. Before shooting a single scene, Spencer vanished—this time for eight days. MGM publicity chief Howard Strickling called Kate in Australia. Did she know where he was? Kate did know—Spencer was calling her two or three times a day, sometimes drunk, always doubt-ridden—but it was up to him to come out of hiding. Given her energy-sapping schedule in Australia, Kate hardly needed this distraction.

Finally, she managed to coax Tracy back to work. But when he did show up, he complained about the high altitude (Montrose's elevation was eight thousand feet), insisted on working only half days, and demanded that his meals be prepared especially for him at his hotel by the assistant director.

Wise had had enough. With Dore Schary's backing, Tracy was fired from the picture. Back in his motel room Tracy collapsed in tears. "It's the end of my career," he sobbed to Wise. "I'm finished. It's never happened to me before."

Tracy's firing from *Tribute to a Bad Man* marked a sad end to his twenty-year career at MGM. Yet Spencer was spared a public humiliation. News of his dismissal was kept out of the papers by the MGM publicity machine, which planted stories about his continuing involvement in the picture even while it searched for his replacement.

Fortunately for Spencer, all the moviegoing public knew was that he was still going strong on the heels of his Academy Award nomination for *Bad Day at Black Rock*. He got an added boost when he was named Best Actor at the Cannes Film Festival. And so many months had passed once Wise began shooting *Tribute* again with James Cagney in Tracy's role, no one in the press seemed to notice.

By the time she returned from her triumphant Australian tour, Kate was satisfied that as she had always suspected, she was indeed skilled at her profession. The tour, she said, "gave me a seal of approval as an actress. I needed that."

Secure in her talent, she turned her attention back to the care, protection, and nurturing of Spencer Tracy. Publicly Kate lauded his wisdom, strength, and moral courage. Privately she knew that he was confused, weak, and self-destructive. He could stray; that had been proved time and again. Beautiful, glamorous young women like

Gene Tierney and Grace Kelly could momentarily bolster his ego, but none of them would have put up with playing nursemaid.

Kate not only was willing to do the job but reveled in it. She promised Tracy that she would never leave him for such an extended period again. In the future she would not tour unless he could accompany her, and they would travel together whenever location shooting was required.

After her five-month absence Kate was alarmed to see how much Spencer had deteriorated physically. In addition to his drinking, Tracy's doctors were worried about the amount of weight he had gained and what seemed to be a complete lack of exercise. Kate took charge of his diet and made sure they resumed their healthy habit of taking long walks together.

When he tried to give up his pack-and-a-half-a-day smoking habit (usually at night, while reading murder mysteries), it was expected that she would also kick the habit. This was one concession to their relationship Kate was not willing to make. While he struggled with his nicotine addiction, Kate merrily puffed away on any one of a dozen brands. "I'm not choosy," she said. "I'll smoke anything but Camels."

Spencer Tracy had become such a full-time occupation that even Kate knew she could not handle the job alone. After Constance Collier's death, Kate hired Phyllis Wilbourn as her secretary-companion. An orphan, Phyllis had been totally dedicated to Collier. Her relationship with Kate became even more intense.

From 1955 on, the prim, painfully proper Phyllis would be a constant presence in the lives of Hepburn and Tracy. In keeping with his habit of mercilessly teasing those he loved most, Spencer delighted in mimicking Phyllis's upper-class British accent. For full effect he would wait until Phyllis was in mid-sentence before delivering his devastating impersonation. "Aeeeeoh! Miss Hepp-bunn," he'd gush as his victim turned beet-red, "how viddy viddy kind!"

"Mr. Tracy and I really got on very well," Phyllis recalled. "At first I must admit I was rather, well, bewildered. It did not strike me as funny, not in the least. But we understood each other, I suppose. Next to Miss Hepburn, I think I understood him as well as anyone possibly could. Which is to say not at all . . ."

In 1955 Paramount finally gave the green light to Spencer's pet project, *The Mountain*. This time Kate and Phyllis followed Tracy to the film's location in Chamonix, twelve thousand feet high in the French Alps. On the way there they stopped in London, where they spent an evening with Edward Dmytryk, *The Mountain*'s director. Dmytryk later recalled what happened when they went to Tracy's hotel suite after dinner. Spencer took off his jacket and, complaining of a pain in his neck, lay down on the couch. "Without saying a word, Kate gave him a very professional massage, then made him some coffee. It was absolutely amazing to me how she took such good care of him, because this woman, who could be so tough on everybody, was so tender and solicitous with him. He just sat there like the lord of the manor while she ministered to him."

In the months since Kate returned from Australia, Spencer had been on his best behavior. When she decided to leave him in Chamonix and return to Paris, she was reasonably confident that he was not about to backslide.

After the *Tribute to a Bad Man* debacle Tracy was careful not to complain about the altitude. He didn't have to. Reluctant to take any chances with his star, Dmytryk did not require Tracy to accompany Robert Wagner, who played Spencer's brother, to the top of Aiguille du Midi, one of the highest peaks in the Alps.

Nevertheless, when Tracy saw that Wagner, whom he had taken under his wing during the filming of *Broken Lance*, was reluctant to take the perilous tram ride to the top, he volunteered to go along. Halfway up, the enclosed car's wheels slipped off the cable, and they jolted to a stop. Hanging by a thread several hundred feet off the ground, the car began to swing back and forth so violently that the windshield shattered. Everyone on board, including Tracy, was convinced they were going to die.

Incredibly, a rescue team was able to get the car's wheels back on track, but the car could not return to the base camp. Instead Tracy, Wagner, and the rest had to proceed all the way to the summit before making the journey back down. Tracy, shaken, had to be held up as he staggered off to the car that was to take him to his hotel. "The whole thing was such a nightmare," Wagner told journalist Bill Davidson, "that I can't blame Spence for what he did that night."

What he did that night was set out to drink himself blind at the hotel bar. "Strangely, he was very talkative and friendly, actually charming," recalled makeup man Frank Westmore, who along with Wagner joined Spencer for a drink. Tracy told them "all sorts of fascinating Hollywood stories even as his head sagged lower and lower on his chest."

Tracy ordered another round, and as they talked, the waiter approached with a trayful of drinks. It was then, without warning and for no apparent reason, Tracy picked up his empty glass and threw it at the waiter's face. Wagner reached up and grabbed the glass before it found its target, shattering it and badly cutting his hand. As blood spurted from Wagner's wound, a barely conscious Tracy was restrained and carried to his room. When he awoke the next morning, he recalled nothing of the incident.

As soon as Kate learned of Spencer's violent outburst, she dispatched Phyllis to the scene. Spencer's brother, Carroll, arrived a few days later. There were no more problems until it was time to return home. Spencer got drunk at the farewell party and on the drive to the airport in Geneva began tossing empty beer bottles out the car window. He resumed drinking after takeoff. When he arrived in Los Angeles, the plane taxied to a closed-off area, where Louise and their daughter, Susie, were waiting to pick him up. Airline personnel carried him to their waiting car. Now that both Tracy children were grown, Louise had moved to a smaller house on a hillside in Beverly Hills, not far from Mary Pickford and Douglas Fairbanks's fabled Pickfair. Louise took Spencer to Cukor's house instead of hers.

With Kate out of town for a few days, Spencer was free to celebrate with Anna Kashfi, one of his fellow actors in *The Mountain*. Tracy and Kashfi, who later married Marlon Brando, hit several Los Angeles nightclubs over the next few nights before he vanished altogether. It was two more weeks before Spencer reappeared at his quiet cottage on the Cukor estate.

Once Kate returned to Los Angeles, she decided to raise a little hell of her own with her old pal Irene Selznick. After Selznick had sold her house in 1953, the two women made a habit of barging in on friends and asking to use their pools. "We'd swim our way across town, from one pool to another," Selznick recalled, "until we reached the surf at Malibu." They also sneaked inside Selznick's former house on Summit Drive—entering through an unlocked door near the pantry—"to see how it was faring. . . . We felt like Tom Sawyer and Huck Finn. For two people so passionate about privacy, this was a hell of a thing to do. We knew better, but somehow felt entitled. Justice was served, because we got caught red-handed—and by the owner no less. As we were inspecting the bedrooms, we heard a woman's voice, shrill and frightened, from below: 'Who's there? Who's there?' I turned to jelly.

"Kate, instantly mobilized, called out, 'We'll be right down. It's all right, I assure you.' She brushed past me down the stairs, all contrition and good manners, hand extended. 'My name is Katharine Hepburn,' as if it needed telling. . . . the trespassers were made welcome." Added Selznick, "Looking back, it seems to me that anything unconventional I ever did, I did with Kate."

Because the remainder of *The Mountain* was to be shot on the Paramount back lot, Kate gladly accepted the female lead in a Paramount film that would be shooting nearby. In *The Rainmaker*, she played another spinster—Lizzie Curry, the southwestern farmer's daughter who falls for a spellbinding con man (played by forty-two-year-old Burt Lancaster).

At first Kate disliked the self-absorbed, humorless Lancaster, then at the height of his fame. The first day of shooting the compulsively punctual Kate arrived on the set in makeup and costume precisely at nine-thirty. When Lancaster arrived twenty-five minutes late, she stood up before the entire company. "Mr. Lancaster," she declared, "we have all been here, but you have not been here. If this is to be your pattern for the rest of the production, kindly let us know and we shall *all* get here at nine fifty-five. Otherwise we expect you to be here on time."

Kate's main reason for begrudging Lancaster his tardiness was Spencer. She wanted to spend every spare moment with him. During the making of their respective films—*The Mountain* and *The Rainmaker*—on the Paramount lot, each strolled over to the other's set several times a day. Spencer was his crotchety old self but managed to stay off the bottle.

Once Kate finished up *The Rainmaker* in mid-December 1955, they flew to Connecticut to spend a tense Christmas with her family at Fenwick. Someone had sent a Tracy family Christmas card to the Hepburn house—the same one that went to scores of movie industry folk and supporters of the John Tracy Clinic. It was signed "Spencer and Louise Tracy."

Unlike *The Mountain*, a critical and commercial disaster, *The Rainmaker* struck the same poignant chord *Summertime* had. By getting her to tone down her Connecticut Yankee accent and soften her appearance, director Joseph Anthony somehow managed to transform Hepburn into a reasonable facsimile of a lonely farm girl. Kate was nominated for another Oscar but lost to her old nemesis Ingrid Bergman in *Anastasia*.

In January 1956 Kate and Spencer flew to London, where she fulfilled an earlier promise to Robert Helpmann to star opposite Bob Hope in *The Iron Petticoat*. Throughout the filming Tracy, unbeknownst to the press, holed up at Clar-

idge's. The *Ninotchka*-like plot concerned a female Soviet officer assigned to an American air
base in Germany. The movie was so bad that
writer Ben Hecht, who left after Hope's gag writers kept adding jokes to the script, asked to have
his name removed from the credits. Hepburn
clearly hated being Hope's straight man. Yet
even under these difficult circumstances, she
managed a convincing imitation of a Russian aviator—accent and all. Hope, on the other hand,
was lambasted for simply not being funny.

Captains Courageous would always be Kate's favorite Spencer Tracy film. So it was only logical
that, after reading Ernest Hemingway's 1952 no-
vella *The Old Man and the Sea*, she told Spencer
it would be a perfect vehicle for him. When
Kate's old flame Leland Hayward, now divorced
from Margaret Sullavan and married to Howard
Hawks's ex-wife Slim, offered Spencer the title
role in the Warner Brothers production, he
jumped at the opportunity.

Tracy had originally met with Hemingway to
discuss the project back in 1953, and they had
gotten along famously. But now in April 1956,
Spencer, experiencing his usual preflight jitters,
had to get bombed to get on the plane to Cuba.
When he arrived there with Kate, she hustled
him off to their fourteen-room rented villa to sober up.

There were few men in the world who had the
power to intimidate Spencer Tracy. Hemingway
was one of them. "Papa" was famous for his sa-

distic streak, and when he saw how "soft" Tracy had become since they had last met, he began needling the actor. He was also contemptuous of Tracy's glaringly obvious inability to hold his liquor.

"Have a drink!" Hemingway ordered Spencer.

"No, thanks."

"Go on, have a drink!" Papa pressed.

"I'd just as soon not."

Hemingway exploded. "What are you? A rummy? Can't you just have a drink or two? Do you have to go till you're insensible? Is that your problem?"

It was, of course, and Hemingway's hectoring only aggravated the situation—as did the director, Fred Zinnemann, with whom Tracy simply did not get along. Unable to stop him, Kate merely watched as Tracy, abetted by Hemingway, went on one of his biggest benders in years.

News of Tracy's erratic behavior filtered back to Hollywood, and Warner Brothers chief Jack Warner was livid. Ernest Borgnine and journalist James Bacon were playing golf at the Riviera Country Club when Borgnine was called away by his agent. He returned with the news that Tracy and Hemingway had destroyed a bar in Havana, and the studio had to pay the owner $150,000 in damages. Jack Warner was on the verge of firing Tracy and wanted to know if Borgnine was available for the part.

As it turned out, Tracy stayed but Zinnemann departed, replaced by John Sturges. Ultimately it was decided that nothing would be accomplished in Cuba. Everyone was sent back to California, where production was to resume on the Warner lot in August.

It was the opportunity Kate had been praying for. The three-month hiatus now gave them the chance to work together again. This time the property was *Desk Set*, based on a successful 1955 Broadway comedy about the dawn of the computer age and its impact (real and imagined) on the modern work force. Adapted for the screen by Phoebe and Henry Ephron, Twentieth Century-Fox's resident Ruth Gordon and Garson Kanin, *Desk Set* pitted Hepburn's Bunny Watson, the encyclopedic head of a television network's research department, against Tracy's Richard Sumner, the inventor of a wall-size computer that threatens to replace Bunny and her staff.

Everyone involved was warned that as he did with every one of his pictures, Spencer would show great enthusiasm for the project, then try to back out at the last minute. When he did it this time, Kate and the Ephrons and director Walter Lang sat down together and begged him not to withdraw. Ephron "glanced surreptitiously at Kate when Spencer said, 'Yes.' I saw a tear appear in her eye. She was, I think, a little disappointed. It's paradoxical, she needed him for the part, but she realized that he wasn't as strong as she thought, that he could be persuaded so easily. She loved him so goddamned dearly!"

It may have lacked the bite of their earlier comedies, but *Desk Set* contained several classic scenes—most notably a rooftop lunch scene during which Richard Sumner tries but fails to trip up the brainy Bunny Watson. To the fans who had been waiting for years to see them again, the scene had the undeniable ring of truth. "The woman is always pretty sharp," Kate said of the character she invariably seemed to play opposite Spencer. "She needles a man, a little like a mosquito. Then he slowly puts out his big paw and slaps the lady down, and the American public likes to see that. In the end he's always the boss of the situation, but he's challenged by her. That—in simple terms—is what we do."

There was no denying the parallel in their offscreen lives. "To most men," she conceded, "I'm a nuisance because I'm so busy I get to be a pest, but Spencer is so masculine that once in a while he rather smashes me down, and there's something nice about me when I'm smashed down."

As far as Kate was concerned, *Desk Set* was a godsend. Not only did it reunite them professionally, but since it was filmed in Los Angeles, it gave Spencer a chance to rest up before plunging back into *The Old Man and the Sea*.

They had another reason to stay close to home: Their beloved Humphrey Bogart had been fighting a losing battle against cancer of the esophagus, and they wanted to be close by. "Spence and Katie," Lauren Bacall said, "came to visit almost every night—about eight-thirty, after everyone else had gone. . . . He looked forward to their visits, and so did I.

"They behaved as they always had: Spence pulling up a chair at the foot of the bed, using our bench as a table for his coffee—Katie on the floor. Spence telling jokes—kidding around as he always did with Bogie. I don't know how he managed, but he did. Much later Katie told me that he was shattered before each visit and shattered after. While he was there, it was no different from the way we had all been in better days. I loved these people so much—they were both so solid, so complete, so unqualified. They helped me as much as they did Bogie."

On January 22, 1957, a Saturday, they stayed at Bogie's bedside for forty minutes or so. "It was their usual kind of visit, Bogie really enjoying them." But this time Bogie was clearly more tired, less focused.

Before he left, Spencer leaned over and patted his friend on the shoulder. "Good night, Bogie," he said.

"Bogie turned his eyes to Spence very quietly," Kate recalled, "and with a sweet smile covered Spence's hand with his own and said, 'Good-bye, Spence.' Spencer's heart stood still. He understood."

As they got into Tracy's black Thunderbird, Spencer said to Kate, "Bogie's going to die."

The next day he did. Bogart was fifty-seven. The obvious choice for the eulogy was Tracy, but he was too broken up. He phoned Bacall and pleaded, "I couldn't deliver the eulogy—I just couldn't—I wouldn't be able to get through it. I loved old Bogie. I could do it for someone I wasn't that emotional about, but not for dear Bogie. Please understand, darling."

"Of course I understood," Bacall said. "Darling Spence—he was too close—he cared too much."

More than three thousand people lined the streets outside the church where Bogart's funeral was held. Kate, wearing a dress, arrived before anyone else to avoid the press. When she saw on the altar a model of Bogie's sailboat, *Santana*, she broke down weeping.

In the wake of hard-living Bogie's untimely death, Spencer was a wreck. To compound his misery, his son, John, who had worked so hard to overcome his disability, was now in the midst of a bitter divorce. Accustomed to being shielded from the press by a studio, Spencer was upset when Nadine Tracy's testimony against her husband wound up in the newspaper. "John repulsed me after the birth of Joey," she told the court. "If I put my arm around him, he would say, 'Let me alone.' " Tracy used his son's messy marital problems, he later admitted, as an excuse to go on yet another binge.

Tired, ill, and self-pitying, he sank into a deep depression. He still phoned Louise daily and still made frequent trips "up to the Hill" to see her. Now he told Kate that he was updating his will and that his saintly "Weeze" would remain the sole heir to his multimillion-dollar fortune.

It could hardly have mattered to Kate. Dr. Hepburn's careful handling of his daughter's finances—as well as her own shrewd business dealings in Hollywood—had made her significantly wealthier than Tracy. At this point in their relationship she seemed amused that he would bring the subject up. "Good God," she said, "don't you think I have enough?" (Years later she suggested Americans have "lost our wits about money. The lack of it is certainly most unfortunate, but who in the hell wants great *piles* of it? Many of my peers are fornicating on the screen for money, and that is ludicrous. I figure that I've made fifty times the amount of money I should have in my career, but the important thing is that I had fun.")

A couple of months later Irene Selznick told Spencer and Kate that her father, a broken man after having been forced out of the studio he had built, was dying of leukemia. Shortly before his death that spring L. B. Mayer asked to see only one person outside his family: Kate.

It was Mayer's wish that Tracy deliver his eulogy. Spencer was sitting in the anteroom of the Wilshire Temple when the rabbi offered him a drink to steady his nerves—something George Jessel had to take every time he gave a eulogy. "I know," Tracy replied, "but if *I* did, Rabbi, I might bury *you* instead of Mr. Mayer."

Back to filming *The Old Man and the Sea*, Spencer was set to wrestle a giant rubber marlin in a 750,000-gallon tank on Warner's back lot. It was hardly the most propitious time for Kate to tell Tracy she was breaking her promise to stay by his side. The pull of the classics was too great for her to resist; at Lawrence Langner's urging, she headed east to star in *The Merchant of Venice* and *Much Ado About Nothing* at the Stratford Memorial Theater in Stratford, Connecticut. For the thrill of performing Shakespeare, she agreed to be paid only $350 a week. Spencer, meanwhile, would have to fend for himself.

Instead of commuting from New York or even from Fenwick, Kate moved into Langner's red-walled fisherman's shack perched on pilings at the mouth of the Housatonic River. At fifty, she now seemed determined to recapture the wonder and excitement of her Connecticut childhood. In the predawn hours before the local fishermen set sail, she served them breakfast. Then she dived in and swam in the treacherous currents, much to the alarm of her fellow actors. "We'd see her come riding in on her bicycle, hair flying in the wind," recalled John Houseman, one of the company's two directors, "or running along a bridle path in army fatigues, breathing hard. Wonderful!"

She was generous and patient with the younger actors, and no one minded when she commented on virtually every aspect of the production from lighting to costumes to set direction. With one exception. Alfred Drake, a leading star of the musical stage and Benedick to Kate's Beatrice in *Much Ado About Nothing*, clashed with her repeatedly.

By now she had quit cigarettes and was, like most reformed smokers, totally intolerant of anyone who dared light up in her presence. Drake's smoking infuriated her. At one point she stormed into his dressing room. "You know, Alfred," she said, "the trouble with you is that you haven't dealt with a costar in a long time. All you've had is leading ladies."

"Well," Drake replied, "at least they were ladies."

Kate's eyes narrowed. "There's nothing you can say to me," she snapped, "that Spencer hasn't said to me—and much more!"

She often mentioned Tracy's name during the most casual conversations and on several occasions excitedly announced his imminent arrival—only to have her hopes dashed at the last minute. To Drake and Houseman it seemed a sad and to some degree pathetic spectacle. Houseman recounted in his memoirs:

Finally, during *Much Ado*, the great day came when Kate, with a young girl's enthusiasm, proclaimed that this time Spencer was really coming. His plane ticket was bought and all arrangements were made. On the evening of his arrival—carefully chosen as an *Othello* day [Kate did not appear in this play]—she drove off alone, in a state of high excitement that she made no attempt to conceal, to the airport to meet him. Soon after she had left there was a phone call from California. Somehow, on the way to Burbank, Spencer had got lost and missed his plane. He never did appear.

Kate's contretemps with Drake notwithstanding, *Much Ado* was such a hit that she decided to tour in it from December to March 1958 with the American Shakespeare Festival Theater.

During the *Much Ado* tour Kate drove herself from city to city with Phyllis and her driver watching the passing scenery from the backseat. When Drake left in the middle of the tour to fulfill another commitment, Kate, who had come to enjoy their verbal jousting, made a moving farewell speech. She also gave him a sterling cigarette box engraved with the names of all the cast members. But what impressed everyone most was the fact that at his going-away party she downed no fewer than eleven glasses of his potent champagne and brandy punch without any apparent effects.

Despite her startling capacity for alcohol, it was one of the few times that Kate drank publicly. "Why should I drink?" she asked. "Stone-cold sober, I find myself absolutely fascinating."

Even after Alfred Drake's departure there was plenty of backstage intrigue during the *Much Ado About Nothing* tour. In February actor Stanley Bell, who had also appeared with Kate the previous year in *The Merchant of Venice*, walked out on Kate during a performance of *Much Ado* in Washington, D.C. Several days later Bell, forty-one, jumped to his death from the eighth floor of a Boston hotel.

Stunned and saddened by Bell's suicide, the company pressed on nonetheless. Hepburn, in particular, was hell-bent on finishing out the tour as planned. Even when she contracted pneumonia and was running a temperature of 103, Kate refused to miss a single performance.

When she returned to California in early March 1958, Kate found a happy, if physically shaky, Spencer on the set of his new film for Columbia Pictures, *The Last Hurrah*. A year earlier she had learned that their old friend John Ford was directing the screen version of Edwin O'Connor's bestselling novel and asked Ford to hire Spencer for the role of Frank Skeffington. With a little prodding from Kate, Tracy had come to the realization that he was perfect for the role of Skeffington, the wily Irish-American pol based on flamboyant Boston Mayor James Curley.

Kate had been anxious to return to California immediately after her *Much Ado* tour for one overriding reason. Not only had Ford been one of Tracy's two-fisted drinking buddies, but several members of the cast—including Pat O'Brien, James Gleason, and Frank McHugh—had been carousing with Spencer since the 1930s. Hepburn was relieved to discover that, to one degree or another, all had seriously cut back on their alcoholic intake.

With nothing on her own plate, Kate was content to sit in the shadows knitting while Spencer worked on *The Last Hurrah*. Tracy would have stormed off the set had he known that Kate had briefed Ford on his star's deteriorating condition. Spencer would have to break for naps occasionally, Kate informed the director, and long afternoons were out of the question.

A constant but largely unseen presence off camera, she materialized between takes, a glass of water in one hand and medication in the other. As Spencer sat slumped in a chair, she massaged his neck or knelt down to rub his feet like a trainer tending to his boxer between rounds. He gulped Maalox to calm his ulcers. "So," she would say, a look of deep concern on her face, "ya feeling OK, old man?"

She had always been Tracy's personal cheering section. Just because Ford had known both Hepburn and Tracy for nearly thirty years, the director was not spared Kate's usual spiel concerning the "mahvelous" Spencer Tracy. "Isn't he *incredible*?" she would say to Ford between takes. "Totally honest. How does he *do* it?"

The Last Hurrah ends with Skeffington dying of a heart attack after losing a tight race for mayor. It left Tracy thinking that maybe now it was time to retire. "I'm superstitious—you know that's part of being Irish—and I'm back with John Ford again for the first time since I started out with him twenty-eight years ago. I feel this is the proper place for me to end. Even the title is prophetic."

Paradoxically, the making of *The Last Hurrah* had the opposite effect. Tracy had delivered one of his most spellbinding performances. In release at the same time as *The Old Man and the Sea*, it offset the negative reaction to Tracy's Hemingway fiasco. "Spencer Tracy is a man of many moods," wrote *Time*'s critic, "and he is rich and famous enough to indulge them—even while the cameras are rolling. In one (*The Last Hurrah*) of two new pictures he worked hard and gave a performance that may well win him an Academy Award. In the other (*The Old Man and the Sea*) he sulked at the director and hardly bothered to act." The review went on to say Tracy played the Skeffington role "with more Celtic charm than a carload of leprechauns."

Tracy was nominated for an Academy Award that year, but for *The Old Man and the Sea*, not *The Last Hurrah*. The academy had not only ignored a performance he considered one of his finest but honored him for one that he thought mediocre at best. Boycotting the ceremonies, he stayed home with Kate and watched them on television. When David Niven won for *Separate Tables*, Tracy applauded. Kate, who had still hoped that her man might win in an upset, was clearly disappointed. "Why shouldn't I clap for Dave?" he told her. "I voted for him!"

Over dinner one evening with Kate, the Kanins, and Edwin O'Connor at the Turtle Bay house, Spencer asked the author of *The Last Hurrah* what he was working on.

"Well, I never like to talk about a work in progress," O'Connor replied, "but I'll say this much: It's the story of a priest. A middle-aged, American priest . . . And . . . the priest happens to be an alcoholic."

Tracy looked pensive. "I see," he said. "Well, yes—I think I could handle that."

Her love kept him alive. No question about it.

— STANLEY KRAMER

It was not a one-sided affair. He was as good for her as she was for him.

— GEORGE CUKOR

Spencer made me live beyond my potential.

— KATE

Nine

❧

In the ten-year period prior to 1959 Spencer Tracy had announced his retirement at least a dozen times. Whenever he completed a film, he vowed it would be his last. No one took him seriously—until *The Last Hurrah*. He was not yet sixty, but it was clear to everyone that Tracy was a very, very sick man. All the old medical problems were still there, and the breathing difficulties were now officially diagnosed as emphysema. It was equally clear that if Tracy retired, his lover/nurse/best friend/soul-mate would follow him into the sunset. She would always, it was understood, put his interests before hers.

But Kate was convinced that work, not the lack of it, remained Spencer's salvation. She put her own career on hold while she actively sought out roles for him. When Stanley Kramer, part of a new wave of independent producer-directors, approached the venerable Mr. Tracy with a project, Kate urged Spencer to listen. Kramer, who numbered among his films *Champion, Death of a Salesman, High Noon,* and *The Defiant Ones,* had bought the movie rights to the hit Broadway play *Inherit the Wind.* The play was based on the celebrated Scopes Monkey Trial of 1925, when William Jennings Bryan and Clarence Darrow squared off in a southern courtroom over the right to teach evolution in the schools. Kramer could think of no one better to play the part of the suspender-tugging Clarence Darrow character, "Henry Drummond," than Tracy. "A delicious idea, Spence," Kate told him. "I think you should do it."

It would be several months before Kramer could begin filming *Inherit the Wind,* and that opened a window of opportunity for Kate. Producer Sam Spiegel had offered her the role of Violet Venable, the mother in *Suddenly Last Summer,* Tennessee Williams's lurid tale of murder, madness, homosexuality, and cannibalism—with Oedipal overtones. Although Kate thought Williams's use of language was unparalleled, she objected to the story's excesses. Spiegel promised that Gore Vidal's screen adaptation would be considerably toned down. He also told her that George Cukor would direct and that all the filming would take place in Los Angles so she could remain close to Spencer.

She soon realized that Spiegel was up to his old tricks; nothing had changed since he had talked her into doing *The African Queen.* Vidal's script was every bit as sensational as the original play, Joseph Mankiewicz was hired to direct instead of Cukor, and to cut costs, *Suddenly Last Summer* would be shot at the Shepperton Studios in England.

It was all but predestined that *Suddenly Last Summer* would become Kate's least favorite moviemaking experience. Her long friendship with Joseph Mankiewicz was already strained. A decade earlier he had used a backstage meeting with her during the run of *As You Like It* as the inspiration for a key scene in his film *All About Eve*. She recognized Bette Davis's portrayal of aging actress Margo Channing as an imitation of her and felt betrayed.

But Kate saw the possibilities in the venal Mrs. Venable and at first looked forward to working with costars Elizabeth Taylor and Montgomery Clift. The story begins with the wealthy New Orleans matron trying to persuade psychosurgeon Dr. Cukrowicz (Clift) to perform a lobotomy on her niece Catherine (Taylor). It seems that the summer before, Catherine and her cousin Sebastian—Mrs. Venable's son—were vacationing in Spain when Sebastian suddenly died under mysterious circumstances. As the story unfolds, it is revealed that on his travels Sebastian had used Mrs. Venable and then Catherine as bait for young boys and that one day a pack of them ended up actually "devouring" him.

Kate clashed with both Taylor and Mankiewicz as soon as the cameras began to roll. "Liz kept us waiting," recalled cinematographer Jack

Hildyard, "and *nobody* kept Katharine Hepburn waiting." Mankiewicz explained to Kate that Taylor was suffering from an impacted wisdom tooth, but by the time Liz finally had the tooth pulled, "Kate, out of exasperation, had taken to directing portions of the film. Joe became so infuriated that on one occasion he threatened to close down the production. 'We will resume shooting, Miss Hepburn,' he screamed, 'when the Directors Guild card which I ordered for you arrives from Hollywood.' Kate stormed into her dressing room and refused to return that day."

Taylor's husband at the time, Eddie Fisher, remembered that "Hepburn was very cool and distant; she and Elizabeth hardly spoke to each other on the set, and we never met socially. . . . She often spoke of Spencer Tracy. 'Spence is coming over next weekend,' she would tell us, or the week following, or the week after that. He never came."

Adding to the mounting production problems was the drug-ravaged Montgomery Clift, who had not fully recovered from the near-fatal car crash that shattered his jaw. Shaking and blinking and blowing his lines, "psychosurgeon" Clift would have made a more convincing mental patient.

Because of her own extensive experience with Spencer, Kate was sympathetic to Clift. She gave him the usual pep talks and advice, but they did no good. "I thought he was weak," she concluded. "Simpatico but weak."

Mankiewicz also did what he could for Clift. "Kate thought I was being too tough on Monty," the director said, "but she didn't realize that I was reassuring him *constantly*, on the set and off. I'd let him stay at my hotel until he sobered up. But the more he leaned on me, the worse he got. We had to shoot every scene eleven, twelve times. He was such a disaster I just gave up." When Sam Spiegel considered replacing Clift, both Hepburn and Taylor jumped to Clift's defense.

By the end of *Suddenly Last Summer*, said Hildyard, "Hepburn and Mankiewicz were mortal enemies"—but for reasons that had nothing to do with either of her costars. Kate had no illusions about the character she was playing. From the moment she makes her entrance descending in a gilded elevator, Venable is a study in refined decadence.

However, Kate did not intend for Mrs. Venable to become a grotesque caricature ("I do *not* do horror films"). Without her knowing it, Mankiewicz and Hildyard conspired to photograph Kate's wrinkled, liver-spotted hands in close-up and without makeup. These shots were to be shown at the climax of the film to illustrate, said Mankiewicz, how the grisly truth about her son "destroyed her illusion of youth."

Being shown in an unflattering light was one thing—Kate was scarcely photographed to her best advantage in *The African Queen* or *The Rainmaker*—but duplicity was another matter entirely. Before long she had figured out the scheme.

On the final day of filming Kate walked up to Mankiewicz in front of the entire cast and crew and smiled. "Are you finished with me?" she asked.

"Absolutely," the director said, thanking her.

"You're quite sure you don't need me for re-takes or dubbing or additional close-ups?"

"I've got it all, Kate," he replied, "and it's great. *You're* great."

"You're absolutely certain that I'm through with this picture?" she asked again.

"Absolutely."

"Then," she said, "I just want to leave you with this." And as everyone gasped in disbelief, she spat directly into his face. She then spun around, strode into Spiegel's office—and did precisely the same thing.

"I was stunned, of course, totally shocked," recalled Mankiewicz. "It was totally unexpected. I never understood why she was angry with me and I *still* don't understand."

Mankiewicz's positive assessment of the film was accurate. Not only did reviewers heap praise on both Taylor and Hepburn for their bravura (if slightly demented) performances, but *Suddenly Last Summer* proved to be one of 1959's most profitable films. Even in a movie she despised—Hepburn never saw *Suddenly*—Kate, along with Elizabeth, would receive an Academy Award nomination as Best Actress. It was Hepburn's eighth.

After her ordeal in London Kate fled back to Spencer's side. They resumed their usual routine of quiet dinners, drives through the countryside, and strolls around the grounds of the Cukor estate. They now seemed to enjoy one unexpected pastime more than any other. On weekends Spencer Tracy and Katharine Hepburn could be spotted on the beach at Malibu or up in the corduroy-textured hills, gazing up at their colorful kite as it soared and dipped in the breeze.

Once she was confident that he was healthy enough to withstand another of her brief absences, Hepburn returned to Stratford for another summer season—this time in *Twelfth Night* and *Antony and Cleopatra*. By the time she got back to California, Spencer was drinking again.

Kate sobered him up in plenty of time to start *Inherit the Wind*. Both Tracy and Hepburn shared a deep respect for Stanley Kramer, but Tracy was determined to let him know who was boss. On the first day of shooting, Tracy mumbled his lines, and Kramer asked for a second take. "He looked at me," Kramer said, "for a full minute with the glance that withers. And I mean a full minute—not fifty-five seconds. . . ."

Once the cast and crew had quieted down, Tracy spoke. "Mr. Kraaaamer. It has taken me thirty years to learn how to speak lines. If you or a theater arts major from UCLA want to do this speech, I am quite willing to step aside." Satisfied that his director had been duly chastised, Spencer added, "All right, we ought to try it again."

At first Spencer demanded a closed set. "Tracy didn't want a bunch of idiots clambering all over the place," Kramer said. "One week later it was like Las Vegas. Everybody was there to see him: bookies, ballplayers, fighters, and press, along with a million actors just there to watch. He loved to get hold of a small press group and disagree with everything asked or said."

Fredric March and Tracy went nose to nose in lengthy courtroom confrontations, hamming it up at every opportunity. "They really chewed up the scenery trying to top one another," said reporter James Bacon.

"Every take brought down the house," Kramer said, "and their escapades were something to see. They teased and goaded each other with every trick they had learned over the years." Whenever Spencer started one of his lengthy monologues, March frantically fluttered a large straw fan. Tracy did not have any props at his disposal, but he got his revenge. Everyone broke up when Tracy, sitting directly behind March, picked his nose throughout March's impassioned summation.

"I finally stepped out of my class," said Gene Kelly, who took the supporting role of a journalist just to appear with the two old lions of the business. "I just can't keep up with this pair."

For most of the filming Kate stayed discreetly

out of sight knitting, usually a sweater for Spencer. She emerged from her spot tucked behind the cameras and booms to remind him to take his pills or adjust his collar. Her respect for Kramer was such that she tried to restrain herself. But before *Inherit the Wind* started filming, the irrepressible Hepburn had quietly done her own research into the hair and clothing styles of the time and even into matters of courtroom procedure in the South. When she had an opinion about the staging of a scene or a line of dialogue, she felt duty-bound to share it.

"Spence cared a great deal about what Kate thought," Kramer said. "If we were talking over some change in the script or the way we wanted to shoot a scene, he would often say, 'Let's see what Kate thinks.' We did, and she was always right."

The competition between the two leading men (March's wife, Florence Eldridge, played his wife in the film) was so intense that Kate did everything she could to stay out of it. Once she inadvertently entered the fray by leaning over to March, who had spent much of his long career on the Broadway stage, to explain why Tracy found it so easy to memorize his lines. "It's his concentration," she said, "his theatrical background, you know."

"Well, thank you," March thundered back, "*Mrs. Shakespeare!*"

Kate could not watch Spencer all the time, and

Tracy took advantage of her periodic absences from the set to drink.

"Tracy got a little drunk on the set of *Inherit the Wind* one day," Bacon said, "and he pulled me aside. Kate wasn't around, and he wanted to show me something. So he led me around the set to this high wall directly behind the judge's bench. And there, behind the wall, was this *mountain* of empty half pint whiskey bottles. There had to be one hundred and fifty of them. Then he turns to me, still a little tipsy, and says, 'So, how many of these are *yours*?"

When it was released before the Christmas holidays in 1960, *Inherit the Wind* was trumpeted as the clash of the theatrical titans that indeed it was. *Newsweek* declared that Kramer had "put on the acting battle of the year, heavyweight division: Spencer Tracy, who gives a classic demonstration of how to speak worlds even when silent and almost motionless vs. Fredric March, who by contrast achieves a kind of magnificence of overacting. . . . *Inherit the Wind* is that rare combination—a thoughtful, honest movie that is a grand show besides." For Spencer it also meant a seventh Academy Award nomination. He was gaining on Kate.

Both Kate and Spencer had boundless faith in Kramer, whom Tracy likened to a modern, less money-crazed Irving Thalberg. Before the end of the shoot, they embraced Kramer as a full-fledged member of their inner circle.

After a day's filming, Kramer would be invited

to the cottage for dinner. Kate always cooked—usually a steak and a salad. The dessert—hot fudge sundaes—never varied. Before anyone else—including whichever ladies might be present—Kate always served Spencer first. After dinner Tracy slumped in his favorite chair, and Kate assumed her customary after-dinner position, sprawled out on her stomach on the floor. "Helps the digestion," was her explanation.

"They always played a sort of verbal tennis," Kramer recalled. "She would make some comment about the atomic bomb or some other heavy subject, and then he would shoot back with 'Oh, there's another subject you know *all* about.' She would just laugh, like a little girl. 'Oh, Spensuh . . .' Then he'd groan."

Their faith in Kramer was justified when he brought them a script about war crimes trials in postwar Germany. Once they finished reading *Judgment at Nuremberg*, Kate made her feelings known. "Spence, you've got no choice this time. You've *got* to do this one."

Shooting on location in Berlin and Nuremberg could not begin for at least nine months—more than enough time for Spencer to take on another assignment. In the winter of 1960 Kate and Spencer journeyed to Hawaii to make Mervyn LeRoy's *The Devil at Four o'Clock*.

Several years earlier Tracy had told *The Last Hurrah* author Edwin O'Connor that he "could handle" playing an alcoholic Irish-American priest. He got his chance as Father Matthew

Doonon, who with the help of three convicts manages to evacuate a children's hospital before it and the island are blown to smithereens in a Krakatoa-like volcanic explosion.

Now at the height of his career, Frank Sinatra, who played one of the convicts in *The Devil at Four o'Clock*, stated that Spencer Tracy was the only actor to whom he would ever take second billing. Indeed, if Spencer had never agreed to share top billing with Kate, he was not about to with Sinatra. But Tracy was quick to concede that Frank Sinatra was the real star of *Devil at Four o'Clock*. "Nobody at Metro," he said, "ever had the financial power Frank Sinatra has today." Recalled James Bacon: "I went to interview Tracy on the set, and he'd say, 'You don't want to talk to me. You want to talk to the other guy.' That's what he always called Sinatra—'the other guy.' "

Both close friends of Humphrey Bogart's, Tracy and Sinatra had bumped into each other often when they made their visits to the dying Bogie's bedside. They admired each other. Sinatra called Spencer the Gray Fox, and Tracy secretly admired Sinatra's success with women and his copyrighted take-charge, out-of-my-way-or-else attitude. "He would tell with great glee," Kramer said, "how Sinatra walked off one picture and flew to Rome. Or how he made the company rebuild all its sets in California because he didn't want to go to Madrid."

What he did not appreciate, however, were Sinatra's work habits. Most days Tracy had been on the set for hours before Sinatra arrived, usually well into the afternoon. Where Tracy and Hepburn always remained behind to read their lines off camera for other actors' close-ups, Sinatra simply took off. Spencer was left to say his lines to a coat hanger dangling from a broomstick while a script girl read Sinatra's part. "Totally unprofessional," griped Tracy, who later complained that he "got tired of acting with a broomstick."

Kate's trademark costume of khaki pants, a loose man's shirt, and sandals was perfectly suited to the sweltering Hawaiian climate. But from her spot on the sidelines she worried about how the heat might affect Spencer. For most of the picture he wore a priest's black cassock. Sweat poured from his forehead, and between takes Kate rushed up to hand him a glass of water and dab at his face with a wet cloth.

Trying to keep up his spirits, Kate continually praised his work. He refused to look at the daily rushes, but she did, reporting back to him that his performance was—as usual—"magnificent." When LeRoy showed Kate and Spencer several still photographs taken on the set, she was thrilled. "Spence," she said, "these are wonderful character studies!"

Tracy shook his head. "Kate," he said sadly, "those aren't character studies. They're just pictures of an old man."

There were constant reminders that Tracy was part of a dying breed, one of the last of the great lions of Hollywood's Golden Age. Bogie, Ronald Colman, Tyrone Power—all gone. When Clark Gable collapsed and died from a heart attack one day after completing *The Misfits*, Spencer was crushed. James Bacon lived five minutes from Gable's home in Encino and got there just as he was being put in an ambulance. "It was a Sunday morning, so there wasn't much traffic on the freeway," Bacon said. "I got to the hospital ahead of the ambulance. As they wheeled Gable into the emergency room on a stretcher, he looked up with a smile and said, 'How's the food in this joint?' Those were Gable's last words to me. I told Spence. He was so shaken up he couldn't bear to talk about it." At Gable's funeral a *Life* magazine photographer captured the grief etched into the faces of mourners Tracy, Robert Taylor, and Jimmy Stewart.

Just getting Tracy to Germany for the filming of United Artists' *Judgment at Nuremberg* in the spring of 1961 proved to be an ordeal. The location shoot in Hawaii had left him exhausted and sick. As the *Judgment* shoot approached, he began suffering his usual last-minute doubts. He was disappointed that Kramer's first choice to play the German judge accused of war crimes, Laurence Olivier, was unavailable. The part went to the dour Burt Lancaster, whose performance in *Elmer Gantry* had just beaten out Spencer's in *Inherit the Wind* for the Academy Award.

Kate helped talk Spencer through all these issues, but then he began having nightmares about the trip to Berlin itself. The prospect of a trans-atlantic flight terrified him. When Kate reminded him she would be there the entire time, holding his hand, he reluctantly agreed to go.

But when they started to board the German-bound plane at New York's Idlewild, Spencer was suddenly gripped by panic. He turned around at the gate and began to leave. Several United Artists advance men, who had been assigned to make sure he got on the plane, begged him to reconsider. Tracy just shook his head. In what could have been a scene from one of their movies, Kate pulled him off to one side, whispered a few words into his ear, and then they turned and boarded the plane. Everyone breathed a sigh of relief.

A studio car was waiting at the airport in Germany. Once it was a couple of blocks short of the hotel, the limousine pulled up to the curb and discharged Kate. She went the rest of the way on foot, entering the hotel through the rear and riding to her suite in the service elevator.

Tracy was grateful that Kate gave him the strength to overcome his fears. In a part patterned on U.S. Supreme Court Justice Robert Jackson, who had sat on the bench at the Nuremberg Trials, Tracy got to be highly visible without having to do much work. And the all-star cast, which enabled Kramer to get the picture funded, impressed even Spencer. In addition to Lancaster, there were Judy Garland and Montgomery Clift, who both played concentration camp survivors; Marlene Dietrich as the wife of a dead German general who befriends the American judge; Richard Widmark in the role of the Army prosecutor, and Maximilian Schell as the German lawyer who fights passionately to defend his indefensible client.

Spencer Tracy did indulge in a few of his patented outbursts. He stopped in the middle of a courtroom speech and threatened to murder ("He meant it," Kramer said) an actor who sneaked bites of a pastrami sandwich between takes. "How the hell can we be passing judgment on four guys," he shouted, "imprisoning them for life for war crimes beyond comprehension, and, knowing all that, how the hell can you munch on that sandwich?" Another time he lit into AP reporter Bob Thomas for good-naturedly referring to the all-star cast as "hams." Tracy turned his back on Thomas and refused to speak to him for the next six years.

For the most part, however, filming *Judgment* was one of Tracy's most rewarding professional experiences. He particularly enjoyed tormenting Lancaster. Tracy told columnist Joe Hyams Lancaster's precise salary for the picture—a tightly held secret—and told Hyams to confirm the figure with Lancaster, just for accuracy's sake. Tracy looked on as Lancaster flew into a rage. "I thought Burt was going to charge me and attack me on the set," Hyams recalled. "Tracy, watching, just laughed and laughed and laughed."

Tracy and Dietrich had come close to working together back in 1937, when Frank Capra wanted to cast them as George Sand and Chopin in a film biography of the composer. Now she was thrilled to play the proud widow of a dead German general whose house and servants have been requisitioned for the American judge's use during the eight-month trial. She and Spencer provided the film with its only hint of bittersweet romance.

Dietrich was excited at last to be working with Tracy. She called him "a wonderful, wonderful man," and although he referred to Dietrich as "The Kraut" behind her back, he liked her. The proof was in the teasing. Tracy would sidle up to Dietrich, give her a lingering, seductive glance, and then say, "You know, you're really not my type. You're Continental; I'm just an old fart."

Dietrich, all but ignoring Kate in the wings, brought strudel and cookies to Spencer on the set. "The Kraut says she baked them herself," Tracy would tell Kramer, adding matter-of-factly, "She didn't." He would offer them to Lancaster and Judy Garland, who played a concentration camp survivor in the film. "Kate says"—Tracy grinned as Garland bit into one of Dietrich's "homemade" cookies—"they come from a factory she owns in the Valley!"

Seeing Monty Clift in his usual state of agony

put Spencer's troubles in perspective. Kate had told him all about the Clift's inability to "get a grip," and now Tracy was witnessing the sad spectacle firsthand. During testimony in which his character recounts being sterilized by the Nazis, Clift kept forgetting his lines. Her hand over her mouth, eyes welling with tears, Kate watched from the sidelines as Clift tried again and again. Clift, Kramer said, "was literally going to pieces."

It was then that Tracy grabbed Clift by the shoulders. "You are the greatest young actor alive. Look, it doesn't matter to Stanley, or to me, what the words are. Stop trying to remember the lines, and just look into my eyes and tell me how you feel."

Clift took a picture out of his pocket—his mother—and improvised the entire scene. It was one of the most powerful moments in the film and earned Clift an Academy Award nomination for Best Supporting Actor. Kramer credited Tracy with "saving Monty's life—or at least prolonging it a while." (Clift died in 1966 of a heart attack. He was forty-five.)

Once Spencer finished his work on *Judgment at Nuremberg* in the early spring of 1961, he and Kate joined the Kanins at the Raphael Hotel in Paris. They dared stay in the same hotel but occupied different suites. It was the off-season, and for several weeks the four friends roamed the streets and back alleys of Paris without fear of being mobbed by fans.

In his brilliant 1971 memoir *Tracy and Hepburn*, Kanin recounted the night they convinced Kate to make one of her rare visits to a restaurant, the Cochon d'Or. Sticking to their usual routine, Spencer and Ruth Gordon left together out the front door of the hotel and piled into a waiting Columbia Studios car. Kate and Kanin went out the back way and arrived at the Cochon d'Or in a taxi.

Once at the restaurant Kate became self-conscious. She bolted down her food. Then she lit a cigarette. Kanin looked over at her, and she looked "odd. Had she been a television image, I would have reached out and begun fiddling with the hue and color dials under her face. A blue-green tint suffused it as she sat there, smoking happily, and smiling beatifically."

A few moments later she asked Kanin to follow her to the ladies' room. Before she could get there, "Kate stopped suddenly, reached out, grasped a handful of air, and keeled over. Too much strain had led to too much food consumed too quickly."

After she came to, they went out to find Tracy sitting, stone-faced, in the studio car. "I'm *so* sorry," Kate said. "I guess I'm not made for public life, that's all." Spencer sat in stony silence, breaking up only when he discovered that as Garson and Kate walked to the car, a pigeon had left its calling card on the shoulder of Kanin's expensive suit.

Four days later Spencer declared he had found

a new restaurant, Chataignier, where they could dine safely. "The great thing is," he said, "it's so small that when Kathy faints, there's no room for her to fall down." But Kate did not faint in the restaurant that night. Spencer broke a front tooth on a piece of bone, and as a result of the excitement, she did faint again—only this time in the car.

A few days later, *another* restaurant adventure, but of a very different sort. At the end of their excellent but otherwise uneventful meal the entire restaurant stood up to toast the Hollywood legends in their midst. Knowing what so much as a sip of brandy could do to Spencer, Ruth grabbed the brandy glass that had been handed him and downed its entire contents in a single gulp. "Spencer," Kanin recalled, "enveloped her with his look of love."

The Kanins had often protected Spencer, but he suffered withdrawal symptoms whenever Kate was not around. While he was being photographed on his hotel roof for a *Judgment at Nuremberg* poster, Tracy kept wandering off to the edge and peering over the side. "Looking for Kate," he explained to the photographer.

"But why are you looking down at the back of the hotel instead of the front entrance?" the photographer asked.

"Kate always comes in the back way," Spencer said with a shrug. "Got to be discreet, you know."

Once *Judgment at Nuremberg* was finished and

they finally made their way back to California, Kate and Spencer were made the sort of offer *she* could not refuse. Portly Ely Landau had won accolades for his *Play of the Week* productions on public television. Now he wanted Spencer Tracy and Katharine Hepburn to assay two of the meatiest roles in America theater: James and Mary Tyrone of Eugene O'Neill's posthumously produced Pulitzer Prizewinning masterpiece *Long Day's Journey Into Night*.

The idea of a film version of *Long Day's Journey*, directed by Sidney Lumet with Jason Robards and Dean Stockwell playing her sons, was irresistible to Kate. It was Hepburn, after all, who had tried so desperately to convince Louis B. Mayer to make O'Neill's *Mourning Becomes Electra* with herself and Garbo in the lead roles.

"One could never be better than the part," Kate said of the tragic, drug-addicted Mary Tyrone. "O'Neill's knowledge of people, and his analysis of that couple, was really thrilling." Tracy had also been a longtime fan of the playwright's, and everyone agreed he was perfect for the part of James, the Tyrone family's pompous, penurious patriarch.

Landau made the pitch to both of them over breakfast at Tracy's cottage. "It was extraordinary to watch her with Spence," Landau said. "She was a totally different person. She turned really submissive—it's the only word I can use—and hardly opened her mouth, other than introducing us. She smiled, laughed at everything he said—which, by the way, was quite justified. . . ."

Ironically, Tracy made the choice James Tyrone, a stage actor based on O'Neill's own father, would have made. As a matter of principle, Spencer was unwilling to act for the nominal twenty-five thousand dollars Landau could afford to pay. "Look," he told Landau, "Kate's the lunatic. . . . I'm a movie actor. She's always doing these things for no money!" So Sir Ralph Richardson got the part.

Kate also acted according to her principles, which made the whole project more artistically compelling *because* there was no money involved. "The only time I am ever miserable is when I do something *just for the money*," she said later. "Well, that certainly wasn't the case with *Long Day's Journey*, was it?"

Money wasn't the only thing missing from the equation. The other was *time*. When Landau first called her about the project, he told Kate shooting was to start the next month, September 1961. They would then have thirty-seven days in which to complete the film. "Mr. Landau," Kate said, "I think you're nuts." Driving him to Los Angeles International Airport after their initial discussions, she exhibited some odd behavior of her own. She pulled the car over, got out, and burst into sobs. "I don't know whether I can do it," she said through her tears. "I'm fascinated—but I'm terrified! It's so great!"

Spencer's physical condition had improved

slightly over the summer of 1961, and as far as Kate knew, he had not gone on a serious bender in well over a year. Still, she felt some trepidation about leaving him behind as she flew east to begin *Long Day's Journey*.

Long Day's Journey was shot in Manhattan and in a Victorian house on City Island in the Bronx. From the moment she set foot on the set, everyone involved knew Kate was a force to be reckoned with. She ordered Richardson to stop smoking his pipe between takes. When he tried to light up in his dressing room, Kate somehow knew. "You're at it again!" she would yell.

There was an unusual number of heavy drinkers among cast and crew, which in a way made Kate feel right at home. Robards, newly married to Lauren Bacall, was typecast as the alcoholic brother. Kate said nothing to him about his drinking, but when young Stockwell brought a bottle of vodka to the set, she tore into him. "She was so angry at him," Sidney Lumet said, "out of love."

When someone showed up drunk or hung over, Kate showed the same loving concern that she had for Spencer. "She was good to them all," Lumet observed. "One man came in late after being off the picture three days. He showed up looking like something the cat had dragged in, and she took him to her dressing room, cleaned the vomit off, and washed him so gently. She knew exactly what to do. . . ."

"I look terrible in this play—you know, I progress to the nether reaches of insanity in the course of a day," she told a reporter. "But I've never had such a part." Now fifty-four, Kate had dispensed with all vanity. She was playing the mother of two grown sons, addicted to morphine and unable to hold herself or her appearance together. For the first time she refused to see the film shot each day. "If I go to the rushes," she told Lumet, "all that I'm going to be able to look at is this"—she pinched the skin around her neck—"and this"—she grabbed the flesh under her arm. She tried to explain that she could not stand "all that distraction. I need all my energy just to play the part."

Carrying her wedding dress down the stairs in one scene, striking her youngest son hard across the face in another, writhing on the floor in yet another, Kate's Mary Tyrone is a riveting study in dementia. But the character's soul-crushing sense of loss is conveyed even more effectively in smaller ways: Kate's anguished, questioning eyes, her loping stride, and the trembling hands that fly up repeatedly to check her hair.

Kate was reaching far down into her own well-spring of emotions to convey Mary Tyrone's pain. More than ever before, she was revealing something of herself to the world. "The play isn't about dope at all," she said. "It's not even about lost love. It's about losing the most important thing in the world—yourself."

At a cast party afterward Ralph Richardson asked Kate to dance. When they were finished waltzing, Richardson looked at Kate with a wide-eyed stare that bordered on disbelief. "I say," he declared, "you're a very attractive woman!"

Kate laughed off Richardson's remark. But like anyone self-conscious about the inevitable sags and wrinkles brought on by age, she found her spirits were lifted by it. When she repeated Richardson's compliment to Spencer, he smiled. "Ah, Sir Ralph," Tracy said. "Now where do you suppose *he's* been for the last thirty years?"

Because of its length and the weighty subject matter, *Long Day's Journey Into Night* was not a commercial success when it was released the following year. But many critics considered it the finest performance of Kate's career. Pauline Kael of the *New Yorker* now dubbed her "the Divine Hepburn." *Esquire's* Dwight MacDonald, who had always dismissed Hepburn as "mannered, to say the least," now proclaimed her "a superb tragedienne." Arthur Knight of the *Saturday Review* wrote that her portrayal of the haunted Mary Tyrone was "in every way masterful."

Long Day's Journey Into Night earned Kate another Academy Award nomination. And though she lost to Anne Bancroft in *The Miracle Worker*, she now stood at the summit of a miraculous career, or so it seemed at the time. For the next five years Kate did not set foot in front of a camera. She devoted herself entirely to the one thing in her life she valued above all others: Spencer Tracy.

He knew full well the extent of her sacrifice. Despite his posturing and gruff sarcasm, Spencer was fiercely loyal to his Kath. He was lunching at Maxim's in Paris with the Kanins and a famous writer when the writer offered to create a play expressively for them. The "big acting," the playwright said, would all have to be done by Tracy "because we all know that Kate is a tremendous personality but not what you'd call a real actress."

"Not what *who'd* call a real actress?" Tracy exploded.

The playwright cleared his throat. "What I mean to say—"

"I *know* what you mean to say," Spencer interrupted, "you stupid bastard. I heard you . . . What in Christ's name does an actress have to do before she gets the big final okay from you supercilious pipsqueaks? . . . God damn it! Look— don't talk to *me* about acting. . . . I *know* about acting, and I've acted with this girl—a lot—and if she isn't a real actress, then there never *was* a real actress. Thanks for the lunch. It was delicious. I'm going home now to throw it up."

According to Kanin, the playwright regained his composure only after downing two double brandies. "I seem," he said, "to have touched his sensitive spot."

"You're lucky," Kanin replied, "he didn't touch *your* sensitive spot."

Kate had always shunned premieres, and because of his failing health, Tracy had made a practice of avoiding them for years. But in December 1961 Stanley Kramer managed to persuade them that the first official viewing of *Judgment at Nuremberg* in Berlin would be no run-of-the-mill premiere. Far more was at stake, and he wanted all cast members to be on hand to stand behind the film and its sober message.

At the time the Germans, apparently not prepared or willing to face the truth, reacted to the film with stony silence. There was a post-premiere party at the Congress-Halle, a modern structure Berliners nicknamed the "Pregnant Oyster." More than one thousand guests were expected; around one hundred showed up, mostly those involved with the making of the picture.

For Hepburn as well as Tracy, perhaps the most disturbing aspect of this Berlin trip was the sad scene made by a drunken Monty Clift. Arriving at the theater "stoned and drunk out of his mind," as one witness put it, Clift scampered between the aisles on his hands and knees, shrieking obscenities and laughing hysterically. As Spencer entered without Kate (she waited for him at her hotel), Clift sneaked up from behind and leaped on Tracy's back yelling, "Yippee!" More than thirty minutes into the picture and with Clift still making a scene, Spencer left.

By jumping on Spencer's back, Clift apparently aggravated a kidney ailment that had already been giving him trouble. He left the theater in agony and was rushed back to his hotel. No one expected him to make it to a press conference scheduled for the next day, but Tracy was there to defend the picture. "Do you really believe what was portrayed in this picture?" a German reporter asked facetiously. Tracy glared—that glare—at the man for a brief, chilling moment. "Every word," he replied.

Tracy was again nominated for an Academy Award as Best Actor in *Judgment at Nuremberg*, but he told anyone and everyone that he was voting for his costar Maximilian Schell. "I just sat there listening," Spencer said self-deprecatingly of his own performance, "and these other fellows did the work." It did not go unnoticed by his peers that in the film Tracy insisted on performing what was then the longest speech in movie history—thirteen minutes and forty-two seconds—in a single, riveting take. Schell went on to win, but at least Spencer's eighth nomination made him even with Kate. But not for long.

The trip to Berlin looked as if it might have been too much for Tracy. Still plagued by kidney problems, he flew on to London with Kate, hoping to attend the British premiere of *Judgment*. But the pain was too excruciating, and with Kate at his side they returned to California and a relaxing week in Palm Springs instead. As it turned out, they both would be needing the rest.

In January 1962 *Look* magazine hit the stands with a story that stunned Hollywood and its most esteemed couple. Over lunch in a private second-floor dining room at Chasen's, Tracy had been unusually candid with veteran journalist Bill Davidson. With his publicist looking on, he talked openly of his alcoholism. He said he'd "go into blackouts and wake up in some goddam distant city. At first I thought it was that all Irishmen were drunks . . . now I think maybe it's genetic."

Spencer praised both his son John and daughter Susie, who had already published a children's book about a deaf cat and was embarking on a career as a photographer. Yet, to Davidson's surprise, he spoke even more warmly of his relationship with Kate, sprinkling the conversation with affectionate references to "My Kate" and even "My Bag of Bones." He praised her acting and even discussed such intimate moments as their romantic walks along the Seine in Paris.

Totally unaware of the unwritten law that no journalist was ever to write about the Tracy-Hepburn Affair, Davidson used many of Spencer's candid comments in the *Look* piece—including references to Tracy's "mean streak" and the fact that he and Louise had not lived together for years. When it came out, Davidson later wrote, "I was immediately excoriated by writers in Hollywood." It did not help Davidson's case that John Tracy had fallen victim to a number of ailments over recent years and that the saintly Louise had returned to caring for him just as she had when he was a boy.

An angry Tracy did what he always did in circumstances like these: He blamed the wanton press. He promptly informed Louise—he still visited frequently—that the article was a collection of lies. He swore he'd never even *spoken* to Davidson. He merely waved off as more scurrilous gossip *Look*'s observation that he and Kate "were something more than frequent co-stars." In the interest of maintaining her sanity and some semblance of dignity, Louise chose to believe him.

Kate was another matter. She did not hold the *Look* story against Spencer, but that did little to lessen her pain. According to Kanin, it was six months before she fully recovered from the piece.

That year Spencer returned to MGM to narrate the studio's all-star Cinerama epic *How the West Was Won*. Even for this only mildly demanding task, Kate was on hand, knitting in a corner, while he added his familiar, commanding voice to the sound track.

Although she now spent most nights sleeping in the maid's room off Tracy's kitchen, Kate still respected his wish that they maintain separate addresses. Hepburn's current rental was the Aviary, a spectacular, light-filled villa at 1300 Tower Grove Drive that had once been the home of John Barrymore and his bird-fancying wife Dolores Costello. Even when she was at the Aviary and he was visiting Louise or the children, Kate saw to it that Spencer ate properly. Upon arriving home at the cottage, he would find a hamper filled with food Kate had prepared herself and left on his front porch.

For much of 1962 Kate's attentions were divided between the constantly complaining Spencer and her comparatively stoic father. Dr. Hepburn's condition had been deteriorating since early spring, and whenever it looked as if Spencer were strong enough to be on his own for a few days, she flew back to be with her Dad in West Hartford.

Strangely enough, despite his long career in medicine, it was Hep's distrust of the medical profession that contributed to his demise. "Dad could have lived longer," Kate later said, "but he didn't like medical doctors; he just liked surgeons, so he diagnosed himself. He thought he was having a heart attack, but it turned out what he really had was a gallbladder that burst. And that really downed him."

After surviving the burst gallbladder, Hepburn underwent prostate surgery. Hep, who had once insisted on being the one to remove Kate's appendix, would permit only his surgeon son, Robert, to operate on him. In mid-November he developed complications. Lobar pneumonia set in, and on the morning of November 20, 1962, with his surviving children at his bedside, he died. Hep was eighty-two.

The death of Kate's mother, so unexpected, had flattened her emotionally. This time her father's decline had been gradual—painfully so—and she was relieved to see his suffering end.

George Cukor sent chrysanthemums to the house, and Kate responded with a handwritten note dated two days after her father's death. "It was lucky for Dad—too long, too long," she wrote. "He looked so relieved. See you soon and many thanks."

Her father gone and her career on hold—perhaps permanently—Hepburn could now focus all her energy on caring for her Spencer.

Tracy and Hepburn both looked upon Stanley Kramer as a kindred spirit, if not a surrogate son. Without even bothering to read the script, Spencer agreed to play the role of a rumpled, fedora-wearing police captain tailing a loony assortment of treasure hunters in Kramer's *It's a Mad, Mad, Mad, Mad World.*

For his "comedy to end all comedies," Kramer assembled a colorful cast that included Milton Berle, Sid Caesar, Mickey Rooney, Buddy Hackett, Jonathan Winters, Jimmy Durante, Ethel Merman, Buster Keaton, Phil Silvers, Peter Falk, Carl Reiner, and the Three Stooges.

Since much of the film was to be shot under the scorching sun in the Mojave Desert, Tracy's contract limited his workday to six hours. Kramer did not object. His friend "was in poorer health than I could remember," the director said. "He had bad color and no stamina whatever." But, Kramer added, "God, how he loved doing that movie!"

"Everybody on that picture—hell, on *every* picture—was in awe of Spencer Tracy. But whenever they started saying what an honor it was to be working with him, he'd stop them cold. 'Aw, cut that crap' was his usual line. But he knew his worth. He was aware of his stature."

Berle and Winters were virtually tongue-tied in Tracy's presence. "The comedians worshiped him," Kramer said. "Never before or since has a king had the court full of jesters who strove only to entertain him so that His Majesty might say, 'That was funny,' or just laugh or smile. Milton Berle, Jonathan Winters, Buddy Hackett, Jimmy Durante, Phil Silvers, Mickey Rooney, Sid Caesar—they all crowded about him and vied for his affection. They had it. And he talked about them to the very last. He loved them all."

The *It's a Mad, Mad, Mad, Mad World* cast was no less impressed by his nurse. Whenever his ulcer acted up, Kate was there to hand him his current cocktail of choice, a glass containing milk over a single ice cube. (At this point he was not abstaining from liquor entirely: Tracy had convinced his doctors that his system was now so dependent on alcohol he needed a single glass of beer with dinner.) Hepburn also made sure that wherever Tracy went, a small tank of oxygen went with him.

Even though he appeared in less than a quarter of the film, Tracy was the cement that held the extravaganza together. Lauding his performance, *The New York Times'* Bosley Crowther wrote, "It isn't so much that Tracy is funny as it is that he is cynical and sardonic about this wholesale display of human greed. . . . Mr. Tracy seems the guardian of a sane morality in this wild and extravagant exposition of clumsiness and cupidity."

As delightful an experience as it was, the making of *It's a Mad, Mad, Mad, Mad World* left Tracy exhausted and spent. He announced, tongue firmly planted in cheek, that this movie was to be his last. "You know," Tracy quipped, "they say Sarah Bernhardt stopped acting one hundred and seventy-eight times."

Spencer would not stay on the wagon for long. In June 1963 Kate rented a house from publicist Frank McFadden at Trancas Beach several miles above Malibu. She persuaded the ailing Tracy that the sea air would do him good, and so he moved—oxygen tank and all—into the modest house at 30842 Broad Beach Road for the summer.

A few days later James Bacon walked into Romanoff's in Beverly Hills and spotted Tracy at the bar. It was around noon. "Everybody knew Tracy hadn't been well, and I'd been told he was on the wagon," Bacon said. "I went up to say hello, and he asked me to join him for a drink. Well, we had a drink, and then another; he was knocking back double Scotches, no food."

They moved on to lunch. "We sat down at a table, and they served us our food, but of course we kept right on drinking," Bacon said. "We were having this perfectly delightful conversation when all of a sudden, right in the middle of eating, he fell facefirst into his mashed potatoes. Out cold. I actually had to reach over and lift his head up off the plate so he wouldn't smother."

The restaurant's owner, Mike Romanoff, helped Bacon clean Tracy off. "I wanted to be a Good Samaritan," Bacon said, "so I got Mike Romanoff and two or three waiters to help me carry Tracy to my station wagon. I wasn't supposed to know where Spencer lived, but I had talked to Frank McFadden a few days earlier, so I did know that he and Kate had rented the house at Trancas."

Once he arrived, Bacon pulled into the driveway and dragged Spencer out of the car. "He had gotten very heavy, and because he was out cold, he was just dead weight. I was really struggling when all of a sudden Kate came out from behind the house in a rage."

"God damn you, Bacon!" Kate shouted. "You and Gable were always trying to get him drunk. You've always been an evil companion for Spence." With that she reached down and picked up a rock or a brick—Bacon wasn't sure which.

"She was getting ready to throw it at me," Bacon said, "so I dropped Spence right there in the driveway—he hit the pavement like a sack of potatoes—and I jumped in my car and drove off. Kate was still screaming at me." It was the last time Bacon saw Tracy. When Bacon encountered Kate years later, she was still angry and refused to talk to him.

The incident at Romanoff's marked Tracy's

last major bender, but the damage to his health had already been done. Shortly after noon on Sunday, July 21, Tracy suddenly began gasping for air. Kate calmly called the Zuma Beach Fire Department for help as he slipped into unconsciousness. Kate administered mouth-to-mouth and, once he had begun to come to, slipped the oxygen mask over his face.

Tracy was convinced he had had a heart attack and was dying. Panic set in over appearances. If he died at Hepburn's home, there would be no way of concealing the fact that they had been living there together. Knowing how much the charade meant to Spencer, Kate sprang into action. "Quick!" she told Phyllis Wilbourn. "Get the picnic basket and a blanket!" On Hepburn's orders, Phyllis tossed the basket and the blanket into the trunk of Tracy's Thunderbird.

Meanwhile Kate held Spencer's hand and stroked his forehead. She offered gentle, soothing words of encouragement. When the rescue unit arrived at 12:31 P.M. and found Tracy ashen and struggling for breath, they were told that he and Kate had been on their way to an innocent picnic on the beach when he was stricken.

A private ambulance took Spencer to St. Vincent's Hospital in Los Angeles. Kate rode with him in the ambulance, still holding his hand. The press was waiting at the emergency room entrance when Tracy was taken out of the ambulance on a stretcher. As flashbulbs popped, he pulled a sheet over his head.

Doctors at the hospital quickly determined that pulmonary edema (fluid in the lung tissue), not a heart attack, had caused Spencer's symptoms. Kate phoned Louise from the hospital, then disappeared out a back door. Meanwhile news of Spencer's suspected heart attack was carried on the networks. When Garson Kanin called from New York to check on his friend's condition, he was surprised to find Louise picking up the phone in Spencer's room.

It was understood that Louise would be making all official statements. As she left St. Vincent's late that night, she told reporters, "He is doing as well as can be expected. He seems to be coming along very nicely. We hope he will be able to come home in two or three days."

But Spencer remained in the hospital for twelve days, with Kate and Louise visiting him in shifts. It was during this period that, as one left and the other arrived, their paths once crossed in a hospital corridor. It was their first and only meeting during Tracy's lifetime.

Kanin remarked that he and his wife could not "help but marvel at Kate's behavior in this crisis. She gets Spencer into the hospital. As soon as she had done so, she informs his family of the situation and allows them to take over."

At the hospital Tracy was flooded with telegrams and flowers. DEAR SPENCE, cabled Cukor, SEE WHAT HAPPENS WHEN YOU EXPOSE YOURSELF TO THAT FRESH SEA AIR COME BACK TO THE DANK

SMOG OF ST IVES DRIVE AND YOU'LL BE OKAY FOR-
EVER. LOVE, YOUR LANDLORD.

Tracy's pithy pseudo-Irish reply: "H'it's dig-
gin for the rent every bloody month as does
h'it—Maike no mistake about that—"

Once he was finally released from the hospital,
it was agreed that Kate, not Louise, would over-
see his recuperation at home on the Cukor estate.
A nurse from the hospital was on hand during
the first few days, but when she departed, Kate
moved into the maid's room next to the kitchen
full-time. The oxygen tank was now kept at the
ready in the hallway outside Spencer's bedroom,
and the emergency buzzer installed at his bedside.

"Yup, I'm on the blink," Tracy told Kanin during one of their frequent transcontinental phone
conversations. "Well, hell, it's a damn wonder I
didn't come unglued before this. But don't
worry, ol' Kathy's got it in hand. In fact she's out
now taking a treatment for what's the matter,"
he quipped, "and if it doesn't kill her, she's going to let *me* take it!"

Spencer was hospitalized again at the end of
August, this time for tests. Still, he hoped he
could fulfill an obligation to the man who
brought him to Hollywood. It was understood
that *Cheyenne Autumn* would be the great John
Ford's last western, and Tracy had promised him
he would make a cameo appearance in the film.
By December, however, Spencer was still not
strong enough to go back to work, even for a few

days. He dropped out of *Cheyenne Autumn* and was replaced by Edward G. Robinson.

Now Hepburn and Tracy lived in virtual seclusion at the cottage. To regain his strength, Spencer pedaled an Exercycle and joined Kate for their walks in the hills around the Los Angeles Reservoir. To keep Tracy company, dog-loving Kate bought a black German shepherd mix named Lobo. They continued to fly kites on a favorite knoll above the Aviary.

By the spring of 1964 Spencer had made enough of a recovery to accept the role of a card-shark who takes on a young challenger (played by Steve McQueen) in *The Cincinnati Kid*. Tracy was intrigued by the movie's Deep South setting and by the prospect of playing with the taciturn McQueen, then one of the biggest box-office draws in the country.

Shortly before rehearsals, however, Tracy was warned by his doctors that he was not yet ready to go back to work. Spencer pulled out of the project, and as he had done before, Edward G. Robinson stepped into the part intended for Tracy. "I was ready for the fight," a disappointed Spencer told one reporter, "but I couldn't make the weight."

At about the same time Stanley Kramer was in the process of casting *Ship of Fools*, his film based on the best-selling book by Katherine Anne Porter. As fond as he was of Spencer, Kramer wanted to cast a younger actor, Oskar Werner, in the pivotal role of the ship's doctor. The decision did not sit well with Kate, who then turned down the part of the aging society matron Mary Treadwell. Besides, Kate was struck by the fact that the character she was being asked to play had Louise Tracy's highly unusual maiden name.

Anxious to prove that he was well enough to work, Spencer accepted Kramer's standing invitation to show up on the set of *Ship of Fools* and watch the proceedings. Louella Parsons speculated that he was preparing for a career as a director. "I don't have the patience—why, I'd probably kill the actors," scoffed Tracy, who billed himself as "Special Adviser to Mr. Kramer."

Kate, meantime, had her hands full with the actress who did take the Mary Treadwell role, Vivien Leigh. The woman who won Academy Awards playing Scarlett O'Hara and Blanche DuBois was now struggling with alcoholism, manic depression, and recurrent tuberculosis. Along with their mutual pal George Cukor, Hepburn had taken it upon herself to try to keep Leigh on an even keel.

When she was not tending to Spencer's needs, Kate was at Vivien's side—to the point of accompanying Leigh to the periodic shock treatments that enabled her to show up for work. "I don't know where her sense of duty ends and her loving heart begins," Irene Selznick said of Hepburn's unswerving devotion to her friends. "But when you're in trouble, she's Gibraltar. If I said she was noble, she would kill me."

In the spring of 1965 Kate was asked by the editors of the *Virginia Law Weekly* to share her thoughts on the issue of privacy. She had always admired her mother's crusading spirit, and she seized the opportunity to speak out on a topic of no small social importance.

She dashed off the following "article"—sans punctuation—revealing much of herself in the process. Beneath the heading "The Predicament of the Public Figure," Hepburn wrote:

In the beginning of my career—in 1932—I had a right to consider privacy my right—and so I fought for it—a wild and vigorous battle—Quite successful—I thought—I went to a great deal of trouble—I went way—way out of my way—the few people I knew could keep their mouths shut. . . .

Today it is extremely difficult to control one's privacy—even if one is not a public figure—Who are you—How old are you—Who are your father—mother-sisters—brothers-grandparents—Of what did they die—what were they when they lived—What diseases have you had—what is your religion—Have you ever been a communist—What is your income—Whom do you support—How much did your house cost—the furnishings—Your wife's clothes—her jewels—fur coats—how much do you spend on your children's schools—Travel—Entertaining—

Books—Liquor—Flowers—Teeth—Do you wear glasses—Do you still menstruate—Are your periods regular—your bowels—What operations have you had—do you sleep in the room with your wife—and how long has that been going on—Have you ever been involved with the law—do you drink—Let's just have a fingerprint now— ...

Both the public and press feel that they have an absolute right of access to the most intimate details of your life—and by this you must read largely sex life. ... I used to go through the most elaborate schemes to avoid the press—I felt that nothing of my private life was any of their business— ...

Kate also used her piece as a platform to rail against the general decline of civilization as a whole:

Polite pornography is no longer interesting—No more subterfuge—The naked fact—Tell it—Do it—There it is—That is the fact—The truth—the four letter word—the naked body—Nothing withheld—You feel sad—low—take a Benzedrine—You feel too lively—take a sparine—you want to sleep—take a secanol [*sic*]—you feel pain—take some codeine—you are confused—go to a psychoanalyst—Don't hide it—Talk—tell it—It is never your fault. ...

While Kate vented her anger and frustration over the loss of her privacy in a little-read law review, Cukor had managed to convince producer Walter Wanger to do another Tracy-Hepburn vehicle at MGM. At first studio executives seemed willing, but by October the deal had all but evaporated. Tracy's health was the overriding concern, although Wanger made it clear that MGM was always open to any project that involved Katharine Hepburn alone.

Spencer's health continued to slide. In September 1965 surgery to remove Tracy's prostate was performed at Los Angeles's Good Samaritan Hospital. The prostatectomy itself went well, but three days later complications set in. Spencer's kidneys shut down. Hovering between life and death, he was given the last rites of the Catholic Church. Kidney dialysis was in its infancy, and in a desperate effort to restore kidney function, doctors attached him to one of the new machines. Miraculously he rallied; the dialysis had saved his life. Throughout the crisis Louise and Kate again kept their bedside vigils on alternate nights.

Press reports had led the public to believe that Tracy's death was imminent. But after six weeks in the hospital—much of that time on the critical list—he was released into Kate's care. They now faced the hard fact that Spencer was unemployable. With the exception of narrating a documentary on his alma mater (*The Ripon College Story*), he withdrew entirely into the world he shared with Kate.

The same chosen few were allowed a glimpse

into that world. All that their hosts asked—demanded—in return were the juicy scraps of gossip and news on which they thrived. Tracy still sipped his single beer or milk with an ice cube; Kate had recently developed a taste for a particular aperitif. "She liked Dubonnet—a lot," recalled Stanley Kramer's wife, Karen.

"Because they never went out," Kramer said, "they were always dying for the latest news— you know, who was sleeping with who, what deals were in the works, the usual." When the Kramers told them in 1966 that Frank Sinatra was going to marry Mia Farrow, who was twenty-eight years his junior, "they were absolutely floored. Kate said, 'Oh, mmyyy God. You're *kidding*!' Spence just thought it was hysterical." So hysterical that Tracy, who rarely ventured out in public, could not resist attending the Sinatra-Farrow wedding reception.

With the exception of an occasional outing— and Kate's periodic tennis lesson at the nearby Beverly Hills Hotel—the fact remained that Tracy and Hepburn were living in a sort of involuntary exile. He would have jumped at the chance to work. But everyone was so convinced that he was about to die any minute no studio would risk it. And so long as Tracy could not work, Kate refused to.

Their quiet days were spent reading (he now devoured religious tracts), listening to classical music, painting, and sculpting. Spencer was Kate's most difficult subject. "He had the most magnificent lion's head," Kate later said, gazing at the three-inch-high bronze bust she sculpted of Tracy. "God knows I am no professional, but I think I managed to capture the shape." Painting Spencer was another matter. "I've painted dozens of portraits of the people in my life—friends and family mostly," she explained, "but for some mysterious reason I could never quite paint Spencer's face. Oh, I could paint his form, the way he sat, the way he held himself. But that face—there's something about it. So when I painted him reading, I hid his face behind a newspaper."

Tracy did not like to talk about death even when he was relatively healthy. Now he and Kate confronted it and discussed their views. Both were against prolonged, needless suffering and favored euthanasia. "If you have a hopeless disease," Kate said, "no matter how many people are trying to keep you alive, you have a perfect right to do whatever you want to do. . . . I've had friends in the last stretches of cancer who've killed themselves, and I really don't blame them. I thought they were very sensible. But of course it's different for everyone. If you have . . . someone who just adores taking care of you, it's terrible to disappoint her. . . ."

Tracy was more to the point. Conjuring up the specter of his father's death from cancer, he bluntly told Garson Kanin, "Right then and there I made plans. Anything like that ever happened to me, I'd check out. And I will too. . . ."

Disillusioned and palpably afraid of being forgotten, Tracy sometimes took out his frustration on the person who loved him most. Occasionally his put-downs of Kate in front of others seemed unconscionably cruel, even to those who knew them well. Without warning or provocation he often cut Kate off in mid-sentence. Guests squirmed uncomfortably when Tracy snapped, "Did anyone ask your opinion?" or, "For Christ's sake, don't you understand plain English?" During a small gathering at the cottage, she picked up a log and casually tossed it in the fire. "Don't *ever*," Tracy scolded, "do that again in front of company." Kate, blushing, merely smiled and sat down.

Yet to Kate, who had grown up the daughter of a "spanking dad," such rebukes were a sure sign of Tracy's enduring love for her. With the exception of her uniquely subservient attitude toward Tracy, she could be extraordinarily tough on the people she loved the most. Phyllis Wilbourn was an excellent example. Kate, said her friend Alice Palache Jones, "is perfectly dreadful to Phyllis, absolutely awful." She treats her "like a dog. It's just awful, and it's embarrassing. But she adores Phyllis. She thinks the world of her, and she'll tell you she's the most marvelous person and 'how she can stand me, I don't know.' . . . Phyllis just takes it and lets it ride. I'm sure she wouldn't do anything else in the world. It's her life. Absolute total devotion."

Stanley Kramer, meantime, was busy hatching the scheme that would bring Spencer out of forced retirement. In November 1966 William Rose, the writer who had scripted *It's a Mad, Mad, Mad, Mad World*, hit on an idea for a story about a rich English couple whose daughter wants to marry a handsome, intelligent, accomplished black man—someone who was such a prize catch that race would be the only ground on which any prospective in-law might object.

Both Kramer and Rose agreed that the story might just as well be set in America and that Sidney Poitier was perfect for the successful black fiancé. Kramer met with Poitier in New York and asked if he wanted the role. "Of course," replied Poitier. "My God, it's beautiful."

Once Poitier agreed, Kramer paid a call on Tracy's cottage. "Spence sat there with Kate at his feet while I described the story," Kramer said. "She wanted to know everything about the film as it related to Tracy—what the story was like from *his* standpoint." Then Kramer turned to Kate. "Well, Kate," he said, "I want you too." Said Kramer: "She looked surprised that I wanted her in the movie. She *acted* surprised anyway."

The parts were tailor-made for them: he the stubborn patriarch who stands in the way of his only daughter's marrying a black man, she the unshakably loyal but comparatively open-minded wife who helps her husband see the light. But there was a hitch: Spencer Tracy was uninsurable. The studio would agree to make the film only if Kate and Kramer put their salaries—

$250,000 for her and $500,000 for the director—in escrow. If Tracy for some reason could not complete the film, that money would be used to reshoot his scenes with another actor.

It was a huge gamble for everyone, but particularly Kramer. "It was very risky; I had everything riding on the film—my bank account, not to mention my career. My head was going to be on the chopping block, definitely. But I told them there was no way I was going to make the film without them. It was that simple." Kate did not hesitate. Knowing how important it was for Spencer to get back to work, she agreed to the terms immediately. "She's that kind of remarkable woman," Kramer said.

Even then Tracy was frightened. Kramer agreed that Spencer would not be required to work past noon. "I said, 'Are you just going to sit here waiting for oblivion?' Finally he decided he wanted back in the game."

Kramer and Rose went into seclusion at the writer's house on the Isle of Jersey and emerged five weeks later with a script for the film. It now had a title: *Guess Who's Coming to Dinner*.

A few weeks before shooting was to begin, Spencer suffered a severe emphysema attack and collapsed. Again Kate summoned the fire department, and rescue workers administered oxygen. Tracy did not have to be taken to the hospital, but it was enough of a scare to make him reconsider. He told Kramer he had lost sleep worrying about whether or not he could "pull this off."

"It isn't too late to call the whole thing off," Kramer said, "and I will, if you can't make it. I'm not going to make the picture without you, and that's final."

"Okay," Tracy said, looking at Kate. "Let's do it."

On the first day of rehearsal Poitier broke down after Tracy gave his first speech. "I'm sorry," he said, weeping. "I can't go on. Working with the two of you is a dream to me."

Kramer understood why Poitier became emotional. "Hell, we were *all* emotional," he said. "Sidney knew that this was going to be Spencer's last picture. Everybody knew."

On February 15, 1967, the first day of production, Kate and Spencer appeared at a brief press conference to introduce the young actress who was to play their daughter in *Guess Who's Coming to Dinner*. The unknown actress, twenty-three-year-old Katharine Houghton, just happened to be the strikingly attractive daughter of Kate's sister Marion Grant. Kate made it clear that this time, out of deference to Tracy, she was not going to be her usual disagreeable self with the press. "Most people get grumpier in their old age," she told reporters. "I get nicer."

The entire shooting schedule was structured to accommodate Spencer and his flagging energy. His shots were all done between 9:00 A.M. and noon, and he no longer had the stamina to read the lines for other actors' close-ups—not even Kate's. In several scenes where she is supposed to be talking to Spencer, Kate was forced to deliver her lines to blank space.

Even then Kramer had to rely on Kate for hourly bulletins on Spencer's physical state. Tracy, intensely grateful for all the concessions being made on his behalf, fought hard to keep up his energy. "He was really a big teddy bear," Kramer said. "A bowl of Jell-O. He had great warmth, and it came across every day we worked on the picture."

Kate was another matter. Barging onto the set in her usual take-charge manner, she was soon locking horns with the director. "She thinks like a director and a set designer and a makeup man. She has opinions about *everything*," Kramer said. "I'd never encountered anything quite like it."

"Spencer was the exact opposite," Kramer explained. "He did what the director asked him to do. Brilliantly. He could stand there and listen to someone else talking and steal the scene without saying a single word. Now Kate very seldom just did what she was told. She had her own ideas of the way a scene should be shot, where she should be standing, what the camera angle should be. She even objected when she saw we were using a fake fireplace and *demanded* that we rip it out and put in a real one!"

Kramer had an ally in Tracy. "Don't bug him, don't bother him," Spencer would tell Kate.

"Jeez, he's worked it out, for Christ's sake." At one point she had her feet up on a table, and Spencer told her to put them down. She ignored him. He then told her that they would begin working once Kate "learned to sit like a lady." She wrinkled her nose, stuck her tongue out at him—and put her feet down.

Another time Kate was kneeling on the floor in a scene—a favorite trick she used to conceal her "scrawny" neck from the cameras. "What the hell are you doing kneeling?"

"Spencer," she tried to explain, "I just thought it would be appropriate—"

Again a favorite Tracy retort—only this time for the benefit of the entire cast and crew: "*Spensuh*! Christ, you talk like you've got a feather up your ass all the time! Get out of here, will ya?"

"I just thought that—"

"Why don't you just mind your own damn business, read the lines, do what he says, and let's get on with it?"

"She'd make a funny face at him," Kramer said, "but we got on with it. . . . She'd take anything from him. She'd take nothing from anybody else." But, he added, "when it came to the important things—what really counted—he respected her completely. He valued her opinion and considered her an equal. In that sense she *never* took a backseat."

After each shot Spencer would call out "Did you get any of it, Sam?" to the cameraman, Sam Leavitt. Then he would wait nervously for Sam to give him a thumbs-up. The entire time Tracy was in awe of Kramer's courage. "I tell him my life expectancy is about seven and a half minutes," Tracy marveled, "and he says, 'Action!' He's some kind of a nut or saint. Or both."

On March 17 Garson Kanin and Ruth Gordon showed up at the Tracy cottage house for their usual St. Patrick's Day celebration. Everyone was suitably attired in green—Spencer wore the green tie that Kanin gave him every St. Patrick's Day—and dined on corned beef followed by pistachio ice cream. Even "Dog Lobo," as they called him, wore green on his collar. Tracy nursed his single green beer and tapped his foot to the Irish minstrel music playing on the stereo.

As shooting on *Guess Who's Coming to Dinner* entered its final week, Tracy took Kramer aside and—as Kate strained to hear—said, "You know, kiddo, I've been looking at this script, and if I died on the way home tonight, you could still release the picture with what you've got."

In the film's emotional climax Christina Drayton (Kate) looks on, her eyes welling with tears, as Matt Drayton (Spencer) finally tells the parents of their daughter's black fiancé that "in the final analysis it doesn't matter what we think. The only thing that matters is what they feel, and how much they feel for each other. And if it's half of what we felt . . . that's everything."

"Spence was talking about Kate, about their love for each other," Kramer recalled of that moment. "He was paying tribute to her before millions of people and saying good-bye. There wasn't a dry eye in the place."

On May 12, 1967, Kate turned sixty without anyone pausing to notice. She had lied for so long about the date and year of her birth, the public now firmly believed that her birthday was November 8 and that she was only fifty-seven.

Two weeks later, on May 26, Spencer finished his final scene. Kramer yelled, "That's the one!" and rushed to embrace Tracy. Everyone, including Spencer, began to cry. Far too emotional to attend the cast party ("This is it. The Big Wrap-Up"), Tracy went home and opened a beer. Back on the set, after Kramer had toasted Tracy as "the greatest of all motion-picture personalities," Kate stood to thank her colleagues. "I want you to know," she said, "that I shall be everlastingly grateful to you all. And I know that your help made a hell of a lot of difference . . . to Spence."

In New York Garson Kanin picked up the telephone and was stunned to find Spencer on the other end. Out of 250 phone conversations between the two men that year, this was the first one placed by Tracy. "Finished!" he said. "Do you believe it? *I* don't. . . . Did you hear me, Jasper? I finished the picture!"

Guess Who's Coming to Dinner was well worth the risk for Columbia. It proved to be a blockbuster—commercially the most successful film either Tracy or Hepburn had ever made. It would also be nominated for ten Academy Awards, including one each for Spencer and Kate. Yet he would never know this. Two weeks after he completed work on the film, Spencer Tracy was dead.

Kate gallantly stepped aside and allowed Louise to play the grieving widow. There were words of comfort from her friends—Howard Hughes was the first to call with his condolences just four hours after Spencer's death—as well as telegrams and flowers. She joined the Kanins at their summer retreat on Martha's Vineyard, where they did their best to distract her with icy morning swims, sailing, and strolls on the beach.

Yet when she returned to Spencer's cottage, Kate could not bring herself to change a single thing. Spencer's will left his financial assets—described simply as "more than $500,000"—to Louise and the children. But Tracy's toothbrush remained in the stand where he had left it, the books he loved were still stacked up on his desk, and the carved Canada goose still swayed from the rafters. Whenever she wanted, Kate could sit in his red upholstered chair, or lovingly take one of his old flannel shirts out of the closet and put it on, or pad around in his wool socks.

Kate continued to rent the guesthouse from George Cukor for eleven years following Tracy's death. When she was in California, she stayed there, surrounded by precious memories of their life together. In this way he never really left her.

*   *   *

On March 17, 1968, Kate was on the French Riviera filming *The Madwoman of Chaillot*. All day long she wore a green silk tie—Garson Kanin's annual St. Patrick's Day gift. Embroidered on the back were the words "Made Especially for Spencer Tracy."

During the *Madwoman* shoot Kate rented a villa in St.-Jean-Cap-Ferrat. At seven one April morning the phone rang. It was Ida and Willie, her housekeepers, calling from California with the news that Kate had won the Oscar for *Guess Who's Coming to Dinner*.

Louise Tracy had been in the audience to accept her husband's award in the event he won, just as she had twenty-nine years earlier for *Captains Courageous*. "Did Mr. Tracy win it too?" Kate asked without hesitation.

"No, madam . . ."

There was a long silence. "Well," Kate said, "that's OK. I'm sure mine is for the two of us."

Hepburn went on to win two more Academy Awards—for *The Lion in Winter* and *On Golden Pond*—the first and only actor to accomplish such a feat. As the years passed, her stature grew. She became an icon, a living symbol of independent womanhood.

"If you hang around long enough, people love you for it," she once mused. "I'm like the old Flatiron Building. Maybe *it* hasn't been torn down yet, but I have a feeling I'm about to be any minute." Another time she sighed. "I'm not Katharine Hepburn. People think she's a saint, but she's not. She's this monster I've created, and I'm her private secretary. But I'm turning on her. I'm so damn sick of Katharine Hepburn I'd like to kill her. On second thought, people have been so nice to me lately because they think I'm going to die. Think I'll just stick around awhile," she added, eyes flashing, "and make the most of it."

There were still surprises left, and some of them sweet—like the morning in 1983 when Kate was taking her tennis lesson at the Beverly Hills Hotel and a young woman stopped to pet Lobo, the dog she bought for Spencer. "It's Lobo, isn't it?" asked the stranger.

"Yes, it's Lobo," Kate said, slowly realizing that the woman was Susie Tracy. Not long before, Louise Tracy had died at the age of eighty-seven and been buried alongside her husband in the family plot at Forest Lawn Memorial Park in Glendale.

Susie knelt down and pet Lobo some more. "He looks fine."

"Yes, he's fine, Susie." Pause. "Look, Susie," Kate said, breaking the silence, "if you would like to get to know me . . . you know where I live and you know the telephone number. . . ." The next day Spencer Tracy's only daughter called, and the two women became friends "just like that."

Kate and Susie shared a nagging feeling that there was much they did not know about Spencer Tracy the man—things that could never be known. "He would come home every Sunday and play tennis with us and tell wonderful stories," Susie recalled. "He was generous, funny—he loved to kid. But he was also complex and extremely sensitive. You couldn't convey the depth of feeling he did on screen without knowing what pain was personally."

Louise's death finally freed Hepburn to talk of her life with Spencer and to express her grief over the questions about him that would forever go unanswered. One day in 1986 Kate was home at her New York town house when she was suddenly "hit by the feeling I had to write to Spence." She bounded upstairs and, sitting on the edge of her bed, scrawled a four-page letter to him. "It took me ten minutes," she said.

"Living was never easy for Spence," she said. "He was deeply troubled—not at all like that totally confident figure the public saw up there on the screen. But whatever it was that made him so unhappy, he never talked about it—not with me, not to anyone. . . ." Then, she added wistfully, "You never really *know* anybody, do you? I never really knew Spencer, not really. I was very, very close to my mom and dad, but I'm not certain I knew them. We all say, 'I'm going to put this piece of me in a little box and I'll never let anyone see it—not anyone.' "

In her letter Kate asked Spence about the demons that had driven him to the bottle. "Why the escape hatch?" she asked. "Why was it always opened to get away from that remarkable you? What was it, Spence? I meant to ask you. Did you know what it was? What did you say? I can't hear you. . . ."

We were together twenty-seven years. It worked. Why it worked, who knows? But it worked, didn't it?

—KATE

It went against everything we knew about her—and what she had always believed about herself. Headstrong, independent, unwilling to take guff from anyone—male or female—Kate strode across seven decades like a colossus. In pants, of course. The quintessential Connecticut Yankee, she was almost as tough on those around her as she was on herself—with one exception.

To as many millions around the world, Spencer Tracy was the uncomplicated personification of the ideal American male: dependable, rugged, and wise. The image grew with time, masking the tortured, guilt-ridden, and often violent alcoholic underneath. The public never knew that behind the family man facade, the hell-raising Tracy was one of the baddest boys Hollywood had ever produced.

Onscreen they were locked in a constant male-female struggle for dominance, but in real life it was no contest. For twenty-seven years the reclusive Hepburn quietly lived the shadowy existence of the Other Woman—a life spent ducking in and out of service elevators, back doors, and alleyways. Sticking by the mercurial Spencer as he battled his demons and his addictions, Kate sat at his feet—literally and figuratively—and endured his wounding words with an understanding smile.

Yet there was something noble in the subterfuge. "It was important for her to be Mrs. Tracy," Kate said of her rival, Louise. "I didn't care, really, one way or the other." For her part Louise—knowing that Spencer's sense of guilt over their son's deafness would always prevent him from divorcing her—did not stand in the way of his one chance at happiness with Kate. It was a classic triangle, but with a difference: All three were decent people trying their best not to hurt one another. As a result, all three got hurt.

To all who knew Hepburn and Tracy, there was no doubt that Kate was the stronger of the two. She was merely the latest in a long line of tough, morally courageous women who made sacrifices for the far weaker men they loved. But there was also no doubt that Spencer admired and respected and adored his Kath. He needed her, and she needed him to need her.

"You know, I've had a pretty good run of it," said Kate, who would never see *Guess Who's Coming to Dinner* ("Too painful. I couldn't . . ."). More than a quarter century after his death, Spencer's monogrammed bathrobe still hung on a hook in her bathroom. "As a matter of fact, I rather look forward to dying. It's a tremendous relief, isn't it? The Big Sleep." If there is an afterlife? "Well, then I'm just waiting to join Spencer." Sadly, when that moment comes, the final curtain will be drawn on Hollywood's Golden Age.

Did Spencer love Kate? Discreetly, but in his own tortured way, completely. Did she love him? Totally, and forever. Theirs was an affair to remember.

Acknowledgments

❧

I first met Katharine Hepburn more than twenty years ago, in September 1976. In later years she would become more accessible, but at the time, she was—next to Greta Garbo—the most intensely private of public personalities, more inclined to throw a punch at a reporter than invite one into her home. After a full year of peppering her with interview requests, I harbored little hope of success when, without warning, she called and invited me over *"now."*

It took me ten minutes to sprint, notebook in hand, the six New York City crosstown blocks from my office at the Time and Life Building to her town house on East Forty-ninth Street. Kate answered the door and led the way upstairs— two steps at a time—to the second-floor living room. We talked. She showed me her paintings, a small bust of Spencer she had sculpted, some framed photographs of friends. At one point a burning log rolled out of the fireplace and onto the floor. Kate jumped up, kicked the log back in, and kept right on talking as if nothing had happened. When my tape recorder clicked off after ninety minutes, Kate stared at the machine. "It's had enough," she said.

Hepburn's housekeeper and cook, Norah Moore, served us lunch—and later tea, which we shared with Kate's secretary/companion/best friend Phyllis Wilbourn. ("Sometimes it looks as if all we do around here is eat," Kate said.) We talked some more. She bounded upstairs, and we went into her bedroom, where she climbed on a chair to reach a book she wanted me to read—the memoirs of a writer friend. We discovered we shared a passion for Eugene O'Neill—I had once interviewed his widow, Carlotta Monterey—and in return for her generosity, I gave her my copy of Arthur and Barbara Gelb's definitive O'Neill biography.

We went back to the living room and chatted some more. When she showed me out the front door, I fumbled with the wrought-iron gate that opened onto the sidewalk. "You see," she said, grinning slyly as she flipped open the latch and pushed open the gate, "like everything here, it's all an illusion." As I walked back toward Rockefeller Center, I glanced at my watch. We had been talking for more than five hours.

Over the next fifteen years I spent entire afternoons and mornings under Kate's spell as I interviewed her for publications ranging from *Life* and *People* magazines to *Good Housekeeping* and *Ladies' Home Journal*. In between, she dashed off notes to me on her stationery with "KATHARINE HOUGHTON HEPBURN" emblazoned in red across the top. "You make me sound," she wrote after one of my pieces on her ran, "very bright."

At Fenwick Kate could paint beach scenes ("I'm especially good at lighthouses") and torture herself splashing around in the icy waters of Long Island Sound. But she spent most of her time at the Turtle Bay town house, surrounded by mementos of her remarkable lifetime before, during, and after Spencer Tracy.

At the bus stop across East Forty-ninth Street the commuters stood waiting as they did every morning—oblivious to the high-cheekboned lady in beige slacks and black turtleneck furiously sweeping her front step. Once, Kate told me, a woman did break the bus ranks and approach her. "Oh, you are one of my favorites," gushed the fan. "I just love all your movies, *Audrey*."

The French bistro on the corner was replaced by an Indian restaurant, and sunlight now filtered down through granite-sheathed condominiums and office towers. But inside, Kate ruled a timeless world. On the wall to the right of the front door hung a framed cartoon from *The New Yorker*. It showed two mares watching as a third throws back her head haughtily. "Oh, she's been acting that way all day," says one mare to the other. "Someone told her she looks like Katharine Hepburn."

Only a chosen few were allowed into Kate's inner sanctum—all Oriental rugs, plush sofas, and burnished antiques. On one occasion I arrived to find a familiar figure sitting at the kitchen table, hand on her hip as she devoured a steaming bowl of Jerusalem artichoke soup. "You know Betty, of course," Kate said, motioning to the woman, Lauren Bacall. I had interviewed Bacall in her apartment at New York's famed Dakota, but seeing her here with Hepburn brought an added human dimension to the two icons.

Her high-ceilinged living room looked out on a shaded courtyard shared with Garson Kanin and composer Stephen Sondheim, who looked up from his piano late one night to see Kate rapping on his window, demanding that he quiet down. Like the rest of the house, this room is crammed with mementos: Coffee and end tables groan under the weight of cannonballs, crystal balls, splinters of petrified wood, huge chunks of quartz (gifts from George Cukor), a Victorian birdcage filled with dried flowers, a game of Chinese checkers, a Steuben pelican. And hanging from the ceiling: the carved goose that had graced the cottage she shared with Spencer. Her four Academy Awards were nowhere to be seen. One stays at Fenwick; the others are displayed at the Guinness World of Records exhibition in the Empire State Building.

Turtle Bay had been her sanctuary for more than sixty years, but in late 1996 Kate put the town house up for rent. As she approached her ninetieth birthday, ill health forced her to move to Fenwick, where she would be closer to her family.

First and foremost, I must thank Katharine Hepburn for her example and her wisdom and for sharing her memories with me. When I told Kate that I had named my daughter after her, she seemed flattered almost to the point of embarrassment, a touching reaction from a woman who has prompted thousands of parents to name their girls after her.

A daunting amount of research is required for any comprehensive biography, and this is particularly true in the case of *An Affair to Remember*. In addition to Kate herself, over the years I have interviewed hundreds of people who knew Hepburn and Tracy: family members, friends, neighbors, classmates, colleagues, people who worked for them, and the reporters and photographers who covered them. Only a few asked not to be identified, and I have respected their wishes.

I owe a special debt of gratitude to the guiding force behind *An Affair to Remember*, William Morrow editor in chief Will Schwalbe—supremely gifted editor, compelling advocate, friend. Will's associate Rebecca Goodhart, another dedicated pro, also played a key role in making *An Affair to Remember* a reality. Again, I owe thanks to all the wonderful people at William Morrow, particularly Bill Wright, Paul Fedorko, Al Marchioni, Paul Bresnick, Jackie Deval, Sharyn Rosenblum, Karen Auerbach, Jennifer Brawer, Brad Foltz, Deborah Weaver, Lisa Queen, Fritz Metsch, Debbie Glasserman, Deborah Weiss Geline, and Pearl Hanig.

My boundless gratitude, as always, to Ellen Levine—literary agent par excellence and a writer's best friend. I also owe a debt of thanks— yet again—to another longtime friend, Ellen's talented associate Diana Finch, and to Deborah Clifford, Jay Rogers, and Louise Quayle.

Digging deep into the Special Collections archives at the Academy of Motion Picture Arts and Sciences, the American Film Institute, the University of California at Los Angeles Film Archives, and elsewhere, my West Coast researcher Sandy Ferguson did a spectacular job unearthing new and important information. I am also indebted to Kate's sister the late Marion Hepburn Grant, to Lorett Treese and the staff of the Bryn Mawr College Archives, Rob Kyff of the Kingswood-Oxford School, Gerard J. Shorb and the staff of the Alan Mason Chesney Medical Archives at the Johns Hopkins University School of Medicine, Corning Corporate Archives director Stuart K. Sammis, Coke Morgan Stuart of the *Virginia Law Weekly*, Laura Vassell and the staff of the Stowe-Day Foundation, Nancy B. Newins and the staff of the Randolph-Macon College Archives, and Jean Chapin and the staff of the Gunn Memorial Library.

Five days after I finished writing *An Affair to Remember*, I turned my attention to another love story that has stood the test of time: On February 3, 1997, my wife Valerie and I celebrated our twenty-fifth wedding anniversary. We both reacted with disbelief—Is it possible we had been together almost as long as Tracy and Hepburn?—and realized that perhaps that is why their story resonates so deeply with us.

Our daughters, Kate and Kelly, were their usual awe-inspiring selves during the writing of *An Affair to Remember*. And my parents, who along with my wife's parents share this book's dedication, have been living examples of how relationships can, with lots of patience and even more humor, not only endure but flourish.

Additional thanks to Lauren Bacall, Laurence Olivier, Stanley Kramer, Marion Hepburn Grant, James Stewart, Joseph L. Mankiewicz, Angela Lansbury, Susie Tracy, Bette Davis, Cleveland Amory, Henry Fonda, Ginger Rogers, James Bacon, Karen Kramer, Sam Spiegel, Joseph E. Levine, Alfred Drake, Robert Wise, James Cagney, Clare Boothe Luce, Tennessee Williams, Robert Wagner, Joan Fontaine, Gore Vidal, Joshua Logan, Martin Gabel, Jane Fonda, John Bryson, Oleg Cassini, Gloria Swanson, Paulette Goddard, Charlton Heston, Lilli Palmer, Barry Schenck, Roland Winters, C. David Heymann, Yvette Reyes, Caroline Rittenhouse, Bob Cosenza, Gus Johnson, Henry Hathaway, Cranston Jones, Lawrence Mulligan, Paula Dranov, Jeanette Peterson, Joy Wansley, Homer Dickens, Lee Wohlfert, Alfred Eisenstaedt, Theodore Kalem, Betsy Loth, Hazel Southam, Laurie Putnam, Ben Carbonetto, Dudley Freeman, Debbie Goodsite, Don Hutter, Doris Lilly, Eileen Flanagan, Jerome Lawrence, Michael Shulman, Coke Morgan Stewart, Tobias Markowitz, Ray Whelan, Sr., and Gary Gunderson and to the Houghton Library at Harvard University, the Beinecke Rare Book and Manuscript Library of Yale University, the Houghton Library at Harvard University, Columbia University's Rare Book and Manuscript Library and Butler Library, the Corning Glass Company, the Bancroft Library of the University of California at Berkeley, Faye Thompson and the staff of the Center of Motion Picture Study at the Academy of Motion Picture Arts and Sciences, the University Research Library of the University of California at Los Angeles, the Ontario Historical Society of Canandaigua, New York, St. Paul's Parish of Hanover County, Virginia, Ripon College, the American Film Institute, the Columbia University Oral History Project, the Federal Bureau of Investigation, the Roxbury Library, the American Academy of Dramatic Arts, the Woodbury Library, the New York Public Library, the Brookfield Library, the University of Hartford, the Southbury Library, the Performing Arts Research Center of the New York Public Library at Lincoln Center, Smith College, the Players Club, Hartford and West Hartford libraries, Radcliffe College, the Woodbury

Library, the Silas Bronson Library, the Lambs, the Vassar College Library, the Boston Public Library, the New Milford Library, the Buffalo and Erie County Library, the Garrick Club, the Connecticut Public Library Archives, the Associated Press, Wide World, the Corning Public Library, the Baldwin School, the University of Notre Dame, Corbis-Bettmann, Sygma, Globe Photos, Movie Star News, the Kobal Collection, Archive Photos, and the Hampden Theatre Library.

Sources and Notes

The following chapter notes are designed to give a general view of the sources drawn upon in preparing An Affair to Remember, *but they are by no means all-inclusive. The author has respected the wishes of many interview subjects to remain anonymous and accordingly has not listed them either here or elsewhere in the text. The archives, oral histories, and special collections of, among other institutions, the Beinecke Rare Book and Manuscript Library of Yale University, the Academy of Motion Picture Arts and Sciences, Bryn Mawr College, the Johns Hopkins University School of Medicine, Randolph-Macon College, the Bancroft Library of the University of California at Berkeley, Ripon College, the Corning Glass Company, the Connecticut State Library, the Connecticut Historical Society, the American Film Institute, the Stowe-Day Foundation, the Lincoln Center Library for*

the Performing Arts, and Harvard University yielded fresh information and insights. In addition, Katharine Hepburn and Spencer Tracy—individually and as a team—have generated thousands of newspaper and magazine articles over the past seventy years, in publications ranging from *The New York Times*, the *Sunday Times* of London, and *Newsweek* to *Life*, *Time*, *Paris Match*, *Vanity Fair*, and the *Washington Post*. Only a representative sample of those that dealt with their personal lives are referred to here.

Chapters 1 and 2

For these chapters, the author drew on conversations with Katharine Hepburn, Marion Hepburn Grant, Cleveland Amory, Stanley Kramer, Karen Kramer, Bette Davis, Ben Lucien Berman, Caroline Rittenhouse, Cranston Jones, and Susie Tracy. Accounts of Tracy's death and funeral appeared in numerous newspapers and magazines, including *The New York Times*, the *Los Angeles Times*, *Time*, the *Los Angeles Herald Examiner*, the *Washington Post*, the *Chicago Tribune*, *Life*, the *Boston Globe*, *Look*, and *Newsweek* and were carried on the Reuters, United Press International, and Associated Press wires—as well as in Hepburn's memoir, *Me: Stories of My Life* (New York: Alfred A. Knopf, 1991). The Kingswood-Oxford School Archives provided valuable documents and information concerning Katharine Hepburn's early years, as did the Bryn Mawr Archives. This material included the vivid oral history of Kate's friend Alice Palache. Among the books and articles that provided insights into Hepburn's family origins were: *Kingswood-Oxford Today Magazine*, Commemorative Issue, 1909–1984; Oliver O. Jensen, "The Hepburns," *Life* (1940); J. Bryan III and Lupton A. Wilkinson, "The Hepburn Story," *Saturday Evening Post* (November 29, 1941); Marion Hepburn Grant, "The Fenwick Story," Connecticut Historical Society, 1975; "A Sad Death," *Corning Daily Democrat*, October 30, 1892; "A. A. Houghton Shoots Himself," *Buffalo News*, October 30, 1892; "Dr. Hepburn's Son, 15, Hangs Himself While Visiting New York," *Hartford Courant*, April 4, 1921; Helen Horowitz, *Alma Mater* (New York: Alfred A. Knopf, 1984); Christopher Andersen, *Young Kate* (New York: Henry Holt, 1988); Barbara Leaming, *Katharine Hepburn* (New York: Crown, 1995); Ralph G. Martin, "KH: My Life and Loves," *Ladies' Home Journal* (August 1975); *Marion Hepburn Grant 1918–1986, A Biography*, edited by Katharine Houghton Grant (West Hartford, Conn.: Fenwick Productions 1989).

Chapters 3 and 4

Information for these chapters was based in part on conversations with Katharine Hepburn, Laurence Olivier, James Stewart, Joseph Mankiewicz, Ginger Rogers, Marion Hepburn Grant, Theodore Kalem, Barrie Schenck, James Bacon, Selden West, Joshua Logan, Shirley Clurman, James Cagney, Gloria Swanson, Paulette Goddard, John Gielgud, and Alfred Eisenstaedt. Katharine Hepburn's correspondence with

Lawrence Langner and Theresa Helburn is from the Theatre Guild Papers at the Beinecke Rare Book and Manuscript Library of Yale University. These papers also include production files, salaries, casting lists, and related correspondence regarding *The Philadelphia Story, Without Love, As You Like It*. George Cukor's correspondence with Kate as well as the file on *A Bill of Divorcement* is from the George Cukor Papers at the Academy of Motion Picture Arts and Sciences. Published sources for this period include Patrick McGilligan, *George Cukor: A Double Life* (New York: St. Martin's Press, 1991); Larry Swindell, *Spencer Tracy* (New York: World Publishing, 1969); Joan Crawford, *A Portrait of Joan* (Garden City, L.I.: Doubleday, 1962); Pat O'Brien and Stephen Longstreet, *The Wind at My Back* (Garden City, L.I.: Doubleday, 1964); Homer Dickens, *The Films of Katharine Hepburn* (Secaucus, N.J.: Citadel Press, 1971); Slim Keith with Annette Tapert, *Slim: Memories of a Rich and Imperfect Life* (New York: Warner Books, 1990); Brooke Astor, *Haywire* (New York: Alfred A. Knopf, 1977); Peter Harry Brown and Pat H. Broeske, *Howard Hughes: The Untold Story* (New York: Dutton, 1996); Penelope Gilliatt, "Miss Hepburn," *Vogue* (November 1981); Bill Davidson, *Spencer Tracy: Tragic Idol* (London: Sidgwick & Jackson, 1987); Donald Deschner, *The Complete Films of Spencer Tracy* (New York: Carol Publishing, 1993).

Chapters 5 to 7

Katharine Hepburn, Lauren Bacall, Angela Lansbury, Joseph Mankiewicz, Sam Spiegel, Joan Fontaine,

Henry Fonda, James Bacon, Laurence Olivier, Phyllis Wilbourn, Martin Gabel, Doris Lilly, Ruth Gordon, Joseph E. Levine, Irving ("Swifty") Lazar, John Bryson, John Henry Faulk, Roland Winters, Robert Wise, Henry Hathaway, Barry Schenck. Articles and other published source materials include "Hepburn in Hartford," *Life* (May 11, 1942); Frank Capra, *The Name Above the Title: An Autobiography* (New York: Macmillan, 1971); Gary Carey, *Katharine Hepburn: Hollywood Yankee* (New York: Pocket Books, 1975); Garson Kanin, "Woman of the Year: Katharine Hepburn," *McCall's* (February, 1970); Katharine Hepburn, *The Making of the African Queen or How I Went to Africa with Bogart, Bacall and Huston and Almost Lost My Mind* (New York: Alfred A. Knopf, 1987); Anne Edwards, *A Remarkable Woman* (New York: William Morrow, 1985); George Haddad-Garcia, "The Incomparable Kate Hepburn," *Saturday Evening Post* (September 1981); Charles Higham, *Kate: The Life of Katharine Hepburn* (New York: W. W. Norton, 1975); Garson Kanin, *Tracy and Hepburn* (New York: Viking Press, 1971); Elia Kazan, *A Life* (New York: Alfred A. Knopf, 1988); Curt Gentry, *J. Edgar Hoover: The Man and the Secrets* (New York: W. W. Norton, 1991); John Cogley, *Report on Blacklisting*, vol. 1, *Movies* (New York: Fund for the Republic, 1956); Hume Cronyn, *A Terrible Liar* (New York: William Morrow, 1991); Lauren Bacall, *By Myself* (New York: Alfred A. Knopf, 1979).

Chapters 8 and 9

The author drew on conversations with Katharine Hepburn, Stanley Kramer, Karen Kramer, Tennessee Williams, James Bacon, Phyllis Wilbourn, Joan Fontaine, Alfred Drake, John Houseman, Jane Fonda, Jerome Lawrence, Robert Wagner, Clare Boothe Luce, Irene Mayer Selznick, Oleg Cassini. The George Cukor Papers at the Academy of Motion Picture Arts and Sciences and the Katharine Hepburn, Constance Collier, and Theatre Guild papers at Yale University's Beinecke Library were of considerable value, as were the Katharine Hepburn and Spencer Tracy Archives at the Lincoln Center Library of the Performing Arts. Published sources included Gene Tierney, *Self-Portrait* (New York: Wyden Books, 1978); Joan Fontaine, *No Bed of Roses* (New York: William Morrow, 1978); Irene Mayer Selznick, *A Private View* (New York: Alfred A Knopf, 1983); Katharine Houghton Hepburn, "The Right of Privacy: The Predicament of the Public Figure," *Virginia Law Weekly* (1965); Arthur Unger, "Hepburn on Pornography," *Christian Science Monitor*, March 6, 1975; Henry Mitchell, "Dispenser of Wisdom and Toasted Cheese," *Washington Post*, January 30, 1976; Kathy Larkin, "Spencer Tracy: Tribute to a Legend," *New York Daily News*, November 4, 1986; Katharine Hepburn, "Tea and Memories," *New York Times*, January 16, 1976; Liz Smith, "Kate the Great," *Vogue* (September 1991); Michael Freedland, *Katharine Hepburn* (London: W. H. Allen, 1984); Hector Arce, "Hepburn," *Women's Wear Daily* (September 15, 1969); Bill Davidson, "Of Booze and Brilliance," *New York Daily News*, September 3, 1988.

Bibliography

Agee, James. *Agee on Film*, Vol. 2. New York: Perigee Books, 1983.

Andersen, Christopher. *Young Kate: The Remarkable Hepburns and the Shaping of an American Legend*. New York: Henry Holt, 1988.

————. *The Book of People*. New York: G. P. Putnam's Sons, 1981.

————. *Citizen Jane*. New York: Henry Holt, 1990.

————. *Susan Hayward*. New York: Doubleday, 1980.

Bacall, Lauren. *By Myself*. New York: Alfred A. Knopf, 1979.

Bach, Steven. *Marlene Dietrich: Life and Legend*. New York: William Morrow, 1992.

Bacon, James. *Hollywood Is a Four-Letter Town*. Chicago: Henry Regnery, 1976.

Bartlett, Donald L., and James Steele. *Empire: The Life, Legend and Madness of Howard Hughes*. New York: W. W. Norton, 1979.

Bergan, Ronald. *Katharine Hepburn: An Independent Woman*. New York: Arcade Publishing, 1996.

Bosworth, Patricia. *Montgomery Clift: A Biography*. New York: Harcourt, Brace, Jovanovich, 1978.

Brown, Eric. *Deborah Kerr*. New York: St. Martin's Press, 1978.

Brown, Peter Harry, and Pat H. Broeske. *Howard Hughes: The Untold Story*. New York: Dutton, 1996.

Capra, Frank. *The Name Above the Title: An Autobiography*. New York: Macmillan, 1971.

Carey, Gary. *All the Stars in Heaven: Louis B. Mayer's MGM*. New York: Dutton, 1981.

————. *Katharine Hepburn: Hollywood Yankee*. New York: Pocket Books, 1975.

Cassini, Oleg. *In My Own Fashion: An Autobiography*. New York: Simon & Schuster, 1987.

Cogley, John. *Report on Blacklisting, vol. 1, Movies*. New York: Fund for the Republic, 1956.

Collier, Christopher, with Bonnie B. Collier. *The Connecticut Scholar: The Literature of Connecticut History*. Middletown, Conn.: Connecticut Humanities Council, 1983.

Crawford, Joan. *A Portrait of Joan*. Garden City, N.Y.: Doubleday, 1962.

Crofut, Florence, S. M. *Guide to the History and Historic Sites of Connecticut*, vol. 2. New Haven: Yale University Press, 1937.

Cronyn, Hume. *A Terrible Liar*. New York: William Morrow, 1991.

Davidson, Bill. *Spencer Tracy: Tragic Idol*. London: Sidgwick & Jackson, 1987.

Deschner, Donald. *The Complete Films of Spencer Tracy*. Secaucus, N.J.: Citadel Press, 1968.

Dickens, Homer. *The Films of Katharine Hepburn*. Secaucus, N.J.: Citadel Press, 1971.

Douglas, Kirk. *The Ragman's Son*. New York: Pocket Books, 1988.

Eames, John Douglas. *The MGM Story*. New York: Crown, 1982.

Edwards, Anne. *A Remarkable Woman*. New York: William Morrow, 1985.

———. *Vivien Leigh*. New York: Simon & Schuster, 1977.

Falk, Candace. *Love, Anarchy, and Emma Goldman*. New York: Holt, Rinehart and Winston, 1984.

Fisher, Eddie. *Eddie: My Life, My Loves*. New York: Harper & Row, 1981.

Fontaine, Joan. *No Bed of Roses*. New York: William Morrow, 1978.

Ford, Dan. *Pappy: The Life of John Ford*. Englewood Cliffs, N.J.: Prentice-Hall, Inc., 1979.

Frank, Gerold. *Judy*. New York: Harper & Row, 1975.

Freedland, Michael. *Katharine Hepburn*. London: W. H. Allen, 1984.

French, Philip. *The Movie Moguls*. London: Weidenfeld & Nicolson, 1969.

Geist, Kenneth L. *Pictures Will Talk: The Life and Films of Joseph L. Mankiewicz*. New York: Da Capo Press, 1978.

Gentry, Curt. *J. Edgar Hoover: The Man and the Secrets*. New York: W. W. Norton, 1991.

Gottfried, Martin. *Jed Harris: The Curse of Genius*. Boston: Little, Brown, 1984.

Grant, Katharine Houghton. *Marion Hepburn Grant 1918–1986: A Biography*. West Hartford, Conn.: Fenwick Productions, 1989.

Grant, Marion Hepburn. *The Fenwick Story*. Hartford, Conn.: Connecticut Historical Society, 1974.

———. *In and About Hartford: Tours and Tales*. Hartford, Conn.: Connecticut Historical Society, 1978.

Halliwell, Leslie. *Halliwell's Filmgoer's Companion, Ninth Edition*. New York: Scribners, 1988.

Harris, Warren G. *Gable and Lombard*. New York: Simon & Schuster, 1974.

Haver, Ronald. *David O. Selznick's Hollywood*. New York: Alfred A. Knopf, 1980.

Hayward, Brooke. *Haywire*. New York: Alfred A. Knopf, 1977.

Hecht, Ben. *A Child of the Century*. New York: Simon & Schuster, 1954.

Helburn, Theresa. *A Wayward Quest*. Boston: Little, Brown, 1960.

Hemingway, Mary Welsh. *How It Was*. New York: Alfred A. Knopf, 1976.

Hepburn, Katharine. *The Making of the African Queen*. New York: Alfred A. Knopf, 1987.

————. *Me: Stories of My Life*. New York: Alfred A. Knopf, 1991.

Heymann, C. David. *Liz*. Secaucus, N.J.: Carol Publishing, 1995.

Higham, Charles. *Kate: The Life of Katharine Hepburn*. New York: W. W. Norton, 1975.

Horowitz, Helen. *Alma Mater*. New York: Alfred A. Knopf, 1984.

Houseman, John. *Final Dress*. New York: Simon & Schuster, 1983.

Huston, John. *An Open Book*. New York: Ballantine Books, 1981.

Jewell, Richard, with Vernon Harbin. *The RKO Story*. New York: Arlington House, 1982.

Kael, Pauline. *Kiss Kiss Bang Bang*. Boston: Little, Brown, 1968.

Kanin, Garson. *Tracy and Hepburn*. New York: Viking Press, 1971.

Kazan, Elia. *A Life*. New York: Alfred A. Knopf, 1988.

Keith, Slim. *Slim: Memories of a Rich and Imperfect Life*. New York: Warner Books, 1990.

LaGuardia, Robert. *Monty: A Biography of Montgomery Clift*. New York: Arbor House, 1977.

Lambert, Gavin. *On Cukor*. New York: G. P. Putnam's Sons, 1972.

Langner, Lawrence. *The Magic Curtain*. New York: Dutton, 1951.

Lasky, Jesse L., with Don Weldon. *I Blow My Own Horn*. Garden City, N.Y.: Doubleday, 1957.

Leaming, Barbara. *Katharine Hepburn*. New York: Crown 1995.

Loos, Anita. *Kiss Hollywood Good-by*. New York: Viking Press, 1974.

Mackenzie, Midge. *Shoulder to Shoulder*. New York: Alfred A. Knopf, 1975.

Mann, Abby. *Judgment at Nuremberg: The Script of the Film*. London: Cassell, 1961.

McDowall, Roddy. *Double Exposure*. New York: Delacorte Press, 1966.

McGilligan, Patrick. *George Cukor: A Double Life*. New York: St. Martin's Press, 1991.

Merrill, Arch. *Southern Tier*. Interlaken, N.Y.: Empire State Books, 1986.

Minnelli, Vincente. *I Remember It Well*. New York: Berkley, 1974.

Mordden, Ethan. *Movie Star: A Look at the Women Who Made Hollywood*. New York: St. Martin's Press, 1983.

Niven, David. *The Moon's a Balloon*. London: Coronet, 1971.

O'Brien, Pat, and Stephen Longstreet. *The Wind at My Back*. Garden City, N.Y.: Doubleday, 1964.

Pratt, William. *Scarlett Fever*. New York: Macmillan, 1977.

Saint John, Adela Rogers. *The Honeycomb*. Garden City, N.Y.: Doubleday, 1969.

Sarris, Andrew. *The American Cinema, Directors and Directions 1929–1968*. New York: Dutton, 1968.

Schary, Dore. *Heyday: An Autobiography*. Boston: Little Brown, 1979.

Schorer, Mark. *Sinclair Lewis: An American Life*. New York: McGraw-Hill, 1961.

Selznick, Irene Mayer. *A Private View*. New York: Alfred A. Knopf, 1983.

Shipman, David. *The Great Movie Stars: The Golden Years*. New York: Hill and Wang, 1970.

Shulman, Irving. *Harlow*. San Francisco: Mercury House, 1989.

Spada, James. *Hepburn: Her Life in Pictures*. Garden City, N.Y.: Doubleday, 1984.

Taylor, John Russell. *The Penguin Dictionary of Theatre*. New York: Penguin Books, 1981.

Thomas, Bob. *King Cohn*. New York: Bantam Books, 1968.

Thomson, David. *A Biographical Dictionary of Film*. New York: William Morrow, 1976.

Tierney, Gene, with Mickey Herskowitz. *Self-Portrait*. New York: Wyden Books, 1978.

Vidal, Gore. *Palimpsest: A Memoir*. New York: Random House, 1995.

Wansell, Geoffrey. *Haunted Idol: The Story of the Real Cary Grant*. New York: William Morrow, 1984.

Warner, Charles Dudley. *My Summer in a Garden*. Boston: Houghton Mifflin, 1871.

Williams, Tennessee. *Memoirs*. Garden City, N.Y.: Doubleday, 1975.

Wilson, Edmund. *The Forties*. New York: Farrar, Straus & Giroux, 1984.

Index